KYC

# ANIMA MUNDI IN TRANSITION:
## CULTURAL, CLINICAL & PROFESSIONAL CHALLENGES

### PROCEEDINGS OF THE TWENTIETH CONGRESS
### OF THE INTERNATIONAL ASSOCIATION
### FOR ANALYTICAL PSYCHOLOGY

# Kyoto 2016

*Anima Mundi in Transition:*
*Cultural, Clinical & Professional Challenges*

Proceedings of the Twentieth Congress
of the International Association
for Analytical Psychology

Edited by Emilija Kiehl & Margaret Klenck

**DAIMON**
VERLAG

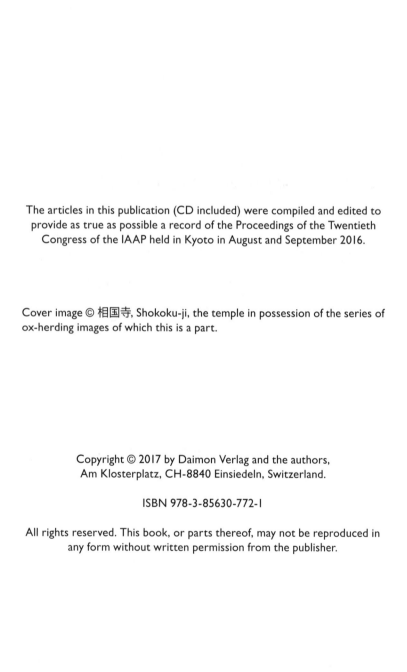

The articles in this publication (CD included) were compiled and edited to provide as true as possible a record of the Proceedings of the Twentieth Congress of the IAAP held in Kyoto in August and September 2016.

Cover image © 相国寺, Shokoku-ji, the temple in possession of the series of ox-herding images of which this is a part.

# Contents

(entries up to p. 210 appear in the print edition, beyond that only on CD)

# Thursday, 1 September

# Friday, 2 September

# Breakout Sessions (on CD only)

# Monday, 29 August 2017

# Tuesday, 30 August 2017

## Thursday, 1 September 2017

# Friday, 2 September 2017

# List of IAAP Committees

*Officers:*

Tom Kelly, President
Marianne Muller, President Elect
Angela Connolly, Vice President
Toshio Kawai, Vice President
Misser Berg, Honorary Secretary

*Executive Committee:*

Pilar Amezaga (SUPA)
Fred Bochardt (SAAJA)
Batya Brosh-Palmoni (IIJP)
Alessandra de Coro (AIPA)
Christine Hajinian (CGIJSF)
George Hogenson (CSJA)
Emilija Kiehl (BJAA)
Margaret Klenck (JPA)
Robert Wimmer (DGAP)

*Standing Committees:*

*Ethics Committee:*

Ann Casement, (BJAA, JPA) Chair
Pwnny Pickles (SAP, Honorary Secretary
Carole Beebe Tarantelli (CIPA)
Paula Boechat (AJB)
Christian Gaillard (SFPA)
Sonoko Toyoda (AJAJ, AGAP)

*Congress Program Committee:*

Toshio Kawai (AJAJ) Chair
Stephan Alder (DGAP)
Alvaro Ancona (SBrPA)
Misser Berg (DSAP)
Angela Connolly (CIPA)
Grazina Gudaite (LAAP)
Tom Kelly (IRSJA, AGAP)
Marianne Muller (DSAP)
Patricia Vasey-McGrew (NESJA)

*Local Organising Committee:*

Yasuhiro Tanaka (AJAJ, AGAP) Chair
Sonoko Toyoda (AJAJ, AGAP)
Masamicji Adachi (AJAJ, AGAP)
Chihiro Hatanaka
Shima Morisaki
Masako Kubota

*IAAP Secretary:* Selma Gubser

# Note from the Editors

The Congress in Kyoto marked a new chapter in the life of IAAP: for the first time in its history, this abundantly creative triennial gathering of Jungian analysts from all over the world took place in Asia, and the scientific and cultural dialogue between Jungians from the "West" and the "East" has entered a new dimension. We can look forward to mutually enriching developments in our thinking and clinical work on both sides of the culturally and, at times, politically different points of view.

The readers of these Proceedings will find that there is more emphasis on the clinical aspect of our work than may have been the case in the past with, as always, the theoretical, philosophical and cultural themes permeating and informing the thinking of the authors whose papers are presented here.

The work on editing the Proceedings has undergone a new approach too and this volume is the result of a truly collaborative effort between Emilija Kiehl, editor of the material published in the printed book, and Margaret Klenck who, with a team of colleagues, edited the presentations on the CD.

I would like to thank all the colleagues who so generously contributed to this endeavor and, as always, my heartfelt thanks to Robert Hinshaw and Robert Imhoff of Daimon Verlag, for our continual warm and friendly working relationship.

We hope that this rich offering of our colleagues' thoughts and ideas will be as stimulating and inspiring for our readers as it has been for us.

Emilija Kiehl

As Emilija mentioned in her Note, we experimented with a new system in the editing of the breakout presentations. Volunteers from around the world joined me in editing the papers as a team. Our task was two-fold: to bring the papers into a standard format (the easy part) and to guide the authors into English usage such that their presentations were grammatically correct while at the same time expressive of their individual voices and cultural realities. This was the hard, but deeply exciting, part of the task. The editing conversations we had with our colleagues took many forms, from email exchanges to Skype sessions. Sometimes third parties generously helped when language and cultural differences could not be easily bridged.

The editing team consisted of myself, nine other analysts and one candidate. At the end of the project, each member expressed gratitude for the opportunity to engage their colleagues' ideas in depth and to converse, in the editing process, in profound cross-cultural and cross-theoretical dialogues. I am grateful to them for their hard work: Penny Boisset, Jill Fischer, Royce Froehlich, Annette Hanson, Dennis Merritt, Margarita Mendez, Arthur Niesser, Susan Schwartz, Ilana Storace, and Nancy van den Berg-Cook.

We hope that you will be affected by the unique, heartfelt ideas and experiences of your colleagues from across the globe as they engaged with the Anima Mundi in Transitions.

Margaret Klenck

# Welcome

*Tom Kelly*
President, IAAP

As President of the IAAP, I would like to extend a warm and hearty welcome to each and everyone one of you at this the XX International Congress of the IAAP. It is an especially auspicious event since it marks the first time that an IAAP Congress is held in Asia. This reflects the ever-growing interest in Analytical Psychology throughout the world and in particular in this region of the world.

The theme of our Congress, Anima Mundi in Transition: Cultural, Clinical and Professional Challenges, is meant to offer us the opportunity in the coming days to explore the challenges we face in these areas of our clinical practice and in the world we live in. We hope the presentations you will hear and the discussions you will partake in will allow you to build bridges to other participants of the congress but especially to open yourself to the discovery of the multifaceted expressions of Anima Mundi in the personal as well as in the cultural, clinical and professional realms.

May this Congress be an opportunity for each of you to meet old friends and to forge new friendships as a result of shared interests. May the discussions and exchanges you participate in in the coming days be stimulating and nourishing and may you come away from the Congress with the impression of having got something special for yourself, feeling enriched and stimulated.

There are many people to thank for their hard work and dedication in making this congress a reality. While I leave this to other presenters, I want to thank our IAAP Group Member host, the Association of Jungian Analysts of Japan, (AJAJ), and especially Toshio Kawai, Chair of the Program Committee, and Yasuhiro Tanaka, Chair of the Organizing Committee for their organizational skills, their boundless energy and for managing to maintain a sense of humour in times of strain and stress.

Without further ado, I would now like to pass the microphone to Marianne Müller, President-Elect of the IAAP, for the Opening Address.

Tom Kelly
President, IAAP

# Opening Address

*Marianne Müller*
President-Elect IAAP

Dear Colleagues, dear Guests, dear Friends,

It is a great honour and a special pleasure to welcome you all to the XX IAAP Congress, here in Kyoto, at one of the historically and culturally most important cities of Japan. The large number of participants from every corner of the world, many of whom have travelled very long distances to participate in this Congress, has exceeded our expectations and makes us very happy. A very warm welcome!

This is the first time the IAAP is holding its International Congress in Asia. We would like to thank the Association of Jungian Psychologists, Japan, AJAJ, for their invitation to host this Congress and their great dedication in making it possible. The IAAP has been present in Asia for many years and is in contact and communication with colleagues from various countries in this region. A lively, reciprocal dialogue between East and West has come into being within our Community and has influenced this as well as supplemented and enriched the theory of Analytical Psychology, and continues to do so.

There are to date two IAAP Group Members with Training Status in Asia: one is here in Japan and the other in Korea. Over the past 15 years Analytical Psychology has spread across the Chinese region and has been met with great interest. In the meantime, six Developing Groups have come into being, each with their own programme, organized by the Executive Committee and in exchange and collaboration with the Individual Members from this region as well as analysts from the USA, Europe and Australia.

It was Professor Hayao Kawai, who first brought Analytical Psychology to Japan 50 years ago, after studying at the C G Jung Institute Zurich in the early 1960's. His influence on the development of Analytical Psychology in Japan cannot be overestimated. Through his numerous publications and scientific books he helped the people in the Far East to better understand the Western way of thinking; and he also sensitized those of us socialized in the West to a better understanding of the East. He was a great and unique bridge builder between East and West in the field of psychology and other areas far beyond. On Tuesday evening, there will be a commemorative ceremony in honour of Professor Kawai and of his seminal contributions to Analytical Psychology.

We know about Jung's keen interest in Buddhism, his fascination with it and his high esteem for Dasetz Teitaro Suzuki's work and contribution to Buddhism. Jung wrote the foreword to Suzuki's *Intro-duction to Zen Buddhism*. Initially, Jung had serious doubts as to whether Zen Buddhism could actually be understood by Western people. Nevertheless, he continued looking for connections and similarities between these two cultures and found it finally in psychotherapy and its teleological orientation. He wrote: "... the psychotherapist who is seriously concerned with the question of the aim of his therapy cannot remain unmoved when he sees the end towards which this Eastern method of psychic 'healing', i.e., 'making whole' – is striving."[1] According to Jung, in the East "methods and philosophical doctrines have been developed which simply put all Western attempts along these lines in the shade".[2]

Jung's contact with Richard Wilhelm and Wilhelm's publications *The I Ching* and *The Secret of the Golden Flower* opened up for Jung not only another reference to the culture of the East, but also, as it is always the case with these encounters, to his own material, in this case the theory of Synchronicity and Alchemy. In the obituary Jung wrote for Wilhelm (1930), he used the concept of Synchronicity for the first time: "The science of the *I Ching* is based not on the causality principle but on one which – hitherto unnamed because not familiar to us – I have tentatively called the *synchronistic* principle."[3] Later, Jung would in collaboration with the physicist Wolfgang Pauli, go on to further develop this principle where matter and psyche are unified and in turn relate to the relativity of space and time.

In his obituary for Richard Wilhelm, Jung again warns against taking over the deep wisdom of the East too rashly "in the hope of finding the right remedy for our sickness."[4] Jung valued Richard Wilhelm for his refined ability to both mediate and interact with a foreign culture. I think his attitude can also serve as a model for our inter-cultural activities. Jung wrote: "Faced with an alien culture of the East, Wilhelm showed a degree of modesty highly unusual in a European. He approached it freely, without prejudice, without the assumption of knowing better; he opened his heart and mind to it. He let himself be gripped and shaped by it, so that when he came back to Europe he brought us, not only in his spirit but in his whole being, a true image of the East."[5]

The many questions that interested Jung in relation to Eastern cultures and which provided abundant stimulation for his own research and insights, will also be themes at this Congress: Ongoing thoughts and experiences in the interchange between East and West, between Buddhism and Analytical Psychology, between spirituality

---

1  Jung, C.G., Psychology and Religion, East and West, CW 11, § 905
2  Jung, C.G., Psychology and Religion, East and West, CW 11, § 905
3  Jung, C.G., Richard Wilhelm: In Memoriam, CW 15, § 81
4  Jung, C.G., Richard Wilhelm: In Memoriam, CW 15, § 90
5  Jung, C.G., Richard Wilhelm: In Memoriam, CW 15, § 93

and individuation and their meaning for the practice of psychotherapy; the widening of the awareness of the differences and mutual influences in psychotherapy; and time and again the significance of symbols for providing a meaningful understanding of psychological processes.

"Anima Mundi in Transition: Cultural, Clinical and Professional Challenges" is the theme that the Programme Committee has chosen. In the discussions that took place about a suitable theme for this Congress it soon became apparent, that the fundamental changes in our time, as they manifest in various areas of life, should be the theme. What we wanted to address are the changes to our world through globalization, through technological possibilities in worldwide exchanges, the opportunities and dangers of these developments and their influence on the individual, on society, on psychoanalysis and on nature. These worldwide changes, the accelerated processes and their consequences cause uncertainty and fear in many people and this in turn has resulted in a variety of individual and collective phenomena such as radicalization, isolation or the flight into consumerism. Dealing with this is one of the major challenges also for our theory and particularly for the practice of psychotherapy. In drafting the programme for this Congress, the Committee's special concern was to place a particular focus on clinical presentations.

Anima Mundi is the central term or concept of our Congress theme, the soul of the world. Even Jungians have questioned its existence, as in our current time one often gets the impression that through modern technology the world is becoming increasingly dehumanised and soulless. This complaint is fairly old: the poet, Novalis, one of the important representatives of German Romanticism, complained at the turn of the 18th to the 19th century in the little poem which became famous that only "numbers and figures" are nowadays "the keys to all creatures". By this, he meant the formulas in mathematics and in science and in general the mentality of rationalism that dominated the so-called period of enlightenment. And anticipating Jung and others, he points to the validity and truth of "fairy-tales and poems" in which "the true world histories" could be discovered. Jung seized on the concept of Anima Mundi, and was referring to the modern human being's isolated psyche, lacking or having lost the connection to an animated, soul-filled whole. Jung also complained about the development that took place since the age of enlightenment with the split of spirit and matter, where the individual acquired significant scientific insights but also lost significant spiritual qualities. Jung's greatest merit is that of making this conscious and highlighting the scientific grasp of this loss and especially the development of his theories such as the Collective Unconscious, Synchronicity and the Individuation Process, which in their multifaceted manner, facilitate the re-establishment of and the connection to something greater, and making this visible. Where do we stand today with respect to this question, since the individual, self-determined route has become increasingly central? What do we as analysts have to offer? To what extent do cultural backgrounds play a central role in the development of new points of reference? These are some of the questions I hope to receive answers to during the course of the Congress.

At this point, I would like to thank the Programme Committee and the Organizing Committee for their significant work over the past three years in the preparation of this Congress in Kyoto. Ahead of us lies a multi-faceted, relevant and up to date programme, scientifically and clinically rich, that is laid out in the Programme Brochure in an aesthetically very pleasing manner, as is everything here in Japan. A number of innovations were included in the programme such as the Pre-Congress Master Classes, brief verbal presentations with the Posters and Zen-meditation in the morning. My special thanks go to Toshio Kawai, Chair of the Programme Committee, and to Yasuhiro Tanaka, Chair of the Organizing Committee, together with his team: Sonoko Toyoda, Masamichi Adachi, Chihiro Hatanaka, Shima Morisaki, and Masako Kubota. They have worked with tireless commitment to realize this Congress. Many heartfelt thanks for their exemplary and reliable work and collaboration with the IAAP over the past three years.

My wish for this Congress and beyond: I hope that this Congress will bring greater awareness of the fact that Analytical Psychology is anchored in all of the world's continents and diverse cultures. Over the next three years the IAAP and I as the future president, see the nurturing of the connections with the Group Members as our central concern. What has been very helpful for these contacts are regional organizations that have come into existence in the past few years like CNASJA (North American Conference of Jungian Analysts and Candidates), CLAPA (Latin American Committee for Analytical Psychology), the European Congress, the China Conference, to mention only a few. Participation in these regional conferences and the contact with regional organizations makes it easier for the IAAP to be in communication and dialogue with each of these groups. The IAAP today is a very complex organization with multifaceted functions and responsibilities towards its members.

It is important for me that the IAAP is not only well networked internally but in addition, it maintains relationships externally with like-minded organizations. In the future we will need to seek to work even more closely together with the scientific world and with universities. This challenges us to critically reassess our theoretical basis and knowledge and potentially also to formulate terminology anew and in an up to date manner, and, it goes without saying, to foster and encourage research further. Jung's legacy is by far not exhausted.

We have in these past years received confirmation of this from various sides and have experienced offers of mutual understanding as, for example, from the neuro-sciences. In addition, I think that we can contribute significantly to the current questions regarding social developments in our time. Only when we are involved and we face reality can we have an influence and make visible our convictions and perspectives. Likewise, we are continuously challenged to understand just how much the psyche and the environment are directly and intimately interconnected. Recognizing the mutual inter-dependence cannot be over emphasized. The importance of nature for humanity can possibly be understood anew right here in Japan. I am thinking of the Logo for this Congress, which is surrounded by nature, and the round form symbolizing Anima Mundi. With this, we are back to the theme of our Congress.

I wish us all a rich and stimulating gathering. Enjoy the Congress and benefit from it.

*Monday, 29 August 2017*

# The Hua Yen Philosophy and its Implications for Modern Psychology and Science

*Shin'ichi Nakazawa*
(Japan, Yamanashi)

## Introduction

The paper argues for a new perspective on the relationship between Buddhism and European psychology, or sciences of the mind, based in the *Kegon Sutra,* a text that emerged in the early stages of Mahayana Buddhism (3rd-5th century C.E.). The basis of European science is *logos* intellection, formalized by Aristotle as following three laws: the law of identity, the law of contradiction and the law of the excluded middle. Logic in the Buddhist tradition, by contrast, is based in *lemma* (meaning to understand as a whole not with language, but with intuition). *Lemma*-based science born in the Buddhist tradition shows that rational perception is possible even without the three laws of *logos.* The *Kegon Sutra*, which explains what Buddha preached only a week after he attained enlightenment, is unified under the logic of *lemma* and can be seen as an effort to create a '*lemma* science of the mind'. The fundamental teaching of the *Kegon Sutra* is explored and its principles are compared with primary process thinking and the unconscious as outlined by Freud and Jung. Jung's research of Eastern texts led him to create a science of the mind that went further than Freud: his concept of synchronicity is given by way of example and can be seen anew within the idea of a *lemma*-based science.

## The *Kegon Sutra*

Buddhism has taken the study of the human mind as its greatest theme. Buddhism begins by asking what people must do to save themselves from worldly desires and self-doubt, and discovers that the source of worldly desires and self-doubt lies not outside the mind but within the mind.

"Three realms are only mind"[1] is the fundamental understanding attained by Mahayana Buddhism. The idea is that the three realms – the realm of desires (desire realm), the realm of material phenomena (form realm), and the latent realm of the non-material (formless realm) – and

---

1 Vasubandhu, (4th-5th century C.E.), *The Treatise in Twenty Verses on Consciousness-only.* The concept is fundamental to all sects of Mahayana Buddhism.

everything that makes up the cosmos is generated from the mind. Buddhism has sought to observe the world's every phenomenon from this "mind-only" perspective. In this sense, I suppose Buddhism could be understood as humankind's oldest form of psychology. In fact, there is no essential difference between the Buddhism that sought to investigate the mind and what we call "sciences of the mind" today.

Sciences of the mind that developed mainly in the West such as psychology and psychoanalysis were quick to grasp the importance of the knowledge of the human mind that was accumulated by Buddhism. Several efforts have been made to bridge the gap between Buddhism and sciences of the mind, such as the "Ajase complex" proposed to counter the "Oedipus complex". Such attempts, however, have been sporadic in nature and, regrettably, no coherent investigation has yet been satisfactorily developed that illuminates the true, inherent relationship between Buddhism and sciences of the mind.

This paper is an attempt to redress this omission. My argument will be grounded in the *Kegon Sutra*[2] a text that emerged in the early stages of the Mahayana Buddhist movement. Presumed to have been compiled in central Asia between the third and fifth century AD, this scripture boasts an overwhelming presence not only because of its tremendous length but also because it encompasses such a broad spectrum of material.

The *Kegon Sutra* freely explores – in the context of their links to number theory, theories of life, and cosmology – subjects that overlap with the main themes of psychology, such as where the mind came from, how the mind works, and where the mind goes in the end. The text, then, offers extremely instructive knowledge to scientists of the mind today who wish to discover a circle of truth linking psychology and material science. Carl Jung researched the structure of time together with physicist Wolfgang Pauli[3]. The issues they sought to resolve were directly related to themes pursued by the *Kegon Sutra*.

In this sense, there is a profound similarity and synchronicity between the investigations pursued by ancient Buddhist thinkers and those upon which we embark, and those of ancient thinkers can sometimes even be seen to have resolved the same issues with greater freedom and depth. That is why I have come to think that I would like to adopt a new perspective in seeking and discover a genuine connection between Buddhism and the sciences of the mind.

---

2 There are a number of modern, annotated translations of the *Flower Ornament Scripture* and its component chapters such as the 'Ten stages *Sutra*' and the '*Sutra* of the entry into the realm of reality'.

3 See Carl Jung and Wolfgang Pauli (1955), *The Interpretation of Nature and the Psyche*.

## Logos and Lemma

There is one serious problem that has stood in the way of the genuine dialogue that should take place between the sciences of the mind developed in Europe and the Buddhism developed in Asia. Even though both Buddhism and the sciences of the mind have each tried their best to establish themselves as "sciences", they differ fundamentally with respect to the essential logic on which they are based. Even when they reach the same solutions about the same subject, therefore, they end up arriving at different expressions that appear utterly dissimilar.

Science as developed in Europe is based on *logos*, while science in Asia where Buddhism was nurtured is run through with the logic of *lemma*. Although ancient Greek philosophers understood the difference between *logos* and *lemma* very well, they valued *logos* and believed that all of the sciences had to be based on it. The logic of *lemma*, on the other hand, was valued in lands east of Greece and spread greatly as it was incorporated into the Buddhist tradition. The difference between science based on *logos* and science based on *lemma* has generated fields of study that seem utterly alien to each other.[4]

Etymologically, I am told, the word *logos* meant "to gather before one's eyes", "to arrange what has been gathered", and "to articulate in words". You gather before you things that are manifest in the world, arrange and organize them, and then describe them using words. This is *logos* intellection. The reason the gathering of things and their arrangement in order has the same meaning as "to articulate in words" is that human language performs exactly the same function. By naming the things that are manifest in the world, human beings gather them in consciousness; by arranging and expressing these things in a linear fashion, they give order to their experiences. Ancient Greek philosophy, therefore, considered *logos* and language to share the same essence.

This led to the notion that "to articulate using the correct words" meant the same thing as "to think correctly", and the idea that through the workings of *logos* "things that were correctly thought were equivalent to the existence of objects that exist" (Parmenides). This is because that which is correctly expressed through language, maintaining the linear order that the deep structure of language follows, is equivalent to the object that exists. This Parmenidean understanding has been of crucial importance to European scholarship; the direction of all the fields of learning developed there from philosophy to Christian theology to modern science has been modeled as the correct performance of *logos* intellection.

---

4 See for example Tokuryu Yamauchi, (1974). *Rogosu to renma* [*Logos and Lemma*]. Tokyo, Iwanami Shoten.

It was Aristotle who formalized *logos* intellection and laid the foundation for "correct logic", according to which *logos* followed three laws; (1) the law of identity (whatever is, is); (2) the law of contradiction ('A is B' and 'A is not B' are mutually exclusive); and (3) the law of the excluded middle (all things can be divided). Aristotle's belief that correct linguistic expression can be achieved by following those three laws was subsequently widely recognized in Europe and remains the foundation of the philosophy of logic and scientific methodology today.

The Buddhist tradition, however, developed a logic quite different from the logic of *logos*: a logic based on *lemma*. *Lemma* has etymological meanings such as "to catch as a whole", "to grab", and "to grasp". It means to understand the whole not with language, but with intuition. Whereas *logos* understands phenomena in the world using the linear structure of language, *lemma* is an expression of the intellection of grasping reality directly without such transformative mediation. Ancient Greek philosophers knew that human intellection included a *lemma* function that differed from *logos*, but they believed that it was *logos* not *lemma* that would bring certain knowledge, and valued only *logos*-based logic.

What happened in Buddhism, however, was the exact opposite. Buddhism valued yoga-based meditation. Yoga brings the constant linguistic activity of the brain to a halt such that the function of *logos* retreats and the intuitive intellect of *lemma* rises to the fore. The reality captured with the intellect of *lemma* was recognized as *tathata* (the ultimate nature of all things). When Buddhism reached the stage of Mahayana Buddhism this subject was pursued even more deeply, leading to the establishment of the "logic of *lemma*".

It was Nagarjuna who created this logic of *lemma*. Nagarjuna tried to establish the logic of *lemma* by struggling against the logic of *logos*. He was, therefore, thoroughly critical of the three laws that support *logos*. The law of identity, the law of contradiction and the law of the excluded middle were all rejected, as Nagarjuna insisted that "true reality" would only be revealed to humankind when the three laws of *logos* were removed from its intellection.

Removing the law of identity leads to "nothing remains the same". Removing the law of contradiction leads to the understanding that "'A is B" and 'A is not B' are mutually compatible'". Removing the law of the excluded middle leads to "all things cannot be divided", and the understanding that "all things are connected (inseparable)". All things are interrelated in this *lemma* way. In Buddhism, this phase of existence revealed when the three laws of logos are removed is called "dependent origination" (*pratîtyasamutpâda*).

Nagarjuna's (2<sup>nd</sup> and 3<sup>rd</sup> centuries C. E.) main book,

*Mulamadhyama-kakarika* [*Fundamental Verses of the Middle Way*], begins with an homage by an anonymous later writer that reads:[5]

> He (Nagarjuna) preached dependent origination
> According to which there is
> Neither ceasing nor arising,
> Neither annihilation nor perpetuity,
> Neither coming nor going,
> Neither singularity nor plurality.

In fact, Nagarjuna thoroughly rejected the four aspects of world phenomena to which *logos* leads: (1) there is arising and ceasing; (2) there is annihilation (discontinuity) and perpetuity (continuity); (3) there is singularity (uniformity) and plurality (diversity); and

(4) there is coming and going. Instead, he reasoned that dependent origination described the true nature of reality characterized by the following four *lemma* understandings: (1) neither arising nor ceasing; (2) neither discontinuity nor continuity; (3) neither uniformity nor diversity; and (4) neither coming nor going.

Nagarjuna's claim seems extreme at first sight, but this is the view one reaches after having thoroughly pursued the logic of *lemma* that courses through Buddhism as a whole. On the basis of the logic of *lemma*, various systems of science have been built within Buddhism, which sought to demonstrate that a solid world could be created using only the logic of *lemma*, without the logic of *logos*. Various "*lemma*-based sciences" were created such as a *lemma*-based theory of the origin of the universe, a *lemma*-based theory of life, a *lemma*-based psychology, a *lemma*-based logic, and a *lemma*-based ethics. Such knowledge was woven into *sutras*.

The *lemma*-based sciences generated in this process were markedly different from the *logos*-based sciences that developed primarily in Europe. Perhaps this is only natural given that *lemma*-based science developed after clearing away the laws of identity, contradiction, and excluded middle that *logos*-based science requires. In modern European philosophy, Kant established a philosophy that cleared away the law of identity and Hegel created a philosophy that cleared away the law of contradiction. Perhaps unsurprisingly, a philosophy that clears away the law of the excluded middle has not yet been established. *Lemma*-based science born in the Buddhist tradition shows that rational perception is possible even without the three laws of *logos*. In fact, human intellection is able to approach reality only after the three laws of *logos* have been cleared away, so *lemma* can be seen as an extension of *logos*.

This paper's main topic, the *Kegon Sutra*, ranks even among such

---

5 Author's translation.

Mahayana Buddhist texts as a *sutra* of great size, depth, and degree of accomplishment. It was compiled with the intention both to reach for an elevated religious state and to establish Buddhism as a "science of the mind". Moreover, the entire work is unified under the logic of *lemma*. In this sense, the *Kegon Sutra* can be seen as an effort to create a "*lemma* science of the mind".

## Mind as *Dharma* realm

At the beginning of the *Kegon Sutra*, it is written that the *sutra* will explain what Buddha preached only a week after he attained enlightenment. It is said that the *sutra* presents how Buddha described his inner experience of enlightenment as it was before developing techniques for skillfully preaching to a large group by teaching to the target audience.

In this *sutra*, Buddha gives a detailed explanation, in the voice of Mahavairocana, of the whole realm of the mind that he traveled through and perceived fully. This realm of the mind is called *dharmadhatu* (the *Dharma* realm). The *Kegon Sutra* was intended to cover the entire *dharmadhatu*, describing, accurately through the use of *lemma* logic, its inner structure and methods for conveying the various truths about the movements that occur there. This was the first such intellectual adventure to be attempted within the Mahayana Buddhist movement. In this sense, the *Kegon Sutra* can be considered the greatest Buddhist scripture of all time.

Next I would like to pick out a few topics related to the *Kegon Sutra* that are important for modern sciences of the mind. In doing so, I would like to make good use of research findings made in China during the period of the Tang dynasty. To tell the truth, the *Kegon Sutra* is truly massive and one cannot help having the impression that its philosophical arguments are scattered throughout rather than ordered systematically. The mission of distilling the ideologically important points from the text and organizing them, then, was left to later generations. It was thinkers of the Chinese Huayan School as represented by Fazang (643-712) who responded to this need. I would like to shed light on the essence of Huayan *lemma* philosophy as found in Fazang's main work, *Huayan wujiao zhang* (*Treatise on the Five Teachings of Huayan*).

According to the *Kegon Sutra*, the *dharmadhatu* – the whole realm of the mind – has the following four kinds of inner structures.

1) The realm of all matter and phenomena, where individual things conflict and combine, and discriminating characteristics are created.

2) The realm of absolute principle, where the laws of discrimination conflict in their details but are equal and unified in their general direction.
3) The realm of non-obstruction between principle and phenomena, where principle and phenomena cross and merge without losing the nature of each, creating a world free of obstacles.
4) The realm of non-obstruction between phenomena, where not only principle and phenomena, but also phenomenon and phenomenon are united, and all is one and one is all, and everything is merged without losing the nature of each and the world is free of obstacles.
(Suetsuna 1957, author's translation)

The realm of all matter and phenomena is the mental world where each thing is separate and independent. This is the layer of mental function that we use as we go about our lives perceiving things in the world objectively. We consider this the realm of all matter and phenomena within "mind = *dharmadhatu*". In the realm of all matter and phenomena, each thing is separate and has its own name. The world that the mind sees in the realm of all matter and phenomena is based on discrimination.

When the realm of absolute principle starts functioning, differences in phenomena (discrimination) remain but one comes to understand that there is something equal in the depth of difference. This is related to what we usually call "abstraction ability". It is like being able to see a concrete building, recognize that it is made of crushed and hardened stone and sand, and understand that, as far as this goes, the artificial and the natural are equal and unified.

The realm of absolute principle is also at work in the minds of organisms other than humans. Organisms transform stimuli that come to their sense receptors into various electronic patterns and convey these to neurons. The neurons find matching patterns among the electronic patterns and categorize them as being of the same class. When organisms act following sensations that have been categorized as, say, "hot" or "cold", we can recognize the workings of the realm of absolute principle. To varying degrees, every organism experiences life and death using a biologic combining the realm of all matter and phenomena and the realm of absolute principle.

In the human mind, flexibility is increased and it can move freely between the realm of all matter and phenomena and the realm of absolute principle. This is nothing other than the function of the realm of non-obstruction between principle and phenomena within the *dharmadhatu*. The realm of non-obstruction between principle and phenomena is set near the surface of the human mind. Things separated in the realm of all matter and phenomena are understood as equal and unified in the realm of absolute principle, but in the realm of non-obstruction between principle and phenomena communication between the overlapping parts of different things or between different things also becomes possible.

The workings of the realm of non-obstruction between principle and phenomena makes it possible to do metaphorical operations that, in linguistic terms, generate new meanings by overlapping different words. Among human languages, only those used by modern humans (*Homo sapiens sapiens*) are believed to be capable of using metaphor. We could say, then, that only when the realm of non-obstruction between principle and phenomena had risen to the surface from where it was hiding in the depths of the *dharmadhatu* mind could an organism with a mind like ours first appear on the earth.

In the realm of non-obstruction between principle and phenomena, the transition from *logos* to *lemma* occurs smoothly. When "principle and phenomena cross and merge without losing the nature of each", phenomena that are separated from each other start communicating with each other through the function of absolute principle. To give an example, this situation is like front and back being connected even though the difference between front and back is maintained. In topology, this is expressed as a "Klein bottle", a precise visual expression of *lemma* intellection.

Retaining the layer of discrimination among phenomena as understood by *logos*, crossed with the lemmatic function of an absolute principle that sees them as equal and unified, leads to the realization of a world where principle and phenomena merge without losing the nature of each. Baudelaire called such a world "a forest of symbols" where all creation sympathizes with one another through the power of metaphor. Indeed, this is nothing but the realm of non-obstruction between principle and phenomena that poetry seeks to realize through the use of "logistic" language.

In Buddhism, however, this is not seen as human perfection. Rather, it is thought that humans can reach the Buddha state – human perfection – only when they are able to open up their own minds to the realm of non-obstruction between phenomena that lies beyond the realm of non-obstruction between principle and phenomena. The emphasis in the *Flower Ornament Scripture*, relative to the teachings of other Buddhist sects, on the mind as the perfection of the *dharmadhatu* has led to it being called *engyo*, meaning "perfect teaching".

The workings of *lemma* intellection reach their peak in the realm of non-obstruction between principle and phenomena. Phenomenon and phenomenon not only cross and merge with each other, phenomenon and phenomenon also *sosoku sonyu* directly. The first part of the word, *sosoku*, means the merging of two things as one without discrimination. The second part of the word, *sonyu*, means the state where forces go back and forth freely between the two. The state of *sosoku sonyu*, then, represents phenomena merging without losing their individuality as one force (one mind) flows through everything.

This state of *sosoku sonyu* appears only with *lemma* intellection. Moreover, because it occurs everywhere within the realm of non-obstruction between phenomena, a change even in a miniscule area spreads throughout the whole in an instant. This is truly a world of "all is one and one is all", one with no obstructions that appears as the whole and the parts merge.

In the *Flower Ornament Scripture*, this state is described using the metaphor of "Indra's net". That is, sacred gems placed at each eye of a net that hangs at the palace of Indra reflect each other such that each gem reflects all others. In the same way, in this realm everything is in a continuous state of *sosoku sonyu* and freely merges without losing the nature of each.

An expression of the human mind, the *dharmadhatu* demonstrates the aspect of the realm of non-obstruction between phenomena when it achieves its highest degree of freedom. The exact same (equal and unified) mind inhabits the mind of every living thing; this mind, as *dharmadhatu*, contains the realm of non-obstruction between phenomena in its innermost part. Only humans, however, are capable of being aware of this, and have the freedom to polish their minds and enter into the depths of the realm of non-obstruction between phenomena. By setting the realm of non-obstruction between principle and phenomena near the surface of mental function, only humans, that is, modern humans with the human mind we know, are capable of opening up the realm of non-obstruction between phenomena in their minds. This is the fundamental teaching of the *Kegon Sutra*.

## Freudian Unconsciousness viewed from the *Kegon Sutra*

The ideas regarding the nature of mind in the *Kegon Sutra* resonate marvelously with sciences of the mind created in modern Europe such as psychology and psychoanalysis. The psychoanalysis of Freud and Jung, in particular, encompassed similar ideas to the Buddhist "*lemma* science of the mind" in that they believed the mechanical application of *logos* rules was not only futile but harmful, and that lemmatic mental functions should be valued.

Both Freud and Jung developed the concept of the unconscious, something that acts not logostically but lemmatically. Freud, for example, considered mental functions to be composed of two different mechanisms: a primary process and a secondary process. Among these two, the secondary process is the function of reason that handles ordinary reasoning. It is based on *logos* intellection, and is the ability to separate things and express them in language in accordance with proper syntax.

The primary process that acts *beneath* it, however, creates images and meanings through direct material processes such as compressing psychic energy or displacing it by moving it to different places. Here, forces whose substance is unclear flow between the words that represent things. Expressions of secondary process, therefore, become transformed and distorted strangely through the influence of the primary process.

From here, Lacan thought that the unconsciousness was structured like a language, and that what Freud called primary process corresponded to the metaphor and metonymy of linguistics. He expressed this idea using topology and arrived at an unconscious with a "Klein bottle" structure, its front and back merged as one.

What Freud called the unconscious shows a surprising similarity with one aspect of the mind as *dhatu* that was distilled from the *Kegon Sutra*: the realm of non-obstruction between principle and phenomena. If you replace "principle" with "psychic energy", and "phenomena" with "words", the unconscious expressing itself through the compression and displacement of psychic energy corresponds to the lemmatic mental function in the realm of non-obstruction between principle and phenomena, one layer of the mind as *dharmadhatu*. It is not, however, called the unconscious in Eastern thinking, including the *Kegon Sutra*.

In Eastern thinking, including the *Kegon Sutra*, there is no discourse on conflict between the conscious and unconscious. Every mental function, including what Freud called the unconscious, is a function of "principle" and, I might venture to say, the conscious. However, the domains where the realm of non-obstruction between principle and phenomena and the realm of non-obstruction between phenomena are centered on *lemma* mental functions, differ from *logos*, and so do not follow the reason of *logos* that drives surface consciousness.

In this way, a vast realm of the Freudian unconscious is subsumed into the realm of non-obstruction between principle and phenomena within the *dharmadhatu*. As Freud actually claimed, the conscious is nothing more than the tip of the iceberg breaking the surface of the human mind. What appears above the surface is the tip of the iceberg that operates under the mental function of *logos*. The essence of the mind of humans as *Homo sapiens* is found in the limitless expanse of the realm of non-obstruction between principle and phenomena and can be seen as a complex body with a structure analogous to that of a "Klein bottle".

## Kegon Sutra and Jung

Reflected in the mirror of the *Kegon Sutra* in this way, we can correctly understand the uniqueness and originality, within the context of European thinking, of the science of the mind created by Jung. After developing psychoanalysis in collaboration with Freud, he later made a decisive break with Freud and went on to create his own science of the mind. As a result, Jung stepped into a realm that Freud would never have been able to approach. I think it was then that Jung discovered the realm of non-obstruction between phenomena that lies beyond the realm of non-obstruction between principle and phenomena, and embarked on its study.

In fact, Jung researched Eastern religious texts such as *The Tibetan Book of the Dead*, *The Secret of the Golden Flower*, and the Gnostic scriptures with great interest. He also travelled to study and conduct fieldwork on Native American religions. What we must not forget here is that these texts and rituals in which Jung was interested assume a "sacred" character and often depart considerably from everyday norms.

Whether Native American or Tibetan, human society is based on linguistic communication so it operates through the agency of the realm of non-obstruction between principle and phenomena as described in the *Flower Ornament Scripture*. What shamans, ascetic monks, and mystics have sought to do in these societies, however, is to transcend societal norms and dive into the hidden layers at the depths of the human mind. By traversing the whole of the human mind in a cross-sectional way, they have sought to attain the ultimate freedom of mind, freedom from control by anything but themselves.

This greatly distinguished Jung's studies from those of Freud and Lacan. All these founders of the sciences of the mind had a deep interest in the lemmatic intellection that is continually active in the depths of the mind, but whereas Freud and Lacan only went so far as to pursue the realm of non-obstruction between principle and phenomena, Jung stepped into the realm of non-obstruction between phenomena.

This can be confirmed from a variety of aspects. Here, let us look at one: the structure of time. The *Kegon Sutra* proposed the realm of non-obstruction between phenomena as a perfect, peaceful mental universe where everything is connected through dependent origination and merges without loss of individuality as one force flows through everything. There, as described in the following passage from Fazang's text, the structure of time appears different than how it is experienced in the realm of absolute principle and the realm of non-obstruction between principle and phenomena.

Time appears to be both synchronous and distinct. That is, time and existence are not separate from each other. The ten worlds are: the three worlds of the past, future, and present, each of which has a past, future, and present, leading to nine worlds. Moreover, these nine worlds adapt to and enter one other, creating one panoptic expression. This panoptic expression and its individual expressions together make up the ten worlds. These ten worlds retain their individuality, simultaneously revealing themselves and making dependent origination possible, such that they are able to adapt to and enter into one another. And so, in the *Kegon Sutra* it is said: put a long *kalpa* [a measure of time in Buddhist cosmology, said to be very long] into a short *kalpa*, or a short *kalpa* into a long *kalpa*, or consider one thousand and one hundred great *kalpa* to be one *ksana* [another measure of time in Buddhist cosmology, this one very short], and one *ksana* as one hundred *kalpa*, or put past *kalpa* into future *kalpa* and put future *kalpa* into past *kalpa*'. In this way (in the realm of non-obstruction between phenomena), time comes into existence through mutual adaption and merging with each other without any obstruction'.

(Fazang op.cit., p. 120, author's translation)

In the realm of non-obstruction between phenomena, where all phenomena and things merge without loss of individuality as one force flows through everything, time does not flow linearly. Naturally, then, one cannot determine causal associations among phenomena. One can only apply the doctrine of causality that has functioned as the basis of modern science as far as the realm of non-obstruction between principle and phenomena, but not as far as the realm of non-obstruction between phenomena. In the *Kegon Sutra,* these ideas are derived through a thorough deduction of yoga experience and *lemma* logic. A *lemma*-based logic has the potential to profoundly expand the concept of time and space as based on *logos* logic.

In this way, Jung's concept of synchronicity can be seen anew within the idea of a *lemma*-based science. Doing so, Jung's ideas – which seem terribly isolated in the modern world – can instead be seen as important ideas that stand on the side of the future of science. A *lemma*-based science is neither a pipe dream nor a delusion, but achievable human intellectual potential. When realized, the *lemma*-based science will itself surely become aware of having merged with the *Kegon Sutra* of ancient times without loss of individuality as one force flows through everything.

## References:

Fazang. (7th century C.E.). *Huayan wujiao zhang* [*Treatise on the Five Teachings of Huayan*], trans. Kiyotaka Kimura, 1989. Tokyo: Chuo Koronsha.

Suetsuna, J. (1957). *Kegonkyo no Sekai* [*The World of the Flower Ornament Scripture*]. Tokyo: Shunjusha

# Panel

# The Emergence of the Ecological Mind in Hua-Yen/Kegon Buddhism and Jungian Psychology

*Harald Atmanspacher*
(Collegium Helveticum, ETH and University Zurich)

Nakazawa's comparison of Buddhism and the traditional approaches to the science of the mind is based on different types of logic, which are well known in mathematical (formal) approaches to logic. Aristotelian logic is there called Boolean logic. Its truth values are limited to true and false, nothing in between is possible. Boolean logic has dominated almost all of psychology over many decades.

But there are non-Boolean alternatives, which permit more than the two truth values of Boolean logic and thus give up on the law of the excluded middle. This approach has been explicitly and successfully used in quantum theory for almost a century now, and it gave rise to exactly the feature that Nakazawa highlights: wholeness. In this sense, quantum physics became a top-down theory in which decomposition is prior to the bottom-up compositional principle that dominates classical physics. This is algebraically mirrored by the difference between non-commutative and commutative operations.

In recent decades, a number of psychologists, cognitive scientists, and philosophers of mind began to realize that this decompositional picture is also highly relevant for mental functions; for details and further references see Busemeyer and Bruza (2012), Wendt (2015). If psychoanalysis (in particular the Jungian brand) with its holistic features had been better recognized in academic psychology, this could have been discovered much earlier.

Vice versa, the new insight that holistic features subsist even in conscious processing might be a key to integrate Jungian psychology, which has held on to holistic reasoning for a long time, into mainstream academic studies of consciousness. A particularly interesting area, also indicated by Nakazawa, is the problem of the difference between sequential and non-sequential time (Primas 2017), which has been raised by Bergson, James, Husserl, Whitehead in philosophy, and is covered by the concept of temporal nonlocality in recent work in physics and cognitive science (Atmanspacher and Filk 2010).

Needless to say, all this also emphasizes the decompositional move in dual-aspect monism, where the emergence of mind and matter, of the mental and the physical, is seen as a symmetry breakdown of an underlying (holistic) reality without the mind-matter split (Atmanspacher 2017).

Joe Cambray, in his ecological approach, stresses the metaphor of the rhizome in its relation to the collective unconscious of analytical psychology. Such a relation was expressed by Jung himself at a few passages in his work. Remarkably, the rhizome also plays a significant role in the philosophy of Deleuze, who uses it to describe an organization of concepts that transcends hierarchical and/or regular structures (very much like in mathematical network theory).

Recently, there has been some discussion on similarities and differences between Jung's and Deleuze's ideas about holism (Kerslake 2007). While Jung is mostly interpreted to refer to a *transcendent* notion of wholeness (which is regarded empirically and experientially inaccessible), Deleuze argues in favor of an *immanent* notion of wholeness that is or can be subject to concrete experience, even though this would not be conceptual or discursive. There are possibilities of bridging the gap between these two options.

On the surface, a rhizomatic structure has distinct nodes and links, so it escapes a radical version of wholeness in the sense of ultimate undividedness. However, one may arrive at a more subtle picture by studying subsets of a rhizome ("plateaus" in Deleuze's parlance) in relation to "levels" of archetypes, from fairly refined ones to very elementary ones. Then, Jung's *unus mundus* would be the limiting case of an archetypal level without distinctions: the "unspeakable" − but maybe "experiencable" nevertheless?

Addressing an immanent reality without distinctions offers another perspective on ecology, which Naess (1977) proposed in his article "Spinoza and ecology" that has been pivotal for the "deep ecology" movement. I think it can be cogently argued that, if everything derives from such a reality at base level, there is ultimate interdependence between all minds and bodies, and thus ultimate responsibility as well

## References

Atmanspacher, H. (2017). Contextual emergence in decompositional dual-aspect monism. Mind and Matter 15(1), 111-129.

Atmanspacher, H., and Filk, T. (2010). A proposed test of temporal nonlocality in bistable perception. Journal of Mathematical Psychology 54(3), 314-321.

Busemeyer, J., and Bruza, P. (2012). Quantum Models of Cognition and Decision. Cambridge University Press, Cambridge.

Kerslake, C. (2007). Deleuze and the Unconscious. Continuum Press, London.

Naess, A. (1977). Spinoza and Ecology. Philosophia 7(1), 45-54.

Primas (2017). Knowledge and Time. Springer, Berlin..

Wendt, A. (2015). Quantum Mind and Social Science. Cambridge University Press, Cambridge.

# Joe Cambray
## (USA, NESJA)

## Rhizomes in Jungian Psychology

Depth psychology's affinity with the unseen aspects of ecological systems, its nascent ecologizing, is reflected in a well-known quote from *MDR*:

> Life has always seemed to me like a plant that lives on its rhizome. Its true life is invisible, hidden in the rhizome. The part that appears above ground lasts only a single summer. Then it withers away – an ephemeral apparition. When we think of the unending growth and decay of life and civilizations, we cannot escape the impression of absolute nullity. Yet I have never lost a sense of something that lives and endures underneath the eternal flux. What we see is the blossom, which passes. The rhizome remains.
>
> (Jung 1961, p. 4)

There is a similar quote in the article on the Visions of Zosimos:

> The psychology of the unconscious has to reckon with long periods of time...for it is concerned less with the ephemeral personality than with age-old processes, compared with which the individual is no more than the passing blossom and fruit of the rhizome underground.
>
> (Jung 1937, para. 120)

Here the emphasis on the psychology of the unconscious begins to offer a model for the collective unconscious; that it is structured similar to a rhizome.

A rhizome is "a somewhat elongate usually horizontal subterranean plant stem that is often thickened by deposits of reserve food material, produces shoots above and roots below, and is distinguished from a true root in possessing buds, nodes, and usually scalelike leaves" (www.merriam-webster.com/dictionary/rhizome, 24 September 2016). Some common, well known examples are: bamboo, ginseng, aspen trees, ginger, lotus, and so on. In the west a famous medieval rhizomatic plant that captured the folkloristic imagination was the mandrake. Mandrakes contain hallucinogenic alkaloids and the roots have bifurcations, or divisions, which can cause them to resemble human figures. According to legend, when the root is dug up it screams and kills all who hear it. Literature of the period includes complex directions for harvesting a mandrake root in relative safety, e.g., using dogs tied by their tails to the plant to pull them up, while the owners remained out of earshot (bestiary.ca/beasts/beast1098. htm, 24 September 24, 2016). The symbolism suggests that bringing the uncanny rhizomatic network system into awareness was overwhelming to consciousness of the time.

The notion of the rhizome as a botanical entity goes back to the 19th century, derived from the Greek term ριζα translated as root. The dense underground network of a rhizome can be quite extensive, with many smaller roots in a network converging in spots to produce the nodes which are associated with the above ground, observable growth. Further, certain rhizomes tend to also interact with numerous other root systems in their vicinity forming vast numbers of connections, creating an ecological system, as we shall see.

A contemporary psychological application derived from Jung's use of this simile is the study of the complex networks of unconscious connections which extend and support various individual representations above ground, e.g., ordinary conscious perceptions of self emerge from a non-local psyche. The psyche analogized as a highly entwined, non-local network, is mostly invisible at the surface level of consciousness, but profoundly distributed beneath, and by implication, is again embedded in a larger ecological system. Ancillary to this view, seeming boundaries between mind, body and world become much more fluid. Psyche's networks conjoin us all in cultural and the natural worlds.

A consequence of such interconnectedness is that we can begin to recognize the possibility of grasping truths about nature through empathy and intuition. The sharp distinctions between subjective and objective aspects of phenomena no longer hold sway at this level, as the network transcends the apparent division of inner and outer. Similarly, the usual parsing of the world by ego consciousness, a convenient and even necessary fiction, can be appreciated as an isolated focus on what has emerged from the rhizomatic world, while secretly, invisibly and even hermetically being tethered to it.

The radical interconnectedness of mind and nature is something shared by various religions, especially in Asia (Buddhism and Taoism being obvious examples). In the western scientific traditions this view first emerged with the German Romantics, who were not only literary people but most had strong scientific educations of their day. Previously I've detailed a few examples relevant for depth psychology, in particular Alexander von Humboldt and Ernst Haeckel, who each had a significant influence on Jung (Cambray 2014; 2015a). Haeckel coined our term 'ecology', from the Greek οικοσ – home, meaning where we live; the organism in its environment. Parenthetically I would also note that Jung's non-linear writing style can be understood as a rhizomatic form of expression, engendering a complex network. Similarly individuation as a process of psychological maturation can be seen to go by rhizomatic pathways, its richness emerging from the vast interconnected world it opens into.

The association of individuation with rhizomatic conceptualization was made explicit in Jung's essay on "The spirit Mercurius":

> The alchemists described their four elements as radices, corresponding to the Empedoclean rhizomata, and in them they saw the constituents of the most significant and central symbol of alchemy, the lapis philosophorum, which represents the goal of the individuation process.
>
> (Jung 1942, para. 242)

As the first of the pre-Socratics to articulate the four element (earth, air, water and fire) theory, Empedocles identified these "elements" as rhizomata in describing the composition and transformation of the phenomenal world. Philosopher David Macauley follows the cosmological threads from Empedocles' four rhizomata to Aristotle's reading of them as $\alpha\rho\chi\alpha\iota$, noting "The elements too are gods (Aristotle 333b20)" (Macauley 2005, p. 284-285). For Empedocles the rhizomata were considered uncreated and eternal and in a holistic manner comprise the totality of his cosmic sphere universe. Psychologically these ideas had powerful resonance with Jung's theory of archetypes which compose the universe of the psyche.

While philosopher Gilles Deleuze openly acknowledged his inspiration from Jung for using the psychological simile of the rhizome (see Henderson 2014, p. 113 and reference therein), he disagrees with the implications of the hierarchical, immutable nature of this vision. Macauley, for example, explores how Deleuze rejected hierarchical arborescent structures in favor of a strictly rhizomatic view:

> 'We're tired of trees. We should stop believing in trees, roots and radicles', they [Deleuze and Guttari] write. 'They've made us suffer too much'. In their view, we live in an arborescent culture – from biology to linguistics, from anatomy to theology and all of philosophy – which is founded on tree and root metaphors.... 'Nothing is beautiful or loving or political aside from underground stems and aerial roots, adventitious growths and rhizomes' (Deleuze 1987: 15).... In contrast to roots and trees, rhizomes are anti-genealogical, nonhierarchical, acentered, nonsignifying multiplicities that are made of 'plateaus' which are connected to other multiplicities.... Unlike Empedocles' rhizomata, they are not eternal or divine.
>
> (Macauley 2005, p. 306)

This polemical rejection, while one sided, does shift the discourse from superordinate structures to the complex networks which operate below the surface of phenomena, supporting as well as often bringing them into existence. By following this reorientation of consciousness, we may need to reconsider our understanding of symbolism.

## Ecosystems, classical symbolism, and beyond – complexity of real world

Ecology professor Suzanne Simard has for the past several decades been studying the lives of forests in the Canadian northwest. Her work on Douglas fir trees has been popularized and points to a convergence of the symbolic and the ecological (Frazier 2015). Seeking to understand how fir seedlings survive during their growth to reach the forest canopy to harvest adequate sunlight for the photosynthetic process they survive upon, Simard followed a hunch. She placed an air tight plastic bag on a large, adult fir tree nearby some seedlings. She introduced some $^{14}C$ labelled $CO_2$ into the bag. Over the course of the next few days she followed the absorption of the labelled $CO_2$ into the tree, as it was incorporated into sugars made through photosynthetic pathways. These labelled sugars were then seen to be transported through interlocking root systems to the seedlings. At the risk of anthropomorphizing, we can see here, what seems a maternal care-taking of youthful offspring. This is consistent with various mythic/symbolic readings of certain kinds of trees. If space permitted I would give other counter-examples from ecological studies.

Simard has gone on to do some even more remarkable work in her study of mycorrhizal networks: fungal rhizomatic systems that are not only extensively non-local but can grow to enormous dimensions: one was discovered in the western US which constitutes the largest known organism on earth, see www.scientificamerican.com/article/strange-but-true-largest-organism-is-fungus/. It is reported to occupy 2,384 acres (about 10 square kilometers); its longevity is also impressive, between 2,400 and 8,650 years old!

However, what is most remarkable is not only their capacity to form such massive organisms, but the ways these humble fungi interact with the trees in their vicinity. Douglas fir regularly "makes and delivers food to the fungus; the fungus, in turn, dramatically increases the plant's water and mineral absorptive powers via its vast network of filaments. They provide far more surface area for absorption than the meager supply of short root hairs the tree could grow alone" (Frazier ibid.). Furthermore, these networks operate to transport nutrients for storage/distribution, e.g., dying trees will download their nutrients into these mycorrhizal networks which have infiltrated tree roots without injuring them, and will then move these nutrients to other members of the network, at times even to other species of trees. Similarly the network differentially distributes phytohormones used in defense/warning signals, e.g., against herbivores such as insects (beetles, caterpillars, etc.).

The mycorrhizal networks serve as a conduit and communication pathway between trees of varying species, allowing cooperative coordination previously undetected between the components of the network. From an ecological perspective these multi-organism systems have a sophisticated communication and distribution network that causes some ecologists to speak about learning *How Forests Think* (Kohn 2013).

More recently, Simard has been investigating the role of mycorrhizas in stabilizing the forest soils in the face of climate change and how their network have scale-free topologies and act as fundamental agents of self-organization in the complex adaptive systems (CAS) of forest ecosystems (e.g., Simard and Austin 2010; Simard, et al. 2012).

From these detailed scientific explorations on plants, we have hints of how profoundly complex the psyche must be – if fungi and trees have such a rich communal interconnected life, what then of sapient beings with their cortices of neural nets engaging with one another and their worlds. Should we not be learning from the ground up about the way biological intelligence has evolved methods of communication that foster cooperative, integrated modes of engaging with others?

## From Rhizome to Cosmos and the Vision of Hua Yen/Kegon Buddhism

Cosmologists have established that much of the "stuff" of the universe is made of dark matter, a mysterious, unknown and invisible substance that can't be directly detected by any known means. Dark matter does not interact with light as other forms of matter do, its existence is inferred solely by the gravitational pull it exerts on surrounding objects. This dark matter is envisioned as existing in a vast network of filaments throughout the universe, pulling luminous galaxies into an interconnected web of clusters, interspersed with seemingly empty voids containing an even more mysterious force of repulsion, the opposite of gravity, dark energy. While this can be detected only at the largest scales of observation (see, e.g., www.sciencedaily.com/releases/2015/12/151202132934.htm), the morphological parallel to rhizomes is striking. It is as if the rhizomatic structure has truth in extraordinarily diverse dimensions. Further, the realm of the visible is minuscule in comparison to what is out there: ordinary matter comprises less than 5% of our universe; dark matter about 24%; and dark energy more than 70% – as if the universe were a galactic rhizome, most in the dark "below ground" as it were.

Scientific truth seeking has brought us beyond the previous bounds of our commonsensical imaginings. The fundamental picture of the type of universe we live in is being radically re-envisioned as the invisible, ungraspable aspects of reality weigh in, and stagger us with their bulk. We are brought to visions of and about nature which reflect back our unknown and at times unacknowledged need for radical new imaginings of our world, ones that we cannot so easily bind to our current understanding, but reintroduce us to awe and confusion. In this sense there are clear parallels with the jolt that depth psychology brought to 19th century sensibilities.

This tricksterish side of the new "dark" explorations began with our contemporary scientific creation myth, the "Big Bang". In logically following through the implications of this originary event, we now become enshrouded again at the edges of our reality in a Hades-like realm of dark invisibles that ultimately hold the fate of our world – whether it ultimately disappears into nothingness, or collapses back in on itself, disappearing to possibly re-emerge phoenix-like in another "Big Bang", or being just one of many universes in a "multiverse".

Re-sizing the imagination of the cosmos can be understood psychologically as a kind of modern alchemy of the world. Does this require a new imagining of the *Anima Mundi* which has been entrapped in the concrete, literal realm of ordinary matter? The newly discovered realm of darkness forces attention onto invisible, mysterious presences that give form to our universe.

Compare a small portion of the large scale structure of the cosmos with the image of a thin section of mammalian cortices (see www.sciencenews.org/article/'-cosmic-web'-weaves-tale-universe's-architecture?mode=archive&context=191406 for a striking example). Neuronal fibres form interconnected networks which serve as the biological foundations of mind and presumably of aspects of the psyche. When examined, these images all have distinctly rhizomatic qualities in their tangled networks. The remarkable similarity in morphology of root systems with brain neurology, an important part of the somatic basis of mind, with the structure of the universe may be wholly coincidental, but the very nature of these parallels requires us at least to re-imagine and entertain possible significances (such as fractal processes in complex systems generating similar emergent forms, even though at vastly different scales). There may be meaning in these similarities even if the objects are not in themselves overtly, causally linked. The coincidence would in this sense be more synchronistic, with meaning supplied by human imagination, which might be on the cusp of realizing its objective aspects through such imagery. We are moving, at least in imagination, from a clockwork, mechanistic universe to one that much more closely resembles sets of networks capable of engendering "intelligence" or mind in many forms that are profoundly non-traditional to western scientific thought.

The new science of the "dark" also offers a potentially fruitful area for bridge building between science and some aspects of religious phenomena. For example, a detailed comparison of dark energy with the Buddhist conceptions of "nothingness" or "emptiness", as discussed in Hua Yen (Chinese) or Kegon (Japanese) schools of Buddhism. Hua Yen doctrine became the theoretical foundation for the practice of Ch'an Buddhism, better known in the west by its Japanese name, "Zen". Hua Yen was transmitted from China to Japan in the 8th century, where it was adapted and integrated into Japanese Buddhism, becoming known as Kegon (Odin 1982, pp. 11-13). The essential feature for our present purpose is the interdependent, co-origination of all aspects of reality. As has been recognized for more than 40 years, this portrayal of reality is profoundly ecological in its vision of the network of interdependence of all being. Since there is no independent origination of anything, the vision is of emergence out of a fecund nothingness, a seeming paradox that sounds curiously like some discussions of the singularity envisioned as the point of origin in modern cosmology; I have discussed this in several recent publications (Cambray 2015b; 2017).

## Conclusion

Cosmology has now identified a pervasive force permeating the entire universe, previously unrecognized, until mapping the sectors of darkness revealed regions of voidness and their evolution in time. The results point to a new, unknown force, "Dark Energy", generating increasing regions of relative "no-thing-ness" and producing the intricate patterns of the Cosmic Web.

Even though the details may reveal differences with the insights of Hua Yen cosmology, we are left to ponder the remarkable capacity of the meditative methods of this school to create such a far reaching vision and more generally how the nature of mind increasingly seems to reflect the universe in which it emerged.

## References

Cambray, J. (2014). *The Red Book*: Entrances and Exits. *The Red Book: Reflections on C.G. Jung's Liber Novus*, ed. T. Kirsch and G. Hogenson, New York & London: Routledge.

— (2015a). Jung, science, German Romanticism: a contemporary perspective. *Jung in the Academy and Beyond: The Fordham Lectures 100 Years Later*, eds. Mark E. Mattson, Frederick J. Wertz, Harry Fogarty, Margaret Klenck, and Beverley Zabriskie. New Orleans: Spring Journal Books.

— (2015b). L'Oscurita nell'immaginazione scientifica contemporanea e le sue implicazioni. *Enkelados: Rivista Mediterranea di Psicologia Analitica*. III (3), 30-46.

— (2017). Darkness in the Contemporary Scientific Imagination and Its Implications', in *The International Journal of Transpersonal Studies,* in press.

Frazier, Jennifer. (2015). 'Dying trees can send food to neighbors of different species', in *Scientific American,* May 9; blogs.scientificamerican.com/artful-amoeba/dying-trees-can-send-food-to-neighbors-of-different-species/

Henderson, D. (2014). *Apophatic Elements in the Theory and Practice of Psychoanalysis: Pseudo-Dionysius and C.G. Jung.* New York & London: Routledge.

Jung, C.G. (1961). *Memories, Dreams, Reflections.* New York: Vintage Books.

— (1937). The visions of Zosimos. *Alchemical Studies. CW* 13.

— (1942). The Spirit Mercurius. *Alchemical Studies. CW* 13

Kohn, E. (2013). *How Forests Think:Towards an Anthropology Beyond the Human.* Berkeley, Los Angeles, London: University of California Press.

Macauley, D. (2005). The flowering of environmental roots and the four elements in presocratic philosophy: from Empedocles to Deleuze and Guattari. *World Views Environment Culture Religion,* 9(3): 281-314. DOI: 10.1163/156853505774841687

Odin, S. (1982). *Process Metaphysics and Hua-Yen Buddhism: A Critical Study of Cumulative Penetration vs. Interpretation.* Albany, New York: SUNY Press.

Simard, S. & Austin, M. (2010). The role of mycorrhizas in forest soil stability with climate change, climate change and variability.

Suzanne Simard (ed.), in Tech, DOI: 10.5772/9813. Available from: www.intechopen.com/books/climate-change-and-variability/the-role-of-mycorrhizas-in-forest-soil-stability-with-climate-change.

Simard, S. W., Beiler, K. J., Bingham, M. A., Deslippe, J. R., Philip, L. J., Teste, F. P. (2012). Mycorrhizal networks: mechanisms, ecology and modeling. *Fungal Biology Reviews,* 26, 39-60.

\* \* \*

## Commentary on Shin'ichi Nakazawa's paper "A Lemma Science of Mind: The Potential of the Kegon (Flower Ornament) Sutra"

Shin'ichi Nakazawa's lucid condensation of key points of the Kegon Sutra for comparison and discussion with depth psychology serves as an excellent opening for new directions in East/West dialogues on the nature of mind and reality. In the midst of a paradigm shift in western science towards formulations couched in terms of complexity, the reintroduction of a more rigorous form of holism, offers a link to an intuitive methodology aimed at grasping the nature of the "whole" which Dr. Nakazawa has shown is located at the heart of the yogic-Buddhist meditative traditions. One approach to expanding the dialogue may be to relativize foreground/background foci of attention of each side (East/West, Lemma/Logos) acknowledging their complementarity which becomes evident when neither is privileged as the sole arbiter of truth.

In the suggested process of "clearing away" the ossified elements in the laws of traditional western logos-oriented philosophy, we've been encouraged to recognize that a few bridges have already been constructed. Thus, the challenge of clearing away the rigidities in the Aristotelian law of contradiction was achieved in part by Hegel. This was significantly expanded by Jung's vision of the reality of the psyche allowing resolution of psychological polarities through manifestation of the transcendent function. The problem of clearing away the excluded middle, has, as stated, not yet fully established, however, advances in ecological understanding of the vast and profound levels of interconnectedness within environments, such as forests, are pointing to structures and process previously unrecognized. Applied to science of mind, an ecology of the psyche may well lead to clearing away, and making porous, the constructed barriers between subjective and objective aspects of phenomena and experience.

It is in its fourth realm, that of non-obstruction between phenomena, where the Flower Ornament/Garland Sutra offers its deepest and most radical vision of reality. In the Kegon version of this sutra the notion of "sosoku sonyu" is key as Dr. Nakazawa discussed. There is another translation of this term that I have found, which presents it as the "mutuality of being and non-being" (clearly a close analog to Dr. Nakazawa's reading). The utility of this translation is that it points towards the cosmogonic myth of the sutra: the interdependent co-origination of the entire world out of a fruitful "no-thing-ness." This bears interesting similarities with the contemporary western scientific creation myth, the big-bang. Further, the fields which emerge out of the proposed singularity between being and non-being, have been shown to allow simultaneous expression, without temporal or spatial constraints, in the phenomena of entanglement at the microphysical level. In depth psychology this realm has been approached through Jung's synchronicity hypothesis together with the Pauli-Jung conjecture as articulated by Harald Atmanspacher. Starting with a theoretical base in complexity theory allowing for manifestations of emergence in self-organizing systems, the empirical observations of synchronistic phenomena can be grasped in a manner indicative of a cosmology with features in accord with this fourth realm of Kegon Buddhism.

*Tuesday, 30 August 2017*

# Supervising Away From Home:
# Clinical, Cultural and Professional Challenges

*Henry Abramovitch*
(Jerusalem, IIJP)

*Jan Wiener*
(London, SAP)

*Jan*: We want to begin our session with an active imagination.

*Henry*: Imagine that you have been invited to a strange country to meet a group of people to whom you must explain the essence of analytical psychology. You set off on this journey...what will happen?

*Jan:* The theme of our paper is Supervising Away From Home. Henry, will you begin and say something about what home is for you?

*Henry:* Home is both a place and a cluster of feelings about that place. It provides a natural container for the Self. When I am feeling most grounded and most at peace, then I am home. The Japanese kanji for home is said to represent a roof over a pig, since nothing is as at home as a pig in its sty.
Home holds together archetypes of both Mother and Father: the security and nest-warmth of the maternal, and boundary separating inner from outer of the paternal; strong walls around the warm hearth. The tension between these masculine and feminine aspects of home is expressed in a poem by Robert Frost. A farmer says to his wife:

> It all depends on what you mean by home.
> Home is the place where, when you have to go there,
> They have to take you in.

But his wife counters that home is:

> Something you somehow haven't had to deserve.
> (Frost [1914] 2002, pp. 164-5).

The archetypal voyage from and to home can be seen in the symbolism of home plate in baseball. Home plate is where we start from and where we seek to return, around the bases of the life cycle to complete our archetypal journey. A haiku by Basho (1976, p. 77), expresses the bonding between origin and homecoming:

> Coming home at last
> At the end of the year,
> I wept to find
> My old umbilical cord.

Jan, what are your associations to "home"?

*Jan:* I think of a heartland where like you, there are archetypal predispositions for feeling safe in an atmosphere of familiarity; the smells are recognizable; there is a shared cultural understanding even in a multi-ethnic atmosphere. Britain is an island and provides a larger container for me around my own experiences of home, especially since my parents were offered refuge there during the 2nd World War. I like the German author and poet, Christian Morgenstern's ([1891], 1918, Chapter 14) idea that, *home is not where you live, but where they understand you.* His sentiments seem similar to your Robert Frost quotation.

The SAP in London has been my professional home – where I did my training, lived in a close (and sometime closed!) analytic community with mostly shared values that have been gradually internalized. I think I am understood there. With Homer's Odyssey in mind and the idea of a challenging journey, I am drawn to Renos Papadopoulos's (2002, p.13) idea that home is made up of two opposites, a longing for the earth, the ground, the land – things which are tangible – but also with less tangible forms, what Papadopoulos calls "the smoke" and what I call "the smells".

Some of my colleagues choose to keep working close to home, in agreement with Jane Austen ([1815], 2014, p. 148) that, "There is nothing like staying at home for real comfort".

For me, the urge to leave home, to explore beyond the familiar, however discomforting, has always been strong; an impetus for adventure and for the challenges of a pioneer, treading new paths and preparing the stony ground for those who may follow. I agree with you that associations to the idea of home are paradoxical; we yearn for it with nostalgia when we are away, but for some of us – and I suspect this is true for us both – the new experiences we have when we leave home, in this case to supervise, can bring rewarding encounters that can be life-changing.

Two books have had a significant influence on me in preparation for this dialogue. Surprisingly, neither are analytic texts. Recently, I read Colm Toibin's (2009) book, *Brooklyn*. The protagonist, Eilis, expresses vividly her experiences of leaving her Irish home and her intense, often physical experiences of homesickness, real fear or dread, or worse, towards the thought that I am going to lose this world forever... that the rest of my life would be a struggle with the unfamiliar (Toibin 2009, p. 29-30).

Homesickness for Eilis went hand in hand with feeling alone. She settled, found a boyfriend, but then returned home when her sister died. Tony, her boyfriend, remarks: "if you go back, you won't come back" (p. 196). This resonates with the tensions when supervising abroad between our homesickness as visiting supervisors and the often unspoken anxieties of those we supervise, "can we be sure YOU will return?" The implications for the kinds of attachments supervisees make to us raise questions for me about our models of work as "shuttle" supervisors.

My second text is William Fiennes' (2002, p. 204) beautiful book, *The Snow Geese*. He writes about managing homesickness when in the presence of homing birds in the Arctic tundra:

> Somehow I had to turn my nostalgia inside out, so that my love for the house, for the sense of belonging ... instilled ... a desire to find that sense of... security and happiness in some other place.

Our conversation about the meaning of home and homesickness provides a central framework for the emotional impact of supervising abroad, working, in what Catherine Crowther and I (2002, p. 286) call "an interactive field of strangeness" or what Renos Papadopoulos (2002, p. 15) calls an atmosphere of "nostalgic disorientation". Henry, how do you feel about your work as a supervisor when away from home?

*Henry:* To cope with interactive fields of strangeness and nostalgic disorientation, I tried to create a symbolic home away from home. During my visits, I would stay at the same hotel, or neighborhood. In retrospect, I realize I was seeking an island of continuity when I was a stranger in a strange land. In preparation, I would try to see films and read, trying to enter into the cultural collective and understand key themes or historical turning points. As an anthropologist who had done fieldwork in exotic places, I knew my task was to make the familiar exotic and the exotic familiar.

Jan, you have written extensively about supervision. What do you think is the essence of supervision?

*Jan:* Supervision has thankfully evolved from what Balint (1948) critically called superego training – telling people how to do it – to a more relational model. The word "super-vision" is really an unfortunate term, implying a configuration of one who knows better working with one who knows very little. I began to supervise too early for my own good, before I had sufficient time to mourn my identity as a trainee and develop a secure style of practice with my patients. It is a pleasure to see now the growth of courses on supervision in the Jungian world; they set off my envy and the nostalgic wish that these had been available when I first began to supervise.

For me, supervision is rather "another vision", and I see myself like a *Bain Marie* (a way of cooking delicate dishes in water in the oven) for my supervisees, hoping that they will "cook" gradually and gently during their training at the right pace and temperature so that when they emerge from the training "oven" and are ready to qualify, they will have internalized their own styles of working and enough of an analytic and ethical attitude to practice independently.

I often find supervising more difficult than analyzing and what comes to mind immediately are Louis Zinkin's (1996, p. 240) words, "supervision can be a delight, but may often be a torment".

I completely agree. With gifted therapists and analysts, supervision is a pleasure, drawing on three archetypal predispositions – *to contain, to play and to initiate* (Perry 2003, p. 193-201). More problematic, is to make distinctions between those trainees who are gifted but need more time to develop and those who may not be suited to therapeutic work. Verena Kast has written about shame in supervision and how exposing it is to present our clinical work to another. This may lead to defences in supervision such as supervisees who hide both themselves and their work; others who compete for who knows best; and those who mimic their supervisors rather than integrate the supervisory relationship.

Supervising is more challenging because I find it more difficult to process my own countertransference affects, uncertain about what comes from the therapist/patient relationship; what from the personal complexes of the supervisee; what from the setting of the therapy and what from my own (hopefully reasonably conscious) shadow, generally involving issues of power and authority.

There is always some auxiliary analysis in supervision. Sometimes, this sits comfortably but on other occasions, skill is needed to disentangle whether supervisees' complexes have been evoked in their transference to me, or whether they are rather enactments from the therapeutic relationship that make themselves felt first in supervision. These are the "hotspots" that make supervision both so interesting but also challenging. I tend not to ask supervisees to take complexes that emerge in supervision to their analysts. These appear in supervision and I try to deal with them in supervision.

If in difficulty, I draw on two key images to help me. First, Hawkins and Shohet's (1989, p. 47) image of the supervisor who requires *helicopter ability*, being able to move in close at times, but also knowing when to pull away to a broader perspective. I draw too on

Henderson's (1998, p. 65) *archetype of the hermit* emphasizing the isolation of the supervisor, especially when carrying responsibility for evaluating trainees' progress. The hermit echoes the loneliness and strangeness we feel when visiting cities away from home where, "we do not know what is supporting and holding us until we no longer possess it." (D'Rozario 2001, p. 215).

Recently, I heard an interview with a talented British concert pianist, Christian Blackshaw, who talked of the tensions between his loyalty to the music on the one hand and his need for a freedom of expression on the other; of how best to combine in his performances, his knowledge with spontaneity. His ideas as a pianist are not so far away from mine as a supervisor.

*Henry:* Jan, I agree that supervision is more complex than analysis and yet I find it easier, more like being a grandmother than a parent. Most of the work I have done in Eastern Europe is group supervision and this adds extra layers of complexity – the group dynamics, their relationship and transferences to me as a supervisor or in my cultural identities as an Israeli, Canadian and Jew with a beard. Also, the goal of group supervision is less focused on helping the trainee understand and manage a specific case, but rather, educational, linking clinical, theoretical and experiential dimensions to help *everyone* in the group to prepare for future cases by stimulating their analytical muscles. Supervising at home, I am relaxed. I can let the process proceed at its own pace. Not every session needs to be dramatic. But away from home, I experience a special, performance-persona anxiety. Coming from far away and carrying group projections as magician or wise old man, I felt an adrenalin-fed impulse to perform the wisdom of the Self and not to disappoint these routers and their passions.

Working across cultures requires clarity about the limits of flex-ibility. The key issue is to know when to be flexible and when not. We all have our Jungian superego, the internalized collective voice of what Jungian analysis should be like. It forced me to clarify my position on many substantive issues and to understand which were essential and which needed to be adapted to local practice. Understanding the power dynamics of supervision may be the greatest challenge when working in different cultural settings.

Managing time in group supervision was often problematic. Trans-lation would cut the time in half. I also wanted to give the presenter enough space to present in depth and to invite the members of the group to actively join in but I have learned that I must leave time for myself, both as a commentator, and supervisor but also to deal with, often strange,    group dynamics. In the beginning I was too "nice" and time expired before I had my say. Now, I try to hold the opposites, thinking, should I be the first to speak, or last to speak, both, or neither? The hardest thing emotionally when doing supervision away from home is when everyone in the group is speaking all at once and I do not know what they are saying or why they are so excited. When things calm down, I say, "Let's all stay together". I ask what has stirred people up; sometimes there is only silence. It has taken time to accept my helplessness. Later, I may come to understand that it is a cultural issue that is difficult to explain to an outsider; sometimes, there are active tensions within the training group; or sometimes it revolves around a key word that is untranslatable.

In your recent book, Jan, I wrote:

> even with the best of translations, visiting analysts have serious difficulty comprehending untranslatable terms and their cultural associations (Abramovitch 2015, p. 62).

It may surprise you that Hebrew has no word for "mind" or "solitude", nor makes a distinction between "envy" and "jealousy". But Israeli Hebrew has a unique style of speaking, called *dugri, or* "straight talk" saying what you really think without worrying too much about the other person's feelings. In many cultures, such straight talk is considered rude. But *dugri* reflects an Israeli cultural complex that relationships are robust and can withstand conflict. In supervision, it happened that I would teach the group the meaning of *dugri* and ask a struggling supervisee, "Say what you mean, *dugri?*" *Dugri* facilitated a refreshing directness in cultures that favor indirectness.

An opposing danger is knowing what is distorted in the translation. Translation hides as much as it reveals. For example, the translator for a Russian supervisee said in English: "her patient said: 'I feel like your friend'". I inquired about the original Russian word and was told, it was *drug.* In Russian, *drug* implies an intense, demanding, enduring relationship that is both exhilarating and exhausting. In Soviet times, your *drug* was the one person one could choose freely. They often took the place of missing brothers and sisters. The transference implications for me as supervisor are profoundly revised when I understand the patient is not talking about a "friend" in the English sense, but a *drug* with all its Russian depth. Such experiences sensitized me to try to comprehend the untranslatable.

Since we are in Kyoto, I will give a Japanese example:

> *Kintsukuroi* – literally "to repair with gold" – the art of repairing pottery with gold lacquer understanding that the piece is more beautiful for having been broken.

*Kintsukuroi*, as a cultural concept, reveals how a wound, whether in ceramics or in the psyche, should not be plastered over or repaired, but rather highlighted and made precious. Understanding the concept of *to repair with gold* would be important when supervising Japanese therapists.

Endings away from home forced me to reflect on the nature of endings and their cultural performance. I came to enjoy the Russian tradition of sitting in silence before my journey home. It made me contemplate my own endings, not only when I left the foreign lands, but later when I returned home and ended each session.

*Jan:* Henry, you raise a number of issues and I would like to comment on four:

## Time for Reverie

Both you and I usually have a great deal of energy but your comments about *time and space* remind me of how tiring it was visiting St Petersburg four or five times a year happening as it did at weekends, alongside our work and patients at home. I wondered about the effect this could have on our Russian supervisees and how the idealizations you mention might have inhibited our supervisees expressing what it was like for them to have to work at weekends and comply with OUR program. Natasha Alexandrova (2011) was a supervisee in St Petersburg, travelling from Moscow nearly every month for her supervision — leaving her young child at home. She compared our weekend visits with the "soviet infant" who in Soviet times was treated in a purely functional, medical way, so that newborn babies only saw their mothers at strictly scheduled feeding times, five times a day, twenty minutes at a time, and breastfeeding mothers could still work in the factories. She talks of "a special maternal conveyor" (p. 642) to avoid any interruptions at work. Alexandrova then comments on the lack of space for mother's reverie running back and forth between factory and baby. It is not difficult to see the analogy here as Alexandrova compares the Soviet factory mother with her experience of our team of six visiting shuttle supervisors as breastfeeding, working mothers,

> like our strong and vigorous mothers, our supervisors...had to get up at 5 in the morning to meet the "feeding" schedule; they flew into a different time zone to have their working day start three hours earlier. And then went back to their London work till the next "feeding break" (Alexandrova, 2011, p. 643).

Under such circumstances, there can be no time for the kind of reverie and creative time-wasting that is of the essence in both analytic work and supervision. What "they" really needed was "us" and our capacity to tune into their needs for time and space. One benefit of working with interpreters was the inevitable slowing-down of the process, so that there was more time to think and for the leisured reverie to which Alexandrova refers.

## Phatic Language

Henry, I like very much your explorations of *language*... Bringing in Israeli "straight talk" led to an association of my own around arrivals and departures; how to meet up and how to say goodbye. I took some Russian lessons and developed a sense of the music of the Russian language, even if my use of it is limited. On arrival, I would smile, make eye contact and say "hello" in Russian; either the more formal *Zdravstvuite* or the less formal *Privet* or *Zdorovo*. When we came to say goodbye, I would say *Do svidaniya* or *Do vstrechi* (till the next time). It felt very important when our arrivals were followed by substantial gaps in time and the next meeting some time away.

I realized that unlike us in the UK, Russians use very little phatic language. Phatic language or "phatic communion" is a term coined by the anthropologist, Bronislaw Malinowski (1923) to refer to what we in English would call "small talk", language that is used to share feelings and establish a mood of sociability – especially important when meeting up and leaving. I believe that the Japanese call phatic language *Aizuchi* and in Persia, it is called *Taarof*.

*Henry*: Canadians often do this by adding an "eh?" at the end of a sentence, eh?

## Analytic Values

*Jan*: I had to discover which of my own analytic values to hold sacrosanct and which to adapt. I had to find out where my supervisees were, psychologically, clinically and culturally and modify my approach accordingly. Like you, I supervised mainly in small groups, believing this would help supervisees listen and learn from each other. However, at the beginning, this was difficult especially in a culture where such high value is placed on didactic teaching. The effects on generations of Eastern Europeans living in oppressive political regimes meant that the internalized dictator was never far from the surface in the individual psyche. Initially, supervisees would stand up to speak in the group, and were intolerant of the clinical presentations of their colleagues. I tried to model a democratic approach of attentive listening with a non-critical, relational demeanor. Inevitably, this did not always work and I became caught up unhelpfully with their dynamics. I valued late night debriefs with Catherine Crowther, my travelling colleague, to reflect together on powerful and puzzling dynamics. I have wondered whether a classically-based Jungian approach is better suited to shuttle projects given our irregular visits. My own largely developmental model emphasizing as it does, the importance of early experiences, of defence mechanisms, psychopathology and on transference dynamics in the service of individuation, seems to work better in situations with greater frequency and continuity of meetings. Recently, when giving IAAP exams in a Russian city, I reflected with amusement about why it was that all the women chose as the theme of their written papers "animus development" and the men "escape from the great mother"!!

Like you, I emphasized the establishment of good boundaries and a sound frame in which an analytic relationship could develop. I do not believe that anyone can be an analyst without understanding transference or indeed countertransference and we tried through giving of *our*selves in clinical presentations to help supervisees to learn to use *them*selves and bear the uncertainties of "not knowing".

Productive meeting points came from comparison between Russian and English fairy tales, which helped supervisees to process the huge amounts of trauma and loss in the Russian patient population. I have been impressed with the work of other visiting supervisors, such as Marta Tebaldi in Hong Kong, who has worked extensively on the development of new and culturally appropriate learning techniques.

### Cultural Complexes and Bi-Directionality

Unlike you, Henry, I have not been trained in cultural compe-tencies. However, cross-cultural encounters in supervision do bring emotionally powerful experiences of turmoil, awe and despair. If they can be survived, they are wonderful opportunities for learning, for "moments of meeting" and for moving forward – both for supervisor and supervisee.

Our thinking about supervising abroad owes a great debt to those who developed the concepts of a cultural unconscious, and cultural complexes (Kimbles and Singer, 2004; Kaplinsky, 2015; Rasche and Singer, 2016). Singer's ([2004], 2016) distinction between a cultural complex, cultural identity and the soul of the country and overlaps between them has great relevance, especially in groups emerging after years of oppression.

### Henry: Supervisors' Responses

As part of our research for this paper, and because we have both supervised routers and others in only a limited number of different countries, we decided to embark on a piece of qualitative research asking the views of a sample of 40 supervisors who had worked abroad in Developing Groups in Eastern Europe, China and Asia, South America and North Africa. We were touched by the enthusiasm with which these supervisors answered the questions we posed, as if all were waiting for an opportunity to express their thoughts and feelings about their experiences. We will write up this research in more detail, but here is a short overview of our findings.

*Jan:* Henry and I were struck that the visiting supervisors began to work without knowing what to expect but with an attitude of curiosity, excitement tinged with anxiety and a real sense of adventure. People talked in their different ways of their first impressions involving experiences of culture shock and how unprepared they felt:

*Henry:* "The deep motivation and passion for Jungian analysis....a slow awakening from years of oppression and a people who were tough and had suffered a lot".

*Jan:* "I was disconcerted by being so hugely venerated…as though I was an exotic creature from another world".

*Henry:* "half the cases I supervised were the children of mid-level functionaries of the Chinese Communist Party at the time of the [Cultural] Revolution and all were, in a way, psychological orphans".

*Jan:* "the social conventions were other and I had to reconsider everything in order to understand clinical situations. I had to forget everything I knew".

*Henry:* "the enormous hunger and gratitude for our hands-on experience of doing clinical work…I was moved by the very recent history of hardship, conflict and social upheaval that all of post-Soviet space has endured".

*Jan:* "the different psychological difficulties in China; the different images that shape them and my own unawareness of the cultural aspects of some of these difficulties".

There were mixed views about the usefulness of supervisors' home training and experience as foundation-stones to take with them abroad:

*Henry:* "training does not prepare us for managing the unexpected or the unfamiliar unless we play defensively with how we conceive of ourselves as analysts".

*Jan:* "the discipline and rigor of my own training and then years of experience to find my own way of working with very different client groups, helped me to be flexible in a culture with was very 'other' to me".

When reading about the effects on supervisors of coming home, it was evident that many felt these encounters with difference affected profoundly their ways of working, challenging long-held clinical practices in their home countries:

*Henry*: "by the end of the program, I think that having been exposed to so many different perspectives and ways of working allowed me to know better how I wanted to work".

*Jan*: "to be more flexible and open-minded about our professional standards...more convinced that the quality of authenticity of the relationship is the most mutative factor for healing".

*Henry*: "I have come to realize that in some areas of my work, I need to be more tolerant and accepting of difference and in others there is a need for greater clarity and implementation of ethical standards and practice".

*Jan*: "the whole experience of encountering difference means that I now feel freer to trust being flexible and to use myself more actively as an analyst and a supervisor".

*Henry*: "you become half a stranger in your own country...your cultural horizon widens and you relativize your culture of belonging".

*Jan:* The clinical and cultural challenges encountered mirror some of those Henry and I have already described but they were expressed in very individual ways. What was clear was how difficult it was for our respondents to separate out whether challenges were specifically clinical or cultural when usually, they were intertwined:

*Henry*: "the awkwardness I felt when entering into aspects of both sexuality and religion".

*Jan:* "the resistance of some trainees who resented being taught by Westerners and used cultural difference as a weapon in a power battle".

*Henry:* "I recalled Gert Sauer saying that supervision in post-Soviet space is done with traumatized patients in a traumatized society".

*Jan*: "difficulties were language, the intensity of their unconscious contents and emotions; the great responsibility towards the complete trust and positive expectation the Chinese have towards a Western analyst".

*Henry*: "fear that beyond my conscious intention I could colonize the mind of the supervisee instead of encouraging him/her to explore the field of the relationship that lay in the in-between of supervision practice".

*Jan*: "the fear of authority to an almost paranoid extent would permeate both trainees' work with the supervisors and with their patients".

Clearly, good interpreters with a grasp of Jungian language facilitated the supervision process. Henry, I think you and other supervisors have illustrated so beautifully the beneficial discussions to be had in supervision about the meaning of words cross-culturally. Similar sentiments were expressed by those supervisors working in countries where neither supervisor not supervisee worked in their first language, making meaning, albeit slowly in a language that was less familiar.

For visiting supervisors then, there was usually an observable process from an initial experience of nostalgia for home and dis-orientation leading to experiences of feeling de-skilled, feelings of not-knowing but somehow a wish to bear this and remain open to unfamiliar experiences. Later, there developed gradual understanding in supervision and the re-establishment of precious values from home and those that needed to be adapted. This provides evidence for Cam-bray's (2015, p. 33) original work on bi-directionality when "we allow ourselves to grow beyond our inherited constraints". Our findings leave questions of how this process affects the ease with which we can evaluate competently the stages of development of supervisees from other cultures and how we can train future supervisors more adequately.

### Henry: Supervisees' Responses

We also surveyed about 30 supervisees, mostly people we knew or had supervised, but we made an effort to contact routers in countries we had never visited, such as China or Taiwan. In the supervisees' questionnaire, we included a particular question: "What have you learned from being supervised by a supervisor coming from abroad that has affected your clinical practice in your home country?"

Almost all supervisees noted how cultural differences impacted on the process of supervision, and "understanding images and symbols from different cultural perspectives". One supervisee from Eastern Europe wrote:

> "it seemed impossible for me to explain the realities of our life to those who never lived here…and the scale of the collective trauma."

Supervisees needed to provide detailed explanations of amplifica-tions used from films, books, songs, myths and their meaning in their culture. Culturally specific issues of formal and informal address, greetings, as you, Jan, discussed, hierarchy and status, holidays, pri-vacy, were also mentioned.

Significantly, these cultural differences made locals more sensitive to their own culture and national myth. One respondent said,

> "I have learned that the supervisor from other cultures could help us be more sensitive and insightful toward our own living culture. The efforts

we make to try to explain and analyze our own culture to the supervisor are helpful for clinical understanding."

Another router wrote,

*"when I work with people from different cultures, even though they speak my language, I try to keep in mind that they may look at things differently... that is, they may see a bright ideal where I see a shadow manifestation or vice versa."*

Another wrote that,

*"supervision with a foreigner helped me accept my cultural identity."*

Supervision provided a place to think. As another router put it, supervision was,

*"where one had a right not to know something."*

Almost all respondents stated clearly that they learned "great respect for therapeutic frames", as well as to work clinically with transference and countertransference and often with archetypal images. Many said they benefited from having supervisors from different theoretical orientations.

Beyond the sometimes disturbing cultural divide, many routers reaffirmed how much is common in the human psyche and how "cultural differences were not unbridgeable."

One wrote,

*"I learned that we are all very similar in our uniqueness."*

and another added,

*"understanding is a process that doesn't have so much to do with the language, culture and way of thinking but rather with deep emotional and intuitive connection with a person you are in relation with and where deepest contents can be shared and understood even without the 'right' words."*

One router who is now a new IAAP member summed up how the supervision process could work at its best,

*"It was an alchemical process of transformation...it was like my birth as an analyst."*


*Ending or Beginning?*

*Jan:* You and I have reflected together on the personal pleasures and pitfalls of this work; our thoughts and feelings, each from our own point of view, with our own cultural style, English and Israeli.

It is striking though that what we are doing here is also part of something larger – an emergent field of strangeness that is perhaps no longer quite so strange! This year, a new book edited by Rasche and Singer (2016) was published called, *Europe's Many Souls: Exploring Cultural Complexes and Identities;* there is Marta Tebaldi's (2016) book written together with a group of routers from Hong Kong (2016), called *Stories of Transcultural Identities: Jungians in Hong Kong';* John Merchant's research evaluating the router programs; and my own book too, edited together with Catherine Crowther (2015) called *From Tradition to Innovation: Jungian Analysts working in Different Cultural Settings.* So, we are not the only ones wishing to process our overseas adventures and evaluate our experiences and cultural competencies when supervising abroad. While some router projects have ended with new Societies forming, there is also something new beginning. There is much to be learned about diversity. In the words of the Italian journalist, Tiziano Terzani (2006):

> only if we look at the universe as a whole in which each part reflects the totality and where the great beauty lies in diversity will we begin to understand who we are and where we are.

When supervising abroad, I have tried to convey my values concerning the essence of Jungian analysis. Struggling together in languages that are not our own, in cities that smell different, and with social mores that have been "other", means that learning is always two-way.

Like Odysseus, returning home to the SAP after these adventures has not always been easy. My encounter with "otherness" has brought a new interest in diversity, a sharper focus on the effects and clashes of cultural complexes and identity in my own consulting room and less allegiance to the theory and practices held sacrosanct in my own institute. I am changed and sometimes this may not be easy for my SAP colleagues. To end with Rilke (2009, p. 56-57),

> for when the traveller returns from the mountain slopes into the valley, he brings, not a handful of earth, unsayable to others, but instead some word gained, some pure word, the yellow and blue gentian.

*Henry:* Jan, your lovely Rilke quote highlights how we have been enriched from our going out and our returning home. That cycle of home-leaving and home-coming reminds me of the Hasidic story of Moishe, a poor Jew who dreams he must travel from his tiny village to the great city of Warsaw and dig under a bridge where he will find a treasure. In Warsaw, he is confronted by a frightening policeman who demands to know what he is doing there. Moishe tells his story; the policeman laughs, "Ah, if I believed in dreams I would have to go to this Jewish village and dig in the backyard of some Moishe's house".

Moishe returns home and finds the treasure that was waiting for him but which he had to leave home to discover.

Before ending, I want to return to the opening active imagination. I am curious what came up for each of you; for me a single word emerged from my imagination. It was not "archetype" or "individuation", but "and". "And" is a word that holds words and things and people and even opposites together. It is accessible and "experience near" and emphasizes an emotional attitude of accumulation and abundance. "And" is a working metaphor that guided me supervising away from home. To add my theory to *their* experience, to add food and depth so routers could grow into themselves.

Elena Bortuleva (2014) describes when a caregiver gives the baby the fullness it requires, drop by drop, to transform *pitanije* (nurturing with food) into *vospitanije* (nurturing with truly human experiences). Our nurturing, allowed supervisees to be nourished, then to nourish themselves and later, to nurture their own supervisees. 'And', so we, the supervisors away from home, have been nourished as well.

Since we are away from home, in Kyoto, I want to end with another poem of Basho (1967) about being in Kyoto:

> In Kyoto,
> hearing the cuckoo,
> I long for Kyoto.

## References

Abramovitch, H. (2015). Pioneers or Colonizers?. *From Innovation and Tradition: Jungian Analysts working in Different Cultural Settings* (Crowther, C. and Wiener, J. Eds). New Orleans, Louisiana: Spring Journal Books. pp. 51-69.

Austen, J. (2014). *Emma*. New York: Black and White Classics.

Basho, M. (1967). *The Narrow Road to the Deep North and other Travel Sketches*. London: Penguin Classics.

Balint, M. (1948). On the psychoanalytic training system. *International Journal of Psychoanalysis*, 29, (3), 163-173.

Bortuleva, E. (2014). Rivers of milk and honey – an exploration of nurturing the self in a Russian context. *Journal of Analytical Psychology*, 59, 531-547.

Cambray, J. (2015). Reflections on the bi-directionality of influence in analytical work across cultures. Chapter 2 in, *From Tradition to Innovation: Jungian Analysts Working in Different Cultural Settings* (Crowther, C. and Wiener, J. Eds.). New Orleans, Louisiana: Spring Journal Books.

Crowther, C. and Wiener, J. (2002). Finding the space between east and west: the emotional impact of teaching in St. Petersburg. *Journal of Analytical Psychology*, 47, 285 – 301.

Crowther, C. and Wiener, J. (2011). Fifteen minute stories about training. *Journal of Analytical Psychology*, 56, 627-653.

D'Rozario, P. (2001). Hymn of the Pearl: a psychological analysis of the process of migration. In, *Landmarks: Papers by Jungian Analysts from Australia and New Zealand,* (Formiani, H. Ed.). London: Karnac Books pp. 205-230.

Fiennes, W. (2002). *The Snow Geese.* Basingstoke and Oxford: Picador.

Frost, R. [1914] (2002). The Death of the Hired Hand. *Robert Frost's Poems.* (Untermeyer, L. Ed.). New York: St. Martin's Press. pp. 160-167.

Hawkins and Shohet (1989). *Supervision in the Helping Professions.* Milton Keynes: Open University Press.

Henderson, D. (1998). Solitude and Solidarity. Clarkson, P. Ed. *Supervision: Jungian and Psychoanalytic Perspectives.* London: Whurr.

Homer (1997). *The Odyssey.* (Fagles, R. translator). Penguin Classics.

Kaplinsky, C. (2015). Cultural Complexes and Working Partnerships. Chapter 5 *From Tradition to Innovation: Jungian Analysts working in Different Cultural Settings* (Crowther, C. and Wiener, J. Eds.) New Orleans and Louisiana: Spring Journal Books.

Morgenstern, C. (1918). Stufen: Eine Entwickelung in Aphorismen und Tagebuch-Notizen. Chapter 14 (Stages: A Development in Aphorisms and Diary Notes).

Papadopoulos, R. (2002). *Therapeutic Care for Refugees: No Place Like Home.* London: Karnac Books.

Perry, C. (2003). Into the Labyrinth: A Developing Approach to Supervision. Chapter 11 in *Supervising and Being Supervised: A Practice in search of a Theory* (Wiener, J. Mizen, R. and Duckham, J. Eds.). Basingstoke: Palgrave McMillan.

Rilke, R.M. (2009). *Duino Elegies* (Mitchell, S. Ed.). New York: Vintage Books.

Singer, T. (2016). Introductions. *Europe's Many Souls: Exploring Cultural Complexes and Identities* (Rasche, J. and Singer, T Eds.). New Orleans, Louisiana: Spring Journal Books. pp. 9-10.

Terzani, T. (2006). *La fine e il mio inizio.* Longanese, Milano.

Toibin, C. (2009). *Brooklyn.* London: Penguin Books.

Zinkin, L (1996). Supervision: The Impossible Profession. Part VI in *Jungian Perspectives on Clinical Supervision* (Kugler, P. Ed.). Switzerland: Daimon Verlag.

# Walking Hand in Hand: Complex in Memory; Mind in Matter

*Aurea Afonso M. Caetano*
(São Paulo, SBrPA)


*Teresa Cristina Machado*
(São Paulo, SBrPA)

## Introduction

Our work was carried out by four hands; it was an exercise in our creative exchange and in the interrelation between two distinct subjectivities, moving forward and intersecting in the construction of this text.

We have organized this work based on the following topics: Jungian attitude and complex psychology; complex, concept amplification; neuroscience and its unfolding; memory; interconnectivity and analytical relationship.

Moving between diverse areas of knowledge can bring forth precious gifts.

Remembering Jung in *The Secret of the Golden Flower* (Jung, CW 13, par. 38): "Movement is only another name for mastery".

## The Jungian Attitude and Complex Psychology

Jung, as we know, was a great walker and he went for walks until the end of his life, always researching. As he walked, he would be revisiting and broadening his concepts, always with a sustained and genuine interest in other fields of knowledge. His attempts at comprehending the psyche in its spiritual aspects, his interest in religions, in physics, in history, and his exploration and expansion of the knowledge of the enigmatic and the unknown, rendered Jung the reputation of not being very scientific, while he enormously widened the scope of his ideas.

Taking movement as our subject of enquiry, we found an approximation to the *Jungian attitude*, or the possibility of a common outlook, in the standpoints of groups that work with transdisciplinarity and complexity.

The term *transdisciplinarity* comes up in 1970, with Jean Piaget, in a meeting of educators who sought to find solutions for expanding knowledge beyond interdisciplinarity and multidisciplinarity in order to break the ties of mechanistic thought.

"Transdisciplinarity is the acknowledgement of the interdependence among all aspects of reality" (Jantsch apud Weill et al., 1993, p. 31). Walking this road and broadening this idea even further, the French sociologist and philosopher Edgar Morin, one of the great researchers on this subject, defines from this standpoint that which would be a new logic: one of complexity (Morin, 2005). Complexity, as presented by Edgar Morin, proposes a logic which opposes the polarized and exclusionary vision between distinctive organizing principles and considers reality to be multifaceted, consisting of an infinity of nuances which cannot be reduced or eliminated, but must rather be respected as inherent to the social reality in which we live. The paradigm of complexity, within this proposition, displays another way of conceiving the world and society, where there is no room for determinism or reductionism.

We acknowledge in this assertion a common attitude – the "Jungian attitude" – as expressed by Jung in his extensive work; the attitude we have regarding facts, regarding the other, regarding knowledge; the attitude we experience and acknowledge in our work as analysts; the attitude which postulates wholeness and diversity, the existence of a relationship which is alive and inseparable between the psyche and the world.

By proposing an unmistakable connection among several aspects of human existence, without a pre-determined hierarchy or value, Jung anticipates Morin's proposition of "complexity". All and every transformation in any part of the whole affects and modifies the whole and its other parts.

> To Jung, the concept of wholeness is intrinsically connected to a dynamic, systemic vision of being and the world, where the parts relate in a compensatory, complementary way in a unique whole. (Penna, 2013, p. 138)

In *Who Owns Jung* (ed. Casement, 2007), the Brazilian analyst Roberto Gambini writes: "Jung was an attitude" (p. 363).

Jung used to say, quoting Terence: "I am a human being; nothing human can be alien to me", expressing a deep openness and curiosity for everything pertaining to nature. This way of understanding and correlating the many possibilities of human expression is contained in Jung's work and is what we call the "Jungian attitude".

## The Complex Psychology

The Jungian attitude takes us to the world of complexities and their interrelationships.

Shamdasani (2005) quotes Jung as saying:

Complex Psychology means psychology of "complexities", which means pertaining to complex psychic systems as opposed to relatively elementary factors (p. 28).

We would like to point out an existing controversy regarding the terminology for Jungian psychology: deep psychology, complex psychology, analytical psychology. Shamdasani remembers:

although at first Jung had used the expression Analytical Psychology to refer to his psychology, in the 30's he renamed it "complex psychology" (p. 28).

Here, Jung clearly shows that he thought ahead of his time, his modernity. The psychology of complexities does not allow for clear separations, much to the contrary, it incites us to work on that which would be the *unus mundus*, the possibility of dealing with reality as proposed by the alchemists:

That which is below is like that which is above and that which is above is like that which is below to do the miracle of one only thing (The Emerald Tablet).

Or in the words of the American physicist Henry Stapp:

Bohm's approach to consciousness brings in an infinite tower of explicated and implicated orders, each one "in-forming" the one below and "in-formed" by the one above (2011, p. 106).

When we use the term Complex Psychology here, we are not talking about the psychology of complexes. We are talking about the Jungian attitude which guides us. The concept of complex embraces the idea of interconnections among the intrapsychic experiences, and carries the same attitude as complex psychology, which means that it also moves among several intrapsychic possibilities, constellating or weaving together several components pertaining to the wholeness of being.

## The Complex

*Structuring*

In one of his first statements about the complex, Jung says that the background of consciousness or of the unconscious consists of complexes which manifest under the form of associations (Jung, CW2 par. 664).

We are aware of the importance of the work done with the Word

Association Test for the development of the concept of complex in Jungian psychology. Together with Perrone, our proposition here, when thinking of the "Jungian attitude" which guides us, is to understand that:

> That which Wundt and his school interpreted as irrelevant "errors" in the analysis of the test results, offered elements for the comprehension of the patient's psychic situation (Perrone, 2008, p. 45).

Thus, errors or flaws considered irrelevant or disposable in the early analyses of results obtained from the Association Tests, paved the way for Jung to sense, with his genius curiosity, that which he will later call pathway or "via regia for the unconscious, architect of dreams and symptoms" (Jung, CW8, p.210).

Like geological shafts showing deep layers of the Earth, the errors in the Association Tests worked as open doors for understanding the deepest expressions of the psyche, allowing for the formulation of the concept of the affective tonality complex.

The Jungian attitude observes numerous phenomena without establishing a hierarchy between them. In this way, we can think with Jung that the error or flaw has its own space, its position and it's structuring.

> [...] I have learnt that life's biggest and most important problems are basically insoluble. They must be, because they express the necessary polarity inherent in all self-regulating system (Jung, CW 13, par 18).

The Jungian attitude encircles the object or fact, in the movement we know as *circumambulatio*. This encirclement furthers the knowledge or acknowledgement of several aspects of the same reality, facilitating a stronger and broader rapprochement. Thus, we enter the world of multiplicity, of complexity, of no linearity.

As we know, Jung proposes that psychic functioning occurs from the movement of energy between polarities. He emphasizes the importance of non-fixation, of motion, and then proposes that the pathology is in fixation, stiffness.

Unbalance or pathology are then linked to the impossibility of movement and not to the pole itself and its contents.

Complexes can be understood as patterns, functional structures, possibilities of psychic and neurobiological organization.

Bovensiepen (2006) suggests that we should concentrate on the relationship between the many complexes in the unconscious rather than on their pathological effects. He says that the theory of complexities is a theory about psyche's operation, and reminds us that, for Jung, the psyche is highly dissociable and the many complexes are its construction blocks, a model aligned with the new findings of neuroscience. Deformities, defects, flaws are constituent elements of our psyche.

Or, as von Franz writes:

It's likely that our personality has originally been construed little by little from these complexes (von Franz, 1997, p.55).

Expressing this same idea in a poetic fashion, the Brazilian writer Clarice Lispector says in a letter:

Even to cut off our own defects can be dangerous. We never know which defects support the whole building.

Quoting Naomi, a character from the book *Norwegian Wood* by the contemporary Japanese writer Haruki Murakami:

[…] we are in here not to correct the deformation but to accustom ourselves to it: that one of our problems was our inability to recognize and accept our own deformities (Murakami, 1990 p.87).

### Network and Landscape Complex

Each of us is a texture, a complex web, a constellation, a landscape. There is no hierarchy – all points are important for every one of our constellations, networks, landscapes, webs.

Verena Kast (apud Bovensiepen, 2006, pg. 452) mentions a "network of complexes" and a "landscape of complexes" which can be revealed in association experiments. Psyche, as we have seen, is not a monolithic construction – it is highly complex and dissociable. Affect is the connecting element between the several building blocks/ complexes. Affect agglutinates several threads, pathways, possibilities, creating our image.

We would like to talk about the landscape, the complex as a nodal point, not as a content but as a dynamic. The image of a landscape brings us to a *whole* consisting of many complexes.

To quote Perrone once again:

The complex, fruit of a constellation, generates new complexes, sets in motion other existing ones and can also be responsible for the constellation of forthcoming secondary associations. Both the consciousness of the moment and the unconscious are fruit of a complex constellation and are agents of constellations (2008, p. 90).

This constellation is a configuration which emerges from the impact of complexes. It is a dynamic movement, for at every moment diverse complexes are activated with different characteristics and different strengths.

We can name every single knot, though what we are interested in is the dynamics which generates the formation of the knots and, in a complex manner, the dynamics which structures the psychic landscape. Complexes as positive nuclei or:

> [...] nodal points in the dynamic psychic life without which we do not want to be; as a matter of fact, they cannot lack, otherwise psychic life would come to a fatal standstill (Jung, CW 6, par. 925).

Constellated complex, landscape of complexes, network of complexes, activation of complexes, nodal points, units of work, building blocks, operation patterns, texture, movement!

> I am always reinventing myself, opening and closing life circles, throwing them aside, seared, full of past. (...) Moments so intense, red, condensed in themselves, which do not need a past or a future to exist. (Lispector, 1980, p. 76)

It is through these images that we comprehend and work with the complex; it is also the way in which nowadays we understand how memory works.

### Complex and memory – mind in matter?

Jung's contemporary, Sherrington, who won the Nobel Prize in physiology in 1932, proposed a new comprehension of neuronal operation and pioneered the principle that the nervous system, including the brain, can be comprehended as an interconnected network. He uses a beautiful metaphor to illustrate the movement of this web.

> [...] the brain is waking and with it the mind is returning. It is as if the Milky Way entered upon some cosmic dance. Swiftly the head-mass becomes an enchanted loom where millions of flashing shuttles weave a dissolving pattern, always a meaningful pattern though never an abiding one; a shifting harmony of sub-patterns. Now as the waking body rouses, sub-patterns of this great harmony of activity stretch down the unlit tracks of the stalk-piece of the scheme. Strings of flashing and travelling sparks engage the lengths of it. This means that the body is up and rises to meet the waking day (Sherrington, 1948, p. 178).

### Neuroscience

At the end of the nineteenth and the beginning of the twentieth century, we see psychology and medicine walking hand in hand, the moment when Freud and Jung begin their studies in medicine. Throughout the twentieth century we observe these two sciences diverting and almost opposing each other, hands that were once united breaking apart. In a way, we can think that they remained together, though not as a sum but rather as two opposing forces.

We go on in an attempt to forget the other science, disqualifying it, rejecting it, not through pertinent criticism, but by avoiding to look at it. Each science rejects the other by not acknowledging it. On the one hand psychology is not acknowledging neuroscience, so long as the latter does not reach the "soul", and "shrinks" the psyche. On the other hand, medicine is not acknowledging the value of the analytic method, since the latter did not use scientific method to validate its interaction with the medical world.

Valuation is a function of consciousness. From its personal, familiar and cultural substrates, the ego valorises the world around it. To appreciate the unknown is always a very hard task for consciousness. It is simpler and faster to dispose of it, to put it aside, or to transform it into a new, idealized God. We do not bother to look in the face of the other in either case, but if we do, we look at it under the same light of the already known field.

As proposed by Jung, when we transit between two poles, we create the possibility of transcending and finding a new unit, a third one; and also, of thinking not only of bridges, but also of transcendence and complexity.

Exercising the Jungian attitude enables us to practice *circumambulation*. Going a little further, however, and starting from complex psychology, we can allow ourselves to review an object under a light originating from another spot, from another subject, from another science – not only to review the object from another perspective but under the nuances of another light.

By shedding light on the psyche through neuroscience we can magnify and create new outlines in our analytical concepts. This is the challenge of complex psychology: to be able to see through the other's light. This is our challenge here today.

As if on a bridge, we transit between two worlds.

Leading Jungians, Miranda Davies, Margaret Wilkinson and Jean Knox were precursors in the stimulating task of bringing together Jungian theory and the new findings in neuroscience. These authors used theoretical models of neuroscientists such as Allan Schore, Daniel Siegel, Antonio Damasio, Erick Kandel and Jan Panksepp, among others, to lay the foundations for this bridge. Since then, the research, both by neuroscientists and by us, Jungian analysts, has been walking side by side, the work of one corroborating and helping consolidate and widen the work of the other in their field of knowledge, thus establishing bridges.

Neuroscience is a broad term, which has been interpreted in diverse ways. We will work with the following definition: neuroscience is the scientific study of the nervous system, aimed at unveiling its operation, structure, development and the possible alterations it may suffer.

Thanks to the massive technological advances that took place during the last 30 years of the last century, we are able to observe and study the brain *in vivo*, and conduct high-tech molecular research. These technological advances provoked changes in paradigms regarding the operation of the Central Nervous System. Several authors propose organizing these changes into two broad areas: molecular and systemic.

The molecular area begins in the late nineteenth / early twentieth century with Mendel and other authors who researched the heredity of information. This field advances when Watson and Crick identify the DNA's double helical structure.

Crick (apud Kandel, 2009) proposes: "The Central Dogma of molecular biology is: DNA produces RNA which produces protein." Epigenetics, however, challenges this dogma. We now know that this mechanism is not that simple.

The term epigenetics was used at first to describe the bridge between genotype and phenotype during development. We know that the epigenome is modified throughout life and is sensitive to environmental cues. Everything we do can alter our genetic expression, as well as that of future generations. This finding caused the definition to be broadened later to include the study of mechanisms which allow for a transgenerational transmission of these modifications without an alteration in the DNA. This will be called "transgenerational epigenetics" (Daxinger et al 2012). Studies from 2015 describe the existence of a third structure forming which is called a triple helix, originating from the relation between DNA and RNA. We have here a third thread.

The other area that underwent a great change is the area called "Systems Mapping". Karl Wernicke (1848-1905) a German doctor – neuropathologist, neurologist and psychiatrist – known for his work on language deficits, proposed that the most complex cognitive functions result from the interconnections between diverse functional sites. He was the first to develop the idea of distributed processing, a principle now central to neuroscience. His proposal is pertinent to both the studies of a particular area and its specificities, and the study of how these areas communicate, modulate. It is not a generalist vision, but rather one which integrates specificities; it is not an indiscriminate relation, but rather interrelation.

Another point which intrigues us is that although Wernicke made this proposal at the end of the nineteenth century, it gained momentum with recent findings in neuroscience. We could say that the twentieth century was predominated by disconnection. Because all things have two sides, we wonder whether this disconnection was necessary for several areas to unfold, mature, and then re-create connections, with the consolidation of their identities.

Will disconnection be necessary for the consolidation of identity?

Together, the molecular component and the systemic component, lay the foundation for the current formulations on CNS's operation. The study of synapses represents this new approach, currently vital for the studies of memory, walking side by side with the studies of neuroplasticity.

During most of the twentieth century, it was believed that the CNS did not undergo alterations throughout life, that its structure and operation were established during the early years and underwent very little change, which we can relate to in psychology with the idea that the psychic structuring is configured in the early relationships of the child. During child's early years, there is a great structuring and maturing of the CNS, but this does not remain unchanged, undergoing changes throughout life based on experiences. The idea of a brain that changes throughout life is very close to the Jungian concept that the activation of complexes continues throughout the whole process of individuation.

The first studies on synapses, which are still valid, were conducted by Cajal (1852-1934), a Spanish anatomist from the early twentieth century. By means of anatomic studies, he formulated his proposal on the morphology and operation of neurons and synapses. Memory formation is imbricated in synapse formation, and many studies of memory walk hand in hand with the studies of synapses. Synapses are areas where neurons interconnect. They are interconnectivity sites, which allow information exchange between diverse areas and modulate this communication. It is mainly through the formation and amplification of synapse connections that the neural plasticity occurs. As synapses are created or disappear, widen or shrink, the brain mapping is redesigned. It is through synapses that the brain gathers strength in its plasticity. We could say that synapses are "ports" where several "routes" integrate and communicate. They are knots where several threads interlace.

## Approaching memory

Memory is the capacity of acquiring and storing information, enabling a more efficient and faster response to the outside world, furthering better adaptation and survival.

Memory is how events from the past affect future functions.

Memories are classified according to duration, and whether or not the awareness of the ego played a part in the evocation.

In implicit memory, there is no participation of the consciousness of the ego in evocation and it may or may not be present in the moment of formation.

But with the explicit or autobiographical memory the awareness of the ego is a pre-requisite in evocation.

Within neuroscience, both are acquired through experiences but the possibilities of connections come *a priori*.

The implicit memory leads us directly to the idea of complexes distant from consciousness which, therefore, show greater autonomy regarding the ego complex.

Neuroscience correlates implicit memories with unconscious memories and proves its automatic quality, independent of consciousness, as Kandel writes, "The unconscious memories are in general inaccessible to consciousness; nevertheless, they exert powerful effects in the behaviour." (Kandel, 2011)

The implicit memory is the source of the fundamental form which defines our manner of being in the world; it involves parts of the brain which do not require conscious processing during storing and remembering phases. It is connected to emotional contents, etched on limbic structures. "The memory's implicit elements are part of the foundations of our subjective sense of self which filters the experience of the moment." (Siegel, 2012).

In line with Knox (2003), we suggest that the model of complex with an emotional tone, used by Jung, is aligned with these mental models or schemes, forms of being in the world, unconscious patterns that organize our perception and our memory.

According to Wilkinson (2010):

> [...] to appreciate the existence of the implicit memory, allows the concept of unconscious to include anatomic structures where emotional and affective experiences, and many times traumatic, pre-symbolic ones, are stored." (pg. 29)

The explicit memory can be either episodic or personal (autobiographical memories) or semantic or factual (what, when and where). For this memory to be registered, a focal attention, a conscious perception is required. For the acquisition of autobiographical memories a sense of self, even if incipient, is necessary. The emergence of consciousness is intrinsically related to the development of memory.

Proust describes well the magnitude of meanings awakened by the smell of Madeleines. We are conducted, in his work, by the recollections, implicit and explicit memories, weaved with sensations and emotions. From these he is led to construe, to reframe his history, his identity (Proust, 1987).

"We are who we are by force of that which we learn and remember" (Kandel, 2009, p. 24)

Besides approaching the issue of dynamism in the complex, we are also going to further a focus on the mechanisms, on the processes which result in memory. Memory is used to be approached as an image/learning which is stored in specific sites, isolated, suffering little alteration throughout time, as a lifeless object that can be manipulated. However, we now approach memory as a living and constant process.

I suspect that the explicit mental images which we evoke come about from the synchronic, transitory activation of neuron triggering patterns which happen in a large scale in the same initial sensorial cortex where the triggering patterns corresponding to the perceptive representations happened in the past. The activation results in a topographically organized representation (Damasio, 1994, p. 128).

A synchronic lighting of several areas representing images, sounds, smells, ideas, emotions which, when being activated/illuminated simultaneously, constellate a memory. Like the image formed on the screen of your computer. All pixels are on the screen, but the activation of a set of specific pixels generates the image, the specific memory.

## Some Current Issues About Memory

In memory formation what we have consolidated is that: experience modifies synapses. Cajal suggested that learning could change the strength of synapses between neurons, thus strengthening the communication between them.

Kandel (2010) proves, through his experiments, that learning leads to a change in the strength of synaptic connections and, therefore, in the effectiveness of communication. Several studies are carried out to understand how the change in the strength of synapse connections is processed, leading to a molecular issue, since the synaptic alteration happens through a protein synthesis. This process is subject to modulation by several channels related to emotions, mood and alertness. Protein synthesis is modulated by the contents and emotional states present in the lived experience. The stronger the emotion, the stronger the activation in the memory consolidation (Izquierdo, 2011).

To us, it also seems possible that: the stronger the emotion, the stronger the activation in the complex consolidation.

In the long-term memory formation two factors are important: the repetition and emotional charge to which this memory is subjected to in its formation and in its evocation processes. These processes of increasing of synaptic strength and protein synthesis do not happen only in the first formation of the memory, but rather at each evocation. Once evoked, the memory suffers all these processes again, it is encoded once again, which means it is associated to other information of the moment, to the affective field where it is re-experienced and, from these new connections, it is updated. In the context of learning, adapting, this reframing permits the constant updating of the learning process. The memory is reframed at each evocation.

This process leads us directly to the idea of the complex and its reframing. It challenges us to rethink our clinical practice. Memories are not lifeless objects; they are living constellations which acquire new outlines with each new lighting. The memory is a living, ongoing system, as is the complex.

Saint Augustine wrote:

> It is abundantly clear that neither future nor past exist, and therefore it is not strictly correct to say that there are three times: past, present and future. Perhaps it might be said rightly that there are three times: a time present of things past; a time present of things present; and a time present of things future. For these three do coexist somehow in the soul, otherwise I could not see them. The time present of things past is memory; the time present of things present is direct experience; the time present of things future is expectation (Saint Augustine, 1964, XI, 20, 1).

### Interconnectivity

If memory leads us to the issue of what is in constant reconstruction, it also brings the interrelation between what we are given *a priori* and what is an outcome of experiences. To quote Kandel again:

> The genetic processes and the development processes specify the connections between neurons, meaning which neurons form synaptic connections with each other and when that occurs. But they do not specify the strength of these connections. The strength – long-term effectiveness of synaptic connections – is regulated by the experience (Kandel, 2010, p. 226).

We are here talking about the concepts of archetype and complex; the archetype is given *a priori*, whereas the complex is the result of our interaction with the outside world. Kandel also relates concepts proposed by Kant and Locke, which used to exclude each other, but now have become part of the same phenomenon – memory.

> The anatomy of the neural circuit is a simple example of Kantian *a priori* knowledge, while changes in the strength of connections in the neural circuit reflect the influence of experience. Besides, in accordance with Locke's idea that practice leads to perfection, the persistence of these changes composes the memory basis (Kandel, 2010, p. 227).

The experience designs us, but the lines are given *a priori*.

Following the interrelation point of view we could argue that several archetypical channels are necessary for the constellation of complexes.

Complexes are crossroads, ports, where several archetypes intersect, intertwine. We propose that there are archetypes with more affinity, which carry *a priori* routes of encounter. For instance, in the ego complex formation we have mother and father archetypes walking hand in hand, intertwining.

Will there be not only archetypes, but also archetypical patterns of interconnection between them? This is thinking of the interconnectivity of specificities and not only of specificities. Thinking of the interconnectivity of archetypes and not only of archetypes.

We also have the interconnectivity of complexes.

If the interrelation of archetypes is the web where the complex is constellated, the interconnectivity of complexes generates the behaviour regarding the stimulus of a certain experience.

Jung presents the issue of interrelation of complexes, though having only the ego as a reference. But, as we think of movement, of intrapsychic dynamics, how could we not think of interconnectivity between them?

In the neurophysiological studies, the interconnectivity between the areas, between neural sites, happens through the activation or inhibition of one over the other. These activations or inhibitions occur all the time among several areas, with varying intensity. It is through these mechanisms that the modulation and the configuration of a given behaviour occur.

Shedding light on our question, we could think that somehow the behaviour manifests as long as one complex appears activated simultaneously with the other's inhibition, not only the inhibition of the ego complex, but also of other complexes which could oppose the complex activated.

Illuminating some areas as well as shadowing others creates the psychic landscape. That brings us to the analytical relationship where we have the landscape of encounter.

## Analytical Relationship

Christian Roesler, German clinical psychologist and Jungian Analyst, published in 2013 an interesting article where he revises some studies, which show evidence of the effectiveness of Jungian psychotherapy. Working with the results of three studies, he shows that, despite being incipient, the data obtained show stable positive effects in a wide variety of disorders. Also, these effects have been proven effective in a six-year post-therapy follow-up and there were signs of important positive changes from the moment the work was concluded (Roesler, 2013).

The American psychologist, Jonathan Shedler, carried out a meta-analysis of a growing research on the efficiency of psychodynamic psychotherapy, citing empirical evidence. In his studies, he observes data which show that while being beneficial, its effects are not transitory; rather, they are long-lasting and can increase as time goes by.

> Psychodynamic therapy sets in motion psychological processes which lead to a continuous transformation, even after the therapy is over (Shedler, 2010).

Which mechanisms anchor these long-lasting changes? Would the analytic process be the field that facilitates and settles the interconnections which further a better intrapsychic transit? The same way that memory is consolidated from an increase of synaptic strength, these paths gather strength from the inter-subjectivity constellated in the relationship.

In the analytical relationship, we remake memories, expand pathways, with error as a conducting wire.

## Memory Imperfections

In the same way that error led us to better understand complex, neuroscience also considers memory errors and imperfections as objects of study. Izquerdo (2005) considers forgetfulness as one of the axes in the study of memory. He says that forgetfulness begins in that which is "chosen" not to be fixed; our work memory and short-term memory assimilate a great deal of information and only part of it is worked out so as to become long-term memory. The persistence or not of a given memory will be determined by the number of times it is recollected, by the affective charge associated to it, and by the possibility of anchoring new experiences. In this way, memories with a low affective charge, not recollected enough, tend to disappear.

It is necessary to forget in order to remember.

Here we are not talking about pathological alterations like Alzheimer Disease, but alterations, *errors,* which constitute our daily life, and further the so-called normal psychic structuring. We are called up to think of other *errors* of memory, of false memories or their imperfections.

> [...] recalling a memory episodically – no matter how important the memory – is not like turning to a photograph in an album. Recall of memory is a creative process. What the brain stores is thought to be only a core memory. Upon recall, this core memory

is elaborated upon and reconstructed, with subtractions, additions, elaborations and distortions (Kandel, 2009, p. 309).

The American psychologist, Daniel Schacter, classified memory imperfections into seven basic categories and called them seven sins, they are: bias, transience, absent-mindedness, blocking, misattribution, suggestibility and persistence. Each one of them provokes interesting issues and can easily be correlated to our practice; however, here we chose to shed light on the issues of bias and suggestibility.

Errors related to bias or filter:

> [...] reflect the powerful influence of our current knowledge and beliefs on how we remember our past. We often edit or entirely rewrite our previous experiences – unknowingly and unconsciously – in light of what we now know or believe" (Schacter, 2011).

Bias or filter explains how the subject encodes an experience from other already consolidated memories; this is very familiar to us. We understand that the complexes determine the reading of new experiences.

This also happens in the technological universe. We know that the algorithms in search tools we use on the internet such as Google, develop from our previous searches. Thus, the same key word can produce different results for different people, according to each one's previous research. Our world vision is reinforced with each new search, meaning we have more of the same. Here, we also have the challenge of reframing and broadening our world vision.

As with suggestibility, it is supported in the relationship with other people. It refers to the tendency to incorporate information from the outside, in general, as a result of questions or suggestions. It is about the influence of others on memory, on how the inter-subjectivity of relationships participates in the formations and reframing of memories, of complexes.

In our practice, we have, on the one hand, the way the patient hears a question, understands the analyst's comments; on the other, we have what the analyst chooses to ask, how he/she construes the question and what they keep from the stories told. What and how we ask, what we forget and what we remember are attitudes conducted by our personal equation. Together with the other we see facts, stories and memories from diverse perspectives, we *circumambulate* the object, pursuing a wider view.

The light guides us in this encounter.

In the analytical encounter, while revisiting a story, we observe what the other chooses to throw a light on. We notice light areas, shadowed areas and blind spots, where there is total darkness.

The play of light and shadow outlines the image. In Caravaggio's canvases, darkness illuminates the face, enhances the image and shows us a lively expression.

We pursue light, but it is darkness that enlightens. We pursue success, but errors give us focus.

The analytical encounter is not only a partnership looking to widen a perception of the self and of the world, it is also there to share the hues of brightness, to revisit the story not only from another perspective but also under another light, its own light, resulting from a personal equation.

Analyst and patient establish a unique relationship at each encounter, at each process. It is a relationship of inter-subjectivity: a state of deep contact, an encounter full of affective resonance which transforms the relationship creating a field which goes beyond this field of the encounter. *"Tertium non datur"*.

Stern talks about "moments of meeting" a moment present to both participants where the inter-subjective field is transformed and the relationship altered. "It cannot be a technical response; it has to be an authentic, specific response, which carries the therapist's signature, as it were" (Stern, 1998), or his/her personal equation.

The unconscious is relational; it is the here and now being transformed at every moment. In the analytical relationship, a true moment of encounter enables the construction of the third channel, the third thread, the third helix.

Memory and complex are dynamic, changeable aspects, living entities in constant transformation. Our working tools are updated by meaningful relationships – the analytical encounter as a promoter in the creation of a third thread from which deep alterations in the mechanisms at the basis of our being can be expressed.

Each experience produces its complex, its memory, and these are the basis and the meaning of development. We walk forth and back, sewing, weaving, connecting roads, constructing ports. Constellating the process of individuation.

## References

Bovensiepen, G. (2006). Attachment-Dissociation Network: some thoughts about a modern complex theory. *Journal of Analytical Psychology, 51*, 451-466.

Casement, A. (2007). *Who ows Jung?* London: Karnack Books.

Cozolino, L. (2006). *The Neuroscience of Human Relationships*. New York: W. W. Norton & Company.

Cozolino, L. (2010). *The Neuroscience of Psychotherapy*. New York: W. W. Norton & Company.

Cozolino, L. (2016). *Why Therapy Works?* New York: W. W. Norton & Company.

Crick, F. H. C. (1994). *The Astonishing Hypothesis*. New York: Touchstone.

Damasio, A. (1996). *O Erro de Descartes*. São Paulo: Companhia das Letras.

Daxinger, L., and Whitelaw, E. (2012). Understanding transgenerational epigenetic inheritance via the gametes in mammals. *Nat. Rev. Genet. 13*, 153–162.

Izquierdo, I. (2005). *A arte de esquecer.* Rio de Janeiro: Vieira & Lent.

Izquierdo, I. (2011). *Memória.* Porto Alegre: Artmed.

Izquierdo, I.; Carvalho, M.; Benetti, F. et al. Memória: tipos e mecanismos – achados recentes. *Revista USP,* São Paulo, n. 98, p. 9-16, junho/julho/agosto 2013

Jung, C.G. (1906/1990). *Experimental researches, CW 2.* New York: Princeton University Press.

Jung, C.G. (1931/1990). *Psychological types, CW 6.* New York: Princeton University Press.

Jung, C.G. (1934/1981). *The structure and the dynamics of the psyche, CW 8.* New York: Princeton University Press.

Jung, c. G. (1935/1989). *The symbolic life, CW 18* . New York: Princeton University Press.

Jung, C.G. (1938/1983). *Alchemical studies, CW 13.* New York: Princeton University Press.

Kandel, E. R. (2009). *Em busca da memória,* São Paulo: Companhia das Letras.

Kandel, E. R. Et al. (2014). *Princípios de Neurociência.* Porto Alegre: Artmed Editora

Knox,J. (2005). *Archetype, attachment, analysis.* London: Routledge.

Lispector, C.. (1980). *Perto do coração selvagem.* Rio de janeiro: Rocco.

Lispector, c. (2002). *Corespondências.* Rio de janeiro: Rocco.

Mazzio, E. A., & Solliman, k. F. (2011). Basic concepts of epigenetics. *Epigenetics.*

Mondal, T., Subhash, R. Vaid, R. et al (2015). MEG3 longcoding RNA. *Nature Communications 6:* 7743. doi:10.138/ncomms8743

Morin, E. (2005). *Ciencia com consciência.* Rio de janeiro: Bertrand.

Murakami, H (1990). *Norwegian Wood.* New York: Vintage International Books.

Penna, E. M. D (2013) *Epistemologia e método na obra de C.G. Jung.* São Paulo: Educ: Fapesp

Perrone, M. P. M. S. B. (2008). *Complexo: conceito fundante na construção da psicologia de Carl Gustav Jung.* Tese de Doutorado, Instituto de Psicologia, Universidade de São Paulo, São Paulo. doi:10.11606/T.47.2008. tde-30072009-135120.

Proust, M. (1987). *Em busca do tempo perdido.* Rio de Janeiro: Editora Globo

Roesler, C. (2013). Evidence for effectiveness of Jungian psychotherapy: a review or empirical estudies. *Behavioral Sciences*(3), pp. 562-575.o Agostinho (1964). *Confissões* XI:20. Lisboa: Lusosofia.net.

Schacter D.L, Guerin S. A, St Jacques P. L. (2011). *Memory distortion: an adaptive perspective.* Trends Cog. Sci. 15:467-474.

Schore, A. N. (2012). *The Science of the Art of Psychotherapy.* New York: W. W. Norton & Company.

Shamdasani, S. (2005). *Jung e a Construção da Psicologia Moderna.* Aparecida, São Paulo: Idéias e letras.

Shedler, J. (2010). The efficacy of psychodynamic psychotherapy. *American Psychologist,* 65, n. (98-109)

Sherrington, C. (1948). *Man on his nature.* Cambridge: Cambridge University Press.

Siegel, D. J. (2012). *The Developing Mind.* New York: The Gilford Press.

Squire, L. R. and Kandel, E. R. (2009). *From Mind to Molecules.* Greenwood Village, Colorado: Roberts & Company.

Stapp, H. P. (2011). *Mindful Universe.* Berkeley: Springer.

Stern, D.N, Sander, L.W., Nahum, J. P., et al. Non-interpretive mechanisms in psychoanalytic therapy the 'something more' than interpretation. *Int. J. Psycho-Anal.* (1998) 79, 903-921

Von Franz, M. (1997). *C.G. Jung – Seu mito em nossa época.* São Paulo: Cultrix.

Weil, P. et al (1993) *Rumo à nova transdisciplinaridade.* São Paulo: Summus Editorial

Wilkinson, M. (2006). *Coming into Mind.* London: Routledge.

Wilkinson, M. (2010). *Changing Minds in Therapy.* London: W. W. Norton & Company.

*Wednesday, 31 August 2016*

# The Dialogue between Jung and Master Hisamatsu – Agreements and Differences

*Ingrid Riedel*
(Switzerland, SGAP)

## Jung's respect for the Asian mentality

Jung's profound respect for the Buddha and the spirit of the East is often detectible in his writings. No great psychologist before him was so thoroughly engaged with the Indian Yoga, with Taoism and with Buddhism – especially with the unique books of wisdom from the East like the *I Ching* or *The Secret of the Golden Flower*. Indeed, Jung himself occasionally compares his idea of the Self to the Purusha or Atman (Young-Eisendrath, 2002, p.116) and he considered the mandala to be absolutely the most appropriate symbol of the transpersonal Self. (CWII, par. 139).

Already during his lifetime, Jung's work was respected in the East – especially in Japan, where a strong affinity between Jung's psychological theories and the Eastern spirit are so apparent (although Jung was well aware of the differences between the Eastern spiritual expressions and his own thoughts which sprang from his Western way of thinking). Jung warned Westerners against a too-quick, naive assimilation and imitation of Eastern spirituality and meditation methods, and called instead for an honest dialogue out of the Western spirit, the spirit which is in the end based upon Christian thought (CWII, par. 905, par. 939). On the other hand, Jung constantly expressed his highest respect for the Buddha and the spirit of Buddhism. Buddha not only taught, but also challenged humanity as a whole. Buddha considered the individual to be a trailblazer for the whole world and called above all for the integration of all gods who have been passed down through cultures in their own unique ways.

According to Jung, archetypes are anthropological constants of human experience, perception, formation, and behaviour. (Kast, 1992, p. 91). A dialogue between Eastern and Western psyche or Eastern and Western religions might be possible if we ask ourselves which archetypic constants of human experience (perception, imagination, formation and behaviour) are expressing themselves in a culturally determined and handed down religious symbol, and which outward expressions of our culture and religion correspond to these. In this way we could achieve some consensus, could also learn something, and moreover broaden our religious horizon and spiritual experience.

Experience as the gateway to religion was absolutely essential for Jung – be it a new experience of the numinous, or be it revitalization of inherited religious symbols through their appearance in one's own dreams or imagination.

Jung therefore considered it possible to come to an inner experience of the divine, to the experience of the "inner Christ" for the Christian mystic, or of the inner Buddha (the „Buddha nature") for the Buddhist. Jung thereby overcame the European incarnational prejudice that God could only exist and be experienced outside the soul. (McGuire and Hull, 1977, p.467).

## How Zen is practised in the West

Since Jung's days the spiritual experience and practice of eastern meditational methods by the Europeans and the Americans has been enormously broadened and deepened. Through the new international culture of travel, through the involuntary worldwide migration and, above all, through the global information network, cultures and culture-specific religions which slowly developed into world religions, are coming closer together than ever before.

The masters of the East are our guests or have come to live among us like, for example, the Vietnamese master Thich Nhat Hanh in Southern France.

Already in my generation it was possible to learn and practice Eastern meditation like Zen with a reasonable degree of authenticity, from Karlfried Count Dürckheim or Pater Enomiya Lasalle, for example, both of whom had lived in Japan for a long time and had learned Zen from the masters there. I do not know whether Jung ever practiced meditation in the Eastern sense. He was intensely interested during and after his stay in India in the theory and symbolism of Kundalini Yoga, which he sought to interpret as a parallel to the individuation process. He therefore held many seminars at the C.G.Jung Institute Zurich around this theme. (Shamdasani, 1998). I also do not know when or where he would ever have practiced Yoga or Zen. His warning against a naive or shallow dabbling in these things is still valid today for those who might jump quickly into Zen in order to discover the unconscious but not adequately attend to their own meditation experiences. (CW 11, par. 905, par. 939). Jung had a great admiration for the engagement of the entire person which Zen practice fosters:

> But since the emptying and shutting down of consciousness is
> no easy matter, a special training of indefinite duration is needed

in order to set up the maximum tension which leads to the final break-through of unconscious contents. (CW II, par. 898).

The East uses the word "Satori" to name the enlightenment experience in Zen. Jung interpreted this word from a depth psychology perspective to mean

> a 'total vision' in potential. It constitutes the total disposition from which consciousness singles out tiny fragments from time to time. (CW II, par. 897).

Or he described the experience of Satori as "a break-through by a consciousness limited to the ego-form, into the non-ego-like self." (CW II, par. 887).

Today, there are Westerners who have achieved the rank of authorized teachers of Eastern meditation through Japanese masters [most prominently Enomiya Lasalle SJ but, today there is also, Niklas Brantschen SJ in Switzerland]. Their experience gives us a new perspective extending beyond Jung's, to a "double belonging" to both Buddhism and Christianity. (Brantschen, 2005).

The dreams of our student analysands from the Oriental countries are certainly interesting in this regard, since they are studying Jung's psychology in Switzerland. One Japanese Christian dreamt of a Catholic priest who walked up to a Japanese shrine as reverentially as a Buddhist priest. Her priest-animus had remained Japanese although she herself had become Catholic. For her unconscious, a shrine belongs together with a catholic priest. Psychologically she brings something together which would otherwise be split: she experiences valid priesthood as an inner possibility of bringing together heaven and earth as much in Christianity as in Buddhism.

In addition to the habitual and careful (we could say "religious") observation of his dreams, Jung's own way of meditation, if you will, was the practice of active imagination. As his article "The Psychology of Eastern Meditation" (CW II, par. 908-949) reveals, he tried to interiorly imagine the imagery depicted in a passage of the Amitabha Sutra (CW II, par. 913-932) so he could begin to interpret it psychologically. (CW II, par. 933-943). Here he says that we in the West (except for the Spiritual Exercises of St. Ignatius Loyola, which are practiced only among a relatively small circle) have not developed anything comparable to Yoga. (CW II, par. 941). He attributes this (among other reasons) to our fear of the personal and collective unconscious, which will undoubtedly come into play if one attempts meditative imagination. Also, entirely unwanted and unexpected by Westerners are the deep moral and religious conflicts which can be set loose. But he did say a few lines further on, "corresponding to our Western prejudice, a medical psychology has developed among us which occupies itself especially with the 'klesas' (the chaotic drives of the unconscious)." (CWII, par. 941). Master Shin'ichi Hisamatsu could relate to this and similar statements when in a discussion with Jung he pointedly asked whether the psychology of the unconscious, specifically the psychoanalytic method, could bring about an adequate experience of freedom as Zen can.

## Dialogue in Küsnacht –Dilemma of the Categories

Despite the different ways of thinking between a Zen master and C.G. Jung, yet due to the points of agreement between them, Master Shin'ichi Hisamatsu travelled to Küsnacht on May 16, 1958 to meet with the 83-year-old Jung. For Aniela Jaffé, who wrote the minutes of the dialogue in German, this was absolutely outstanding. (Hinshaw, 1986). Hisamatsu was the honoured patriarch of the Kyoto philosophers of his time and he had entered a Rinzai monastery. He worked from 1932 to 1949 at the University of Kyoto where he held the Chair of Religious Philosophy and Buddhism. Moreover, he lectured in the USA with Suzuki and there he had met Paul Tillich.

Hisamatsu had heard so much about analytical psychology in the USA that he initiated the meeting with Jung. He wanted to understand more thoroughly the position of analytical psychology and to compare it with Zen.

Jung immediately pointed out a difficulty with this comparison inherent in the comparison categories: a psychologist must argue psychologically, while a Zen master's opinions will be philosophical. Hisamatsu readily agreed, but added more precisely that although Zen is essentially a philosophy, it is very different from general philosophy, which depends on human reason. His definition: "Zen is a philosophy and at the same time a religion, but no ordinary religion. It is religion and philosophy." (Young-Eisendrath, 2002, p.112).

"Under which category should the comparison then be made?" I ask myself, "philosophic, or philosophic-religious?" Where is the place of psychology in this attempt to compare? Would the comparison be possible only if Jungian psychology, like Zen, included both philosophical and theological aspects? And would a comparison then perhaps be possible only along these aspects? But which aspects would they be ... and are they accessible? It was exactly this that Master Hisamatsu was apparently getting at: here lay his interest in Jungian psychology. Jung himself, however, hesitated on this question, pressed by precision. He asked questions explicitly from the psychological point of view: "You want to know, what I think psychologically of the task that Zen poses for us. The task is in both cases –Zen and psychology the same. Zen is comparable with how we deal with Wu-hsin.... (Young-Eisendrath, 2002, p. 112)

## The Unknown Self – Between the Ego and the Unconscious

Jung, both as a person and as a psychologist accepted the challenge of this philosophical-religious problem which Zen poses. (Don't these questions also belong in therapy, although they originally belonged to religious pastors who in the contemporary situation cannot completely fulfil them, Jung asked himself. (CWII, par. 505).

Here Jung saw a comparable problem for Zen and psychology: to figure out just "how we deal with Wu-hsin"? (Young-Eisendrath, 2002, p.112). Jung used here Zen's central concept of Wu – hsin, respectively Mu-Shin – "I mean the unconscious by it" (Young-Eisendrath, 2002,p. 112) – as a bridge of understanding. But: Can Mu-Shin really be compared to the unconscious? Hisamatsu immediately reacted by insisting upon a "true and strict definition for the term from the standpoint of Zen." (Young-Eisendrath, 2002, p.112).

Jung himself understood the unconscious to be "the unknown, that affects me psychologically, the unknown that disturbs or influences me, whether positively or negatively." (Young-Eisendrath, 2002, p.112). Hisamatsu interjected the precise question of whether or not there is a difference between this unknown and the unconscious, whereby Jung denied any.

And then Jung began to talk about the difference between the personal and the collective unconscious. Hisamatsu, however, posed the important question to Jung as to whether or not the non-personal unconscious is more fundamental than the personal. This non-personal unconscious, in relation to the super-personal unconscious, is apparently what intrigued Hisamatsu most (interested in philosophy and spirituality as he was) about Jung's psychology. Here, Jung once again stressed the difference between the personal and the super-personal unconscious: "The personal unconscious develops in the course of life, for example, through experiences, the memory of which I repress. The other, the collective is something instinctually innate and universally human." (Young-Eisendrath, 2002, p.1 12). And here came the decisive sentence in Jung's description of the collective unconscious, to which in his view also the religious imagination owes its existence: "My collective unconscious is the same as yours, even though you were born in Japan and I here in Europe." (Young-Eisendrath, 2002, p. 112). As I see it, in so far as religious-philosophical concepts, as well as those at the basis of Zen, have their origin in the collective unconscious of humanity, they must correspond to collective patterns, which are also established for an European and are from there negotiable. Where does the differentiation of cultural expressions of the collective unconscious begin?

Hisamatsu wanted more precision concerning the expression "the collective unconscious": "Does the collective unconscious involve something common to all persons or something that is beyond the personal.?" (Young-Eisendrath, 2002, p.112). Jung leaned more toward the aspect of commonality:

> One can only say that the collective unconscious is the commonality of all instinctive reactions found around all human beings. The possibility of our speaking with each other intelligently rests on our sharing a common foundation. Otherwise we would be so different as to understand nothing. (Young-Eisendrath, 2002, p.112).

The commonality relates itself here, however well-perceived, not to the formed concepts and contained images themselves, but rather to the commonality of all instinctive psychic reactions. Jung used once again the example of a child, who develops an ego out of a still collective unconscious condition, while the affect life is there like that of an animal's before the conscious life.

Whether these affects are more comparable to the eastern term of Klesas, the chaotic soul drives, as possessions and symptoms of the unconscious, was Jung's question, and he tried to ascertain, whether he correctly understood this eastern term. Hisamatsu, however, answered: "From our viewpoint, Klesas belong to the sphere of consciousness." (Young-Eisendrath, 2002, p.113). With that a great difference between the human image of Jung and that of Zen becomes visible. Buddhism does not know the unconscious, which is a terminus of modern western depth-psychology.

Klesas is understood as an annoyance or obstacle which belongs to conscious people, to the illusory ego, which should be overcome.

Jung seized upon what, according to his view, the role of consciousness in view of the Klesas could be, namely,

> of course consciousness is necessary, otherwise we could not establish that such things exist. But the question for us is: Is it consciousness that creates the Klesas? No, the conscious is their victim. Before consciousness passions already exist. (Young-Eisendrath, 2002, p.113).

Here both held fast to their different terminologies. The debate over the Klesas rans thus: that Jung introduced the eastern term of Klesas, to describe disturbing products and symptoms of the unconscious, which for Hisamatsu in Eastern Buddhist terminology present themselves as something that belongs to consciousness, just as surely as they belong to the unconscious according to Jung's definition. Buddhism simply does not know the unconscious in this way.

## A Light in the Night – the Relevance of the Ego

Hisamatsu's interest in Jung's understanding of the actual Self was very keen: How should the Self be understood in view of the unconscious, in view of the conscious or the observed ego?

Jung replied: "Consciousness refers to itself as 'I'. The Self is the whole personality – you as a totality – consisting of consciousness and the unconscious. This is the whole, or the self, but I know only consciousness; the unconscious remains unknown to me". (Young-Eisendrath, 2002, p. 113). Jung answered with his famous definition that the ego includes only the consciousness of a person; the Self, however, which is much larger than the ego, also contains the unconscious: but with that the Self is ultimately indescribable, ultimately unknown.

Hisamatsu was surprised by this revelation and as a consequence replied further: "So the Self is unknown?" (Young-Eisendrath, 2002, p.114).

To that Jung answered, but again relativising, "perhaps only half of it is known – and that is the 'I', the half of the Self." (Young-Eisendrath, 2002, p.114).

I myself find this picture-like image of C.G. Jung's somewhat misleading, for it suggests the idea of something substantial, like a round cake, which one can cut in half and bring into experience. In other places Jung defines the Self as completely immaterial, and there the unconscious is presented as nothing but a potential.

It became ever clearer during the discussion that Hisamatsu was mostly interested in the possible religious quality of the concept of Self and its comparability with that of Buddhism – yes, but with which concept ? Could one say that it is the concept of what Buddhism calls the "Buddha nature"?

Hisamatsu was keenly interested in how the common, partially-known ego is then connected to the originally unknown Self. What place does the ego occupy in the total personality?

Jung answered here clearly and precisely: "The 'I' is like a light in the darkness of night." (Young-Eisendrath, 2002, p.114). For Jung, the ego-bound light of consciousness surrounding the ego is indispensable for and inseparable from the Self. It is the conscious part of the Self. From the Buddhist perspective, this ego-personality as such is an illusion from which one should be freed. But: is there any Ego at all in the Asian concept of human nature? Have we in the West ever understood this correctly?

When finally the question was asked concerning a common orientation or goal for psychotherapy vis-à-vis Zen, Hisamatsu emphatically stood up for freeing one from the ego into the actual Self (i.e., into the "Buddha nature") which Zen teaches and practices. By this Zen means the Self which must no longer travel through the ten thousand things.

Zen points the way there. And here Hisamatsu clearly spelled out his divergence with Jungian thinking: " Is it necessary to liberate oneself from the collective unconscious as well, or from the conditions it imposes on us." (Young-Eisendrath, 2002, p.116).

From my point of view, this shows that he did not fully understand the Jungian meaning of the collective unconscious: by definition one cannot free oneself from the collective unconscious because it belongs to the Self: certainly a distinction can be strived for through the process of becoming conscious, if not also release. Surprisingly, here Jung accepted Hisamatsu's thought so far as to say that it is really necessary to free oneself from blind obedience to the collective unconscious: "If someone is caught in the then thousand things, it is because the person is also caught in the collective unconscious. A Person is liberated only when freed from both". (Young-Eisendrath, 2002, p. 116). One should free people from "must" – either from running after things, or from blindly obeying the unconscious.

## Suffering – Surmount or Acccept

A further central question which Master Hisamatsu kept asking from the perspective of Zen Buddhism was the value Jung placed upon suffering and overcoming suffering. Starting with the suffering of sick people, he asked whether the release from these sufferings which leads to a state of non-suffering could be the essence of therapy. How would such therapy be connected to the original unconscious?

Jung answered: in so far as the causes of the sickness lie in the unconscious, so far is it possible to alleviate it through making the causes conscious: "For example, there are other causes in which a person already knows that a bad relationship with his father or mother is the cause of his suffering." (Young-Eisendrath, 2002, p.114).

By this Hisamatsu understood that therapy consists in making clear the causes of the suffering and this would, of course, have reminded him of the basic principles of Buddhism concerning the origin of suffering.

Jung confined this within limits: there are also instances in which the causes have been long known, for instance that they lie with the father or mother of the patient. For him, the main point was:

> How can I treat the patient so that he becomes able to cope with his experience, while the father's and the mother's responsibility may be a causal factor. When all is said and done therapy hinges on the final question: What kind of meaning does my life have. (Young-Eisendrath, 2002, p.114).

So far as therapy has to do with becoming free from suffering,

Hisamatsu asked further, which changes in the realm of the unconscious bespeak this freeing?

Again, with this question Hisamatsu apparently did not fully understand Jung's concept of the unconscious: for psychotherapy in the Jungian sense does not seek to change the unconscious, but rather to make contact with the unconscious and bring into consciousness much of what was up till then unconscious. That part, which had been until now unconscious, has succeeded via this experience in becoming conscious, and making possible a change, a great freedom. When the conscious mind comes into contact with the unconscious, the power of the unconscious over consciousness is, by this very action, diminished.

According to Jung, suffering is not only caused by unconsciousness but is also a question of the attitude of the conscious mind. The patient could free herself from the suffering from her neurotic illness if she could achieve an objective perspective vis-à-vis her suffering; if she, for example, could learn to say yes to the suffering. If she could accept this, then it would already lessen her pain, Jung thought. When there is a chance, the therapist must go along with the suffering and even, for example, strengthen the suffering of the neurotic egocentric until the patient learns to ask herself the right questions: the archenemy of egocentrism itself is the via regia (the royal highway) to that stillness which makes possible the primordial religious experience. (CW 11, par. 526).

## Liberation – "all at once"

Hisamatsu did not waver from his line of questioning. With the example of Zen enlightenment in view he asked: "Can psychotherapy liberate us from suffering in one fell swoop"? (Young-Eisendrath, 2002, p.115).

Since Jung hesitated in answering, Hisamatsu underlined his question again: Is there a possibility that psychotherapy can, "in one fell swoop," free someone from suffering? Jung relativized in that he pointed out that in therapy one seeks to lessen the suffering of the person. "We need suffering. Otherwise, life would no longer be interesting. Psychotherapy must not disturb the problem of suffering too much in people. Otherwise people would become dissatisfied." (Young-Eisendrath, 2002, p. 115). "Connected with the practice of psychotherapy Jung often pointed out that suffering from a neurosis, for example, is necessary in order to finally make possible the steps of development: Suffering must even become stronger in order to move the person to transform.

Hisamatsu admitted at this point that suffering is in a certain sense necessary in life: it is, however, the deepest wish of humans to be freed from it.

Jung soberly answered: " The physician strives to reduce suffering, not to put an end to it." (Young-Eisendrath, 2002, p.116). Hisamatsu, however, obviously filled with one of the basic ideas of Buddhism, said that it is the duty of the great religions to alleviate human suffering. He referred to the great religious witnesses – even Christ's, whose intention it was to free humanity from suffering, even from the suffering of death or of the original sin. (I question whether Hisamatsu correctly interpreted the intention of Christianity).

"Is it possible to think," asked Hisamatsu reinvigorated and incisively, "that such a great liberation – as is the liberation from suffering – could be realised in psychotherapy?" (Young-Eisendrath, 2002, p.116). "The Great Liberation" was the title of a pioneering work by D.T. Suzuki about Zen, for which Jung wrote a foreword. (CW 11, par. 877-par. 907).

> What did Jung now have to say to this highly charged question of whether in psychotherapy an adequate liberation could occur, which a Zen master would understand as having a philosophical-religious quality of experience? To Jung it is not inconceivable, if you regard the problem not as personal illness, but as an impersonal manifestation of evil..."The concern of psychotherapy is in many cases to make patients conscious through insight, of the nidana chain, of the unnecessary suffering, fostered by lust, desire and passion. Passion ties us up, but through insight, we are made free. The goal in psychotherapy is exactly the same as in Buddhism. (Young-Eisendrath, 2002, p. 116).

In other places, such as in his essay "Psychotherapists or the Clergy" (CW 11, par. 488 – par. 552) Jung addressed himself much more thoroughly than here to the problem of suffering and the possibility of release through the psychotherapeutic process. Also, he considered religions, especially Christianity and Buddhism, to be healing systems for the suffering of the soul, and he also asked himself the question: "How can we assist the suffering soul to have freeing experiences. What it needs in order to live, namely faith, hope, love, and understanding". (CW 11, par. 500). And he continues: "These four highest achievements of human endeavour have so many gifts of grace which are neither to be taught nor learnt...Since they come through experience, which is an irrational datum not subject to human will and caprice." (CWII, par. 501).

In response to this, Jung reported his many experiences of how a turn-around towards healing could occur at the peak of illness. The so-called archetypes awaken to independent life and take over the leadership. The religious person would say, "God has taken over", but for most of his patients Jung has to say: "The soul's own functioning has been awakened". (CWII, par. 534).

The great turn around succeeds namely at the moment where in dreams or fantasy there arises a content or a theme whose origin in the unconscious cannot be traced. Something foreign, which is not the ego, emerges out of the dark realm of the soul and confronts the patient. It functions in the same way as a great enlightenment. Then one finds again the access to the spring of the blessed life and, with that, healing begins. (CWII, par. 534).

Jung here basis everything upon the personal experience of a possible becoming whole through psychotherapy and the accompanying awakening of contact with the unconscious, which can achieve the experiential quality of emotion. There is no methodological way: however

> Often it is simply the deep impression made on the patient by the independent way the dreams deal with his problem or it may be that his fantasy points to something for which his conscious mind was quite unprepared. But in most cases it is contents of an archetypal nature, or the connections between them, that exert a strong influence of their own whether or not they are understood by the conscious mind. This spontaneous activity of the psyche often becomes so intense that visionary pictures are seen or inner voices heard – a true primordial experience of the spirit. (CWII, par. 535).

For Jung, the suffering from the split between conscious and unconscious mind, separated from each other, creates neurosis, which arises from the rebinding of consciousness and the unconscious, which can release an experience of wholeness. "Such experiences reward the sufferer for the pains of the labyrinthine way. From now on a light shines trough the confusion; more, he can accept the conflict within him and so come to resolve the morbid split in his nature on a higher level." (CW II, par. 536).

## Misunderstandings and Differences

In their last round of talks Hisamatsu steered yet again to the clarification of the term Self . "What we in Buddhism, and especially in Zen, usually call the 'common self' corresponds exactly to what you call the 'collective unconscious', only through liberation from the collective unconscious, namely the common self, the authentic self emerge". (Young-Eisendrath, 2002, p.116).

Hisamatsu here sought to compare the "common self" of Jung, as he called it, with the actual self of Zen. Jung objected and said more precisely that the "common self" which Hisamatsu was talking about corresponds only to Jung's term "ego": "The self of which you speak corresponds for example the Klesas in the Yoga sutra. My concept of Self corresponds, however, to the notions of Atman or Purusha. The personal Atman corresponds to the Self insofar as it is at the same time the suprapersonal Atman. In other words: 'My Self' is at the same time 'The Self'. In my language the Self is a counterpart of the 'I'. What you call the self is what I would call the 'I'. What I call the Self is the whole, is the Atman. (Young-Eisendrath, 2002, p. 117).

Being again corrected, Hisamatsu immediately checked Jung's inaccurate use of the Atman language. With the introduction of Eastern terminology into the talk with Hisamatsu, Jung appeared not to have a lucky hand.

As opposed to the conventional Atman, which Jung was referring to, Hisamatsu repeated towards the end of the talk yet again his conviction, which agrees with the Zen tradition: "In Zen's true self there is no form and no substance, no spiritual nor bodily form"... (Young-Eisendrath, 2002, p.117).

To this Jung confessed the relativity of his own knowledge:

> "So when I compare the Self with Atman, my comparison is an obviously incorrect one. They are incommensurable, because the eastern way of thinking is different from my way of thinking. I can say, that the Self both exists and does not exist, because I really can say nothing about it". ((Young-Eisendrath, 2002, p.117). And he continues: "I cannot know what I don't know. I cannot be conscious of whether the Self hast attributes or not, because I am unconscious of the Self. The whole human person is both, conscious and unconscious...I can state metaphysical matters until I am blue in the face, but fundamentally, I don't know." (Young-Eisendrath, 2002, p.117).

Jung thereby defended himself against using "the Self" as a metaphysical term. Here again the difference between psychological and philosophic-religious terminology and argumentation reveals itself most clearly. However, in other places in his works, such in his essay "Psychotherapists or the Clergy" (CW 11, par. 488 – par. 552) Jung had nevertheless conveyed religious quality of the Self, not least in "Jung Speaking", where he compared the Self with Christ and described it with the same words that have been classically reserved for the image of God, namely: "The Self is a circle, whose center is everywhere and whose circumference is nowhere", and Jung continues: "And do you know what the self is for Western man? It is Christ, for Christ is the archetype of the hero, representing man's highest aspiration". (McGuire and Hull, 1977, p.401). And Jung continues, hese various descriptions of the Self revolve around a question of whether a purely dynamic structure is meant (which is for Jung also without substance and form), or a symbolization with contents. Here misunderstandings are easily possible.

Hisamatsu closed with an affirmation of the true Self which is "without form or substance": ... "and is therefore never bound by the ten thousand things. That is the essence of religious liberation. This is also the religious character of Zen, with its insight into the value of transcending the passions and becoming the formless self". (Young-Eisendrath, 2002, p.117). And he repeats: "That is, why I said at the beginning of our conversation that Zen is both, philosophy and religion." (Young-Eisendrath, 2002, p.117).

He thanked Jung for having discovered the connection between the unconscious and what we have called the true Self. Had this, however, really become clear?

## Conclusion

When we pull together Jung's descriptions of the Self in their essential expressions, we notice that his conception describes a pure potentiality without substance or form – and in this sense it is relatively near to the "true Self" of Zen – as near as conceptions arising from such various cultures and different disciplines as psychology and philosophical theology can be . How in this dialogue, Jung himself mentions repeatedly in his writings, that he had chosen the term "Self" to designate the totality of man, the sum total of his conscious and unconscious contents in accordance with Eastern philosophy?

In his last talk with Miguel Serrano, the then very elderly Jung, recounted the book of a Chinese Zen Buddhist which he had read to the end. Jung said: "And it seemed me, that we were talking about the same thing, and that the only difference between us was we gave different words to the same reality. Thus the word 'unconscious' doesn't matter. What counts is the idea that lies behind the word". (Mc. Guire and Hull, 1977, p. 467).

It is worth pondering that Serrano reported having had this last meeting with Jung in his Küsnacht residence, six weeks before Jung's death, and that Jung was wearing a Japanese ceremonial robe: "Jung was seated beside the window, dressed in a Japanese ceremonial gown..." (McGuire and Hull, 1977, S. 465). What a deep inner connection with the Japanese spirit, with the spirit of Zen, expressed itself in this clothing? Jung was convinced that the encounter between the spirits of the East and the West would intensify in the future, that this contact was necessary and constellated, that it had, moreover, begun long before with Meister Eckart: "I know that our unconscious is full of Eastern symbolism. The spirit of the East is really at our gates". (CW 15, par. 90).

At the gates of the West the spirit of Asia wants to create a break-through, namely a "break-through by a consciousness limited to the ego-form in the non-ego like Self". (CW 11, par.887) Jung was a trailblazer for this opening in the West.

## Note

The Jung-Hisamatsu conversation is translated into English from Aniela Jaffé's original German protocol by Shojo Muramoto, in collaboration with Polly Young-Eisendrath and Jan Middeldorf:

Young-Eisendrath, P. and Muramoto S. (eds) (2002) *Awakening and Insight. Zen Buddhism and Psychotherapy.* East Sussex: Brunner Routledge. In US: New York, Tylor and Francis, Inc.

## References:

Brantschen, N. (2005) *Auf dem Weg des Zen. Als Christ Buddhist.* München: Kösel Verlag.

Jaffé, A. In: Hinshaw, R, Fischli. L.(ed.) (1986) *C.G. Jung im Gespräch.* Einsiedeln, Daimon. p. 176-197.

Jung, C.G., *Foreword to Suzuki Introduction to Zen-Buddhism,* CW 11, par. 877-907.

Jung, C.G., *The Psychology of Eastern Meditation,* CW 11, par. 908-949.

Jung, C.G., *Psychotherapists or the Clergy,* CW 11, par. 488-552.

Jung, C.G., *The Psychology of Eastern Meditation,* CW 11, par. 908-949

Kast, V. (1992) *The Dynamics of Symbols. Fundamentals of Jungian Psychotherapy.* New York: Fromm International Publishing.

McGuire, W., Hull, F. (eds) (1977) *C.G. Jung speaking. Interviews and Encounters.* Princeton and New Jersey: Princeton University Press.

Shamdasani, S. (ed.) (1998), *The Psychology of Kundalini Yoga. Notes of the Seminar Given in 1932 by C.G. Jung.* Zürich, Düsseldorf: Walter Verlag.

# Women in Korean and Japanese Fairytales: "ChunHyang" (春香)

*Youkyeng Lee*
李裕瓊
(Seoul, South Korea, KAJA)

The story of ChunHyang is so popular in Korea that every Korean knows it. ChunHyang is included in the repertoire of the traditional Korean folksongs, Pansori, and the yearly "ChunHyang" festival[1] has been held for many years. Several versions of the film about Chun-Hyang have been made in Korea over the years.

## Synopsis

ChunHyang(春香) was the daughter of a Kisaeng[2] (妓生) and the Namwon Magistrate. She was pretty and wise. When the new Magistrate was appointed, his son, MongRyong, (夢龍) fell in love with ChunHyang and married her without his parents' permission. After his father finished the term as the Magistrate of Namwon, MongRyong had to follow his father back to Hanyang but he promised to come back for ChunHyang upon passing the state examination, where he expected to win the first place. Then the newly appointed Namwon Magistrate arrived and ordered ChunHyang to serve as a courtesan. ChunHyang refused his command and was thrown in prison and tortured, but she resisted to the end. MongRyong came first in the state examination and was appointed the secret royal inspector by the king. He returned to Namwon, punished the brutal Namwon Magistrate and rescued ChunHyang.

Interestingly, apart from the "ChunHyang" festival, which takes place in Namwon every year, there is also a shrine for ChunHyang built at the Gwanghallu (廣寒樓苑, secret garden) in Namwon. Even though ChunHyang is not a historical figure, she has been given a form of a real person who once lived there and is enshrined as sacred. An annual cultural event about "The Arrival of the New Magistrate" takes place in Namwon in spring.

Traditionally in Korea, regions, cities and important voyage vehicles (e.g. ships) are often named after goddesses. A feminine soul such

---

1 ChunHyang festival has been attracting millions of visitors every year and has been held for several hundred years since the Chosun Dynasty.

2 Kisaeng is a female artist(藝人) who can write poetry, play music and dance.

as the Goddess of the Earth or Mother Holy Ghost, represents the power of a region. A goddess of the region may not accept a corrupt king or a ruler who should no longer hold power. ChunHyang has also been regarded as a Goddess of Namwon so that she looks after the region and protects it. Considering the relationship between Chun-Hyang and the local Magistrate, it may be supposed that ChunHyang welcomed the new Magistrate as a soul of the region. The arrival of the new Magistrate is very important in local people's lives because the Magistrate is a leader in the collective life and the collective consciousness, like a king. In this regard, the story of ChunHyang could be understood as her refusal of the soul of the region, (the new the Magistrate, whom she disobeyed) even if the people of the region wouldn't have consciously recognized this.

From the point of view of analytical psychology, male and female figures in "ChunHyang" must not be understood as actual human beings but as autonomous psychic products, namely images. An encounter between male and female figures may bring forth the union of ego consciousness and the unconscious. Love in the story never means simple biological mating. Married couples dream of eternal love. From the point of view of depth psychology, love between a man and a woman may refer to the symbolic event of the encounter of ego consciousness with his or her Self thus raising self-awareness. Therefore, love is a very important experience for modern people by which they can regain their own roots, become whole persons. Jung points out in *The Psychology of the Transference* (1946) that modern people have lost connection to anima and animus because they have lost their own roots. This has caused a great increase in the divorce rate in modern societies through actual marital problems.

Love in "ChunHyang" deals with the spiritual pairing or psychic relationship between ego consciousness and anima/animus. We need to take this psychological point of view to understand love between a man and a woman. Let's look into the story in detail. This story will be interpreted in view of feminine psychology.

The story begins with an old lady, WolMae (月媒), who lived in Namwon with her daughter, ChunHyang. WolMae was a famous former Kisaeng(妓生). Our heroine, ChunHyang, is rooted in the maternal world because she was raised by and lived with WolMae who was a single mother. WolMae represents a typical mother image who serves to bring forth the feminine elements within the psyche and engage the masculine elements for the coniunctio oppositorum.

The character of WolMae corresponds to the very maternal strength which provides every protection and support for the production and acquisition of new feminine elements. Wol (月) means the Moon and Mae (媒) means a mediator. The name, WolMae, has the attributes of the Moon as a mediator. As a Kisaeng, WolMae had a daughter with the then Namwon Magistrate. This suggests that WolMae also has the characteristics of a Soul of the region, a Goddess of the Earth or Mother Holy Ghost, who stands for the reception of the dominant masculine principle which rules the region. We need to keep in mind the fact that in this story the mother image is a Kisaeng not a wife of the Namwon Magistrate.

Traditionally, the noblemen of Korea engaged in a cultural play called Poong-Ryu (風流). In Poong-Ryu, the intellectual noblemen have to sing their own poetry to present, one by one, their philosophy as well as to enjoy the aesthetic value of music and dance. Kisaeng, the woman artist, must join in Poong-Ryu and participate in the play as anima in order to bring forth the emotional aspect, to open up a new horizon of consciousness and ultimately to lead to the unity of opposites. The woman artist had a special role to attract the anima. However, Kisaeng was also treated like a prostitute. A courtesan has the power of a mother goddess to attract masculine elements for the renewal of an old ruler so that he can acquire new consciousness. The special social group, Kisaeng, belonged to one of the lowest social ranks, but they were not under the control of the dominant hierarchical forces so they could act freely enough to have relations with the upper psychic level as well as the lower. These characteristics of the mother image can attract elements of the opposites and forge relationships for the coniunctio oppositorum.

The heroine ChunHyang refers to the new feminine elements of consciousness. She acquires new feminine consciousness and becomes the owner of an individual personality. Let's look at her name: Chun(春) means "spring" and Hyang(香) means "scent" so the name ChunHyang(春香) means energy or scents of the coming spring. Her name reveals the directionality towards a higher level of consciousness or towards realization of a new spiritual ideal, like the coming spring with sprouting leaves against the long-lasting stillness and cold darkness of winter. The coming spring will raise the level of feminine consciousness to join the life of the collective consciousness.

As the daughter of a Kisaeng, ChunHyang could easily have been treated as a Kisaeng herself. This would have been an intentional disparagement of ChunHyang by the dominant part of the collective consciousness or a reflection of a lower level of the less differenti-ated feminine consciousness. The fact that in the story ChunHyang overcomes the social class divide shows us how the newborn feminine elements bring about true ownership of the feminine personality.

MongRyong, the partner of ChunHyang, is the son of the Magistrate who replaced ChunHyang's father. At this point in the story, the figure of the Magistrate corresponds to the collective consciousness as well as being an unconscious support of the individual feminine consciousness. Therefore, the arrival of the new Magistrate with his son indicates the impending change in the feminine psyche. Let's find the meaning of the name MongRyong: Mong(夢) means dream and Ryong(龍) means dragon. Therefore, MongRyong(夢龍) means dreaming, sleeping dragon. In Korea, dragon is a symbol of mail power or strength, like a king or it is a sign at birth of a boy who will later achieve something great. The dreaming, sleeping dragon should reflect characteristics of the masculine element, which corresponds to the animus. It does not aim to attain the new masculine consciousness but aims to act behind the feminine consciousness, as animus.

Considering the son of the new Magistrate as animus brings in the differentiation in feminine personality. However, animus belongs to the Magistrate who represents the collective consciousness. This suggests the possibility that animus would be applied in an extra-verted way. Therefore, the feminine personality is still unconscious or the feminine personality is totally assimilated into the collective consciousness. As long as the feminine ego consciousness is still undifferentiated, the animus plays the role of feminine consciousness.

MongRyong visited Gwanghanru during the traditional Korean spring festival Dano(端午) on April 15th and saw ChunHyang far in the distance, playing on the swing. On Dano, women washed their hair in water boiled with Changpo (a kind of herb) and played on long rope swings to ward off evil spirits and to preserve health and wealth through the year. Using their bodies, women played on the swings to try and reach higher altitudes. The higher the altitude they reached, the wider the scope of the external world they could see. The purpose of this play is to broaden the horizons of consciousness and make a leap towards the external world. Let's look into this moment from the position of depth psychology: feminine consciousness is about to become free from the maternal world and to finally express her interest in the external world. This would be the first step in the differentiation of the individual feminine consciousness. At that very moment, MongRyong appears and attempts to meet ChunHyang. This situation suggests two possible interpretations: one interpretation is that MongRyong, as the son of the Magistrate, would guide ChunHyang to the external world as animus applied in the way of extraversion: women after puberty usually meet the demands of the external world, and then they are unintentionally possessed by the animus. As adaptation to external environment is urgently needed in modern society, it may be considered as quite natural for women to identify themselves with social roles, namely the persona. As we know, identification with social roles can be a cause for activation of animus. Then feminine consciousness would also be guided by animus.

The other interpretation is that animus appears to ask for application introvertedly, when ChunHyang made her first step towards the external world having been freed from the maternal world. MongRyong's attempt to meet ChunHyang is psychologically equivalent to the feminine consciousness beginning to be aware of itself. Through the touch of the animus, feminine consciousness may become able to recognize that she had never been the owner of her personality. MongRyong actively proposed to ChunHyang to marry him. On behalf of the feminine consciousness, the activated animus is working for the development of feminine personality.

MongRyong visited ChunHyang's mother, WolMae, to ask her permission to marry ChunHyang. WolMae gave her permission and they were married. The role of the mother image, WolMae, is essential here. At that moment, the mother image, the root of feminine personality, awakens the inner feminine nature and brings the activated animus into the totality of feminine personality. Now animus belongs to the feminine psyche. By this transition, feminine consciousness acquires the capacity to distinguish inner needs from external social requirements. A new phase begins after the marriage of MongRyong and ChunHyang and the story now goes on to follow the journey of the heroine, ChunHyang.

ChunHyang is now under the spotlight while MongRyong returns to Hanyang (Seoul) with his father. In spite of their marriage, the divide in the social class between them still remains. Psychologically, this means that there exists a divide on the psychic level between the two. Their marriage with WolMae's permission is equivalent to the preparation for the coniunctio oppositorum, the so called "Vornehmen". In other words, the marriage is the preliminary stage before the achievement of the ultimate goal, which is the union of the feminine consciousness and the animus. The fulfillment of this purpose is the feminine consciousness owing itself and intending to find an inner partner. The mother image is always the driving force that turns the gaze of the feminine consciousness back towards its inner nature and origin. Then the animus will not turn to the external world any more.

Back in the story, the newly arrived Magistrate exerts his power over ChunHyang. His command that she should be treated like a courtesan corresponds to the significant sufferings of feminine personality in the position of a heroine: the Magistrate causes the heroine's suffering. Now ChunHyang must choose between the power of the new Magistrate and her love for MongRyong. Owning her feminine personality, ChunHyang proclaims her "single-minded love (一片丹心)" for MongRyong. When she married MongRyong, ChunHyang promised her single-minded love to him by saying that she would never have two husbands. At that moment, ChunHyang's promise acted as a kind of principle to awaken MongRyong, who was living in his higher social class, not to abandon ChunHyang in the lower social class that she belonged to.

Psychologically, the "single-minded love" may be thought of as women's conservative attitude based on the mother image. Living in the maternal world, women are reluctant to connect with strangers from the external world. This conservative attitude helps to create a relationship with the animus by mediation of the mother image in order to follow the demands of the woman's inner world.

MongRyong, who went back to Hanyang following his father, studied hard for the state examination in order to rise in the world. It looks as though the partner of the heroine, or animus, is going to actively participate in the collective consciousness. However, from the perspective of the feminine psychology, it can also be seen that the heroine is going to reveal herself to consciousness with the introverted application of animus. ChunHyang's refusal to follow the command of the new Magistrate and her proclamation of her single-minded love correspond to the thoughtful attitude of listening to the voice of her inner nature and keeping a distance from the demands of the external world. ChunHyang's single-minded love brought about her real ownership of feminine personality.

The story reveals MongRyong's success in the state examination following ChunHyang's refusal to follow the orders of the new Magistrate. A man who succeeded in the state examination must not follow the existing dominant collective ideology but can propose a new ideology. MongRyong's success indicates a state which proposes a universal ideology in the collective human life by introverted application of animus. On behalf of the king, MongRyong can exert influence over the collective daily life. This is the role of true animus. Animus can raise his own voice even if he is not directly involved in the external world. As a secret royal inspector, MongRyong punished the Namwon Magistrate and rescued ChunHyang. The feminine personality can realize universal social value with the help of the animus.

We can get a better understanding of animus in a woman by comparing MongRyong and the Namwon Magistrate. Animus may be substantially blooming after puberty and projected on to boys or men around a young woman. This helps to open her eyes to the external world. When the father image exerts its influence on the values of the collective consciousness, animus fosters development and acts instead of feminine consciousness. The refusal of ChunHyang to obey the command of the Namwon Magistrate means that she can distinguish between her inner demands and those coming from the external world. She is now able to maintain her feminine consciousness in her own way. Furthermore, she can restore her own original value of the individual feminine personality. Introvertedly applied animus can guide the feminine consciousness to realize universal values, which are inherent in human nature. It can also perform a compensatory function to the one-sidedness of feminine consciousness. It will exert a healing effect on feminine personality and on the collective consciousness.

The story ends with the Namwon Magistrate being replaced and MongRyong returning to Hanyang with ChunHyang. The title of the last chapter is: "Lee-Hwa-Chun-Poong (李花春風)", meaning "Spring has come at last". Like her name, ChunHyang, the energy or scent of the coming spring is filling up human consciousness. Spring means new consciousness. That spring has come represents the feminine consciousness being able to freely participate in the collective conscious life, which will lead to the individuation of the feminine personality.

The scene where ChunHyang is oppressed by the tyrannical Namwon Magistrate reminds us of women's condition in modern society. When the dominant principle of the collective consciousness is prejudiced or not properly functioning, women may feel as if the collective consciousness is oppressing them. To solve this problem, women should stick to their own hearts and keep a distance from the demands of the external world. This corresponds to ChunHyang's attitude of single-minded love, keeping her promise to MongRyong against the oppressive Magistrate. This attitude may help modern women connect to their inner psyche and their animus on the unfolding path of individuation.

### References

Hwang, H.J. ed., (2007). *Chunhyang.* Seoul, Korea: Kyelimbook.
Jung, C.G. (1946). The Psychology of the Transference. *CW 16.* Princeton: Princeton University Press, pp. 442-444.

# The Feminine in Korean and Japanese Fairytales: "Princess Kaguya"

*Sonoko Toyoda*
(Japan, AJAJ)

## Princess Kaguya and the Feminine spirituality

The most well-known and the most popular heroine of Japanese old folk tales is Princess Kaguya. She is the heroine of "The Story of the Bamboo-cutter", by an unknown author, originating around the 9th Century. This tale is regarded the oldest written tale in Japan. But the original story has been simplified and, as the fairytale, "Princess Kaguya", it has been handed down for a long time from generation to generation until today. This story's heroine, Princess Kaguya, has been loved by the Japanese people for such a long time that this story must represent a certain peculiarity of the Japanese psyche. At the same time, I believe that this story is essential when we are looking for a feminine quality that is very important yet missing in today's world. Many women of today, without knowing it, are trying to modify themselves in order to comply with social expectations of how they should be, although it might betray their own feminine instinct. Such a tragedy can and does happen because in many cases these expectations are based on men's idealized or biased images of the feminine which were formed during the long lasting social dominance of men. In my view, there must be a feminine quality, which gives dignity to women as they naturally are, and I will call this feminine quality "feminine spirituality." Of course, you can give this quality many different names, but I wanted to express this particular feminine quality, which exists in the feminine psyche, like a sacred spring in a deep forest. The problem is that many women of today have completely forgotten about the existence of this spring in their own psyche, or they cannot believe in it anymore. This has made it difficult for women to have self-confidence, even when they are successful in society. I have worked with many such women in my private practice. The story of Princess Kaguya that I am going to tell you now, will give you an image of this missing feminine quality and perhaps some clues as to what is feminine spirituality.

## Beginning of the story

The story begins when an old bamboo-cutter found a glowing bamboo in the bamboo forest. He cut its trunk and there inside he found a wonderful, shiny baby girl, who was so tiny that he took her home in his cupped hands and raised her carefully with his old wife. Thereafter, whenever he cut a bamboo, he found gold inside.

The girl grew very quickly and in 3 months she became a beautiful woman. Because her luminous beauty lit the whole house, she was named, Princess Kaguya, meaning the Shining Princess.

Bamboo is often seen as a symbol of vital force because it grows very quickly. It is also said that a certain divinity dwells in the hollow of the bamboo. So the girl discovered inside a bamboo would certainly have divine qualities. The name, Kaguya, means not only shining brightly, but it has other connotations, too: the word "kagu 輝" means "shining brightly", and "ya" can be understood as a word of exclamation. But this "ya" is also written with the Chinese character 夜, which means "night". In this case, her name means "shining brightly in the night", and her name is often written in this way. Accordingly, some people insist that all incidents in this story happened in the night. Moreover, in some versions of the story, the word "kaguya" is written with the Chinese characters 赫野, meaning "fire-blazing red" for "kagu" and "field" for "ya". From these various connotations of her name, we can say that she is not only a beautiful shining princess but also that she has many facets.

## The Difficult Tasks for Suitors

To return to the story: having heard of her luminous beauty, many suitors came to Kaguya's house. However, she refused to see them. In the end, only five noble men remained, asking fervently for her hand in marriage. The old bamboo-cutter tried to persuade Princess Kaguya to choose one of them as her husband but she was reluctant. Finally, she asked them to find and bring to her five legendary treasures as a proof of their true love. The five legendary treasures she wanted were: 1) Buddha's stone bowl, 2) a pearl-born branch from a tree of gold and silver on Mt. Horai (the isle of Eternal Youth), 3) a skin of a fire-mouse in China, 4) a dragon's multi-colored ball, 5) a cowrie shell possessed by swallows. To find such treasures is in fact an impossible task. Some suitors tried to cheat Kaguya by bringing her fake treasures. Some tried to get them recklessly, but in the end they gave up having risked their lives for the treasures. Ultimately, no man could have the Princess as his bride.

I think that none of the suitors understood what Princess Kaguya really wanted. All these treasures have certain spiritual values. The

Buddha's stone bowl is a receptacle for all human sorrow, misery and despair as well as joy and happiness. It is a vessel of compassion. Mt. Horai is a legendary Taoist mountain of immortality in China. The tree composed of silver and gold is the union of the principles of Yin and Yang, and the pearls on it are the spiritual fruits of this union. It is said that the skin of a fire-rat is not only burnt by fire but cleansed and renewed in the fire. Here fire works for purification and transformation and not for destruction. A dragon is an imaginary animal which connects heaven and earth. It makes the rain fall, which in turn brings forth the bounty of the earth. The dragon is a controller of water, and the dragon's multi-colored ball might be a symbol of feminine wisdom. The cowrie shell is well known as a symbol of feminine genitalia and fecundity. The swallow is written as 玄鳥 (black-bird in Chinese characters). However, this character, 玄, does not mean just black but it also connects with the dark, mysterious female. A migration of swallows lets us know of the cycle of the seasons. It reminds us of the feminine time cycles. In this way, what Princess Kaguya requested was for the men to seek treasures related to feminine spirituality. In essence, these treasures give us some hints about what feminine spirituality is. Thus, it is quite natural that no man could get these treasures for her. Women have to search for these treasures by themselves, for themselves, within their own deep psyche.

## Emperor's Visit

Another male figure also appears in the story: the Emperor. The Emperor had heard of Princess Kaguya, a woman who trifled with men and refused to marry. He called her to the Palace, but she refused to obey his command at the risk of losing her life. Intrigued, the Emperor unexpectedly arrived at her home, pretending that he was on a hunting expedition. There he saw a beautiful woman in abundant light. He thought that she must be the Princess and grabbed her by the sleeve but she vanished like a shadow. When he realized that he could not enforce obedience upon her, the Emperor apologized to Kaguya and she reappeared in front of him. The Emperor then returned to his palace and began to write letters to Princess Kaguya, and she wrote back. This exchange of letters continued over the course of three years.

As a ruling power, the Emperor is considered as the collective consciousness. Princess Kaguya refused to obey him. She represents a feminine image who has her own dignity and does not obey a masculine power. However, once the Emperor showed that he respected her dignity and accepted that she would keep her own space near nature rather than in the Palace, Princess Kaguya accepted the Emperor and wrote poems in her letters to him. Here the feminine and the masculine are equal in their relationship, and there is certainly a spiritual union between the two.

## The Weeping Princess and the Moon

Then one spring, Princess Kaguya began to sigh deeply while watching the moon. By the summer she was lamenting more and more, shedding tears. When the old couple asked her what was wrong, she revealed: "I am sad, because I must leave you. I am from the Kingdom of the Moon. On the 15th of August, on the night of the full moon, a retinue will come to take me back to the moon."

If we regard Princess Kaguya as an image of feminine spirituality, her relation to the moon is not surprising. The moon is a well-known symbol of femininity. Esther Harding speculates about the importance of the moon as a symbol of the feminine psyche in her book, *Woman's Mysteries* (Harding, 1971). Similarly, Erich Neumann wrote, "Thus the moon manifests (…) in female form as the highest expression of the female spirit-Self, as Sophia, divine wisdom" (Neumann 1994, p. 110). Princess Kaguya was sent from the moon. However, she felt very sad to leave the old couple because she was raised by them. Although from the beginning she had certain divinity, she was humanized enough to feel human affection and emotions.

## Ascent to the Moon

On the night of August 15th, the Emperor sent 2000 warriors to guard the Princess, and the old couple hid her in a secluded room in their house. When the full moon shed an extremely bright light, celestial people in beautiful raiment came down riding on the cloud. The warriors became numbed and lost the will to fight. Then the King of the Moon summoned the old bamboo-cutter and said: "Her Highness, the Princess, has lodged temporarily in the house of a person living in humble conditions like you. This is because she committed a sin. But now she has paid for her sin, so we will take her back to the moon." Then he called Princess Kaguya, "Your Highness, you are not allowed to stay any longer in this contaminated world." Then all the doors sprang open by themselves, and Princess Kaguya stepped out. She said to the weeping bamboo-cutter and his wife: "I have to leave you against my will. Please look at the moon and think of me." She wrote a letter to the Emperor and gave it to his messenger with the elixir of immortality. Then she ascended to the heavens, followed by hundreds of celestial people.

As the King of the Moon spoke to the Princess in a reverential manner, it seemed that he recognized her as a higher being than himself. Who was she? Yes, she might be the Moon Goddess. We can find her features as this goddess in Esther Harding's wonderful book, *Women's Mysteries* that I mentioned earlier. Harding points out that the most distinguishing feature of the Moon Goddess is her virginity. "She is essentially one-in-herself," she writes (Harding 1971, p. 125). This was the way that Princess Kaguya was. Harding also points out the dark side of the virgin Moon Goddess whose coldness is negative and hostile to men. Princess Kaguya's mercilessness towards her suitors may be understood as the dark side of the moon, namely the new moon and the crescent.

We should also consider the light that Kaguya emanated. As her name was often written as "Shining- Night Princess (輝夜姫)", her light is not the daylight, but rather something akin to the moonlight. Harding writes:

> The light of the moon which shines from heaven above and brings enlightenment and wisdom to the earth is frequently personified and represented by a bird, usually a dove. The Sophia, the Holy Wisdom of Gnostics, is in fact, the light of the Heavenly Mother and is equated to the Holy Dove of the Spirit (Harding, p. 52).

We can esteem Princess Kaguya as a kind of Moon Goddess with spiritual value.

Another big question is what kind of sin did Princess Kaguya commit. The story says nothing about it. It is a mystery. I would like to focus on the fact that Princess Kaguya did not want to go back to the moon. She expresses her affection towards the old couple who raised her and also towards the Emperor. She wanted to find her own place on this earth, but she was not allowed to do so.

Here is the comparison between the contaminated human world and the clean moon world. The way of seeing the feminine spirituality largely changed in the 9th Century when this story was written. In ancient Japan the feminine spirituality was respected, and religious rites were carried out by women. After this period, Shintoism was established by male priests based on the doctrine of refinement (removing uncleanliness). In ancient times women's blood at delivery and menstruation were regarded as the source of feminine spirituality, but from this time on it was regarded as unclean and something to avoid. Princess Kaguya's lamentation when she was leaving this world might have been symbolic of the women's sorrow for the gone ancient era because what was essentially feminine became unacceptable in the male-dominated society.

## The End of the Story

After Princess Kaguya ascended to the heavens, the old bamboo-cutter and his wife were overwhelmed with grief and became seriously ill. The Emperor who received the Princess's last letter with the elixir of immortality lamented in his great sorrow: "Now that I have lost Princess Kaguya, such an elixir is useless!" Then he asked: "Which mountain is the nearest to the heavens?" and he commanded that the elixir be burned on the top of that mountain. The Emperor's messenger climbed up this mountain with many soldiers, and this mountain was named, Mt. Fuji (meaning "many soldiers" or "immortality"). It is said that the smoke from the burning elixir still rises up to the heavens. This is how the story of Princess Kaguya ends.

Mt. Fuji is the highest mountain in Japan. This beautiful solitary mountain is nowadays a dormant volcano, but in the 9th Century when this story was written, it was still active, and people always saw the smoke rise up to the sky.

There is also another old story with Princess Kaguya: the story of the guardian deity of Mt. Fuji. In this story, Kaguya (written: 赫野, meaning fire blazing red field ) was also discovered in the bamboo bushes and raised by an old couple. She grew up and married a human but then left him and returned to the top of the mountain. In this story princess Kaguya is regarded a goddess of Mt. Fuji. She is identified as the flower-blossoming Princess, who is a better known goddess of this mountain. We might have different impressions of the red-hot volcano goddess and the cold moon goddess but I think that these two aspects are important, when we regard Princess Kaguya as a symbol of feminine spirituality.

Why did Kaguya have to go back to the moon? Here I have to bring in our Japanese Sun goddess, Amaterasu. In Japanese mythology the supreme deity in the center of the pantheon of gods is the Sun Goddess. But if we read the myth precisely, we soon recognize that she is not "essentially one-in-herself" as Harding says, but a typical "father's daughter" who was born from the left eye of her father, Izanagi. In fact, we can always recognize the existence of the fatherly deity behind her behavior. Although Amaterasu was the supreme goddess, the male dominance in the society had already begun and had influenced the myth.

What is crucial is that Princess Kaguya, who was "essentially all-in-herself" has been loved by the Japanese people for such a long time. The story of Princess Kaguya clearly compensates Japanese mythology in the Japanese psyche. This story also illustrates the deep sorrow for the loss of feminine spirituality. We are severely wounded by this loss. Not only women, but men too. The loss of feminine spirituality is certainly the loss of Anima Mundi. Mt. Fuji is also written in Chinese characters as: 不二 (this represents non-duality, unity). If you have a chance to see this unique mountain, please remember this story.

*Fig.1: A sand play image on the story of Princess Kaguya*

This Japanese story shows a great loss of feminine spirituality in our world and our deep grief resulting from this loss. The Japanese people's longing for this missing feminine spirituality may have something to do with the Japanese esthetic which permeates Japanese culture. However, I think that women of today need to revive the image of Princess Kaguya in our own psyche and to find our spring of wisdom in the deep forest.

## Conclusion

Since 2008, every year, Dr. Youkyeng Lee and I have been giving collaborative seminars on fairytales. Both of us are very interested in feminine psychology and in each seminar we look into feminine stories. On this occasion of the 2016 IAAP Congress, together we chose the most popular story from each of our two countries. As you have seen, the two stories are very different and our approaches are also very different. Dr. Youkyeng Lee emphasized that, in all instances, in our modern society women must be rooted in the maternal world.

Through this condition, women can recover their inner relationship with the animus and keep a distance from the external social demands. On the other hand, with the story about Princess Kaguya, I have tried to reflect on the image of the feminine spirituality, with its main feature being virginity. I have attempted to extract feminine quality, which gives women certain dignity and which is separate from maternity.

Nevertheless, our mutual conclusion is that a woman needs to be "essentially one-in-herself" in order to have an equal relationship with a man (or animus) and to attain the wholeness of her personality.

## References

Harding, E. (1971).*Women's Mysteries: Ancient & Modern*, Shambhala.

Neumann, E. (1950). The Moon and Matriarchal Consciousness, *The Fear of the Feminine and other Essays on Feminine Psychology*, Princeton University Press, 1994.

*Thursday, 1 September*

# Soul in the World: Symbolic Culture as the Medium for Psyche

*Warren Colman*
(London, SAP)

## Plato, Descartes and the split between mind and matter

The idea of the *anima mundi* or world-soul from which this confer-ence takes its theme is an attractive idea with a long history. In its orig-inal incarnation in Plato's *Timaeus* it directly refers to the animation of the world, universe or cosmos. Plato conceives of the world as a living being, endowed with soul and intelligence, encompassing all the living creatures within it (2008, 30b; 30d). This is a vision rooted in a cultural world where science and myth had not yet been differentiated so there was no contradiction between an animistic vision of the physical world and a demonstration of its nature in terms of mathematical geometry. The relation between soul and body also carried ethical implications. Plato considered that the aim of life was to recover the perfect revolutions of the soul from the perturbations caused by the chaos of the senses and this was linked to a belief in reincarnation in a more or less perfect bodily form, a view that nevertheless held humans and other animals to be ontologically equivalent by virtue of their common possession of a soul (Carpenter, 2008). There are thus many linkages between Plato's thought and similar animistic beliefs still found in many cultures all over the world.

Yet there is also a crack in Plato's world that has grown into the great divide between body and soul, matter and spirit that has rent the modern world in two – a split that Jung laboured to heal in the world and himself throughout his life and work. It is not so much that Plato conceives of body and soul as separate, for many animistic cultures have beliefs about the circulation of souls through various cosmic forms; it is rather that Plato sets up a clear hierarchy between the two, made most apparent in the *Symposium*, where he contrasts the love of absolute, divine beauty with the grossly inferior love of physical beauty which he describes as "a mass of perishable rubbish" (Plato 1951, 212).

This notion of the inferiority of the body and the physical world came to play an increasingly dominant role in the Christian world, exemplified by St. Paul's view that "the desires of the flesh are against the Spirit and the desires of the Spirit against the flesh" (Galatians 5: 16-17), a much more extreme conflict than we find in Plato. The more that soul is seen as the true and only source of life, the more the material world comes to be seen as devoid of life and divorced from spirit. This trend became clearly apparent in the scientific revolution of the seventeenth century and found its philosophical expression in the work of Descartes. Descartes' explicit intention was to rid philosophy of the old Aristotelean (and latterly Christian) idea of things in the world having the teleological qualities of soul (Descartes 2009, p. 163) The aim of this deanimation was to clear the way for science to explore the world in terms of purely physical mechanisms. Since the body is part of the physical world, then surely it too must be purely mechanical, thus giving rise to the problem of how mind and brain are connected. Over the past two centuries, this trend has gone even further: not only have we come to see the mind as separated off from the material world but we have come to doubt whether the mind has any kind of soul at all or is merely an expression of the physical activity of the brain.

The scientific method developed in the 17th century has been spectacularly successful as a means of understanding the natural world and harnessing its forces for industrial and technological transformation. Yet this has come at a high price, often described in terms of the desacralisation and pillaging of the natural world, together with the alienation, isolation and loss of meaning that characterise Western societies. These concerns are clearly evident in the theme of this conference with its references to climate change, ecological crises and the "dissociation from *Anima mundi*".

## *Esse in anima* – Jung's solution to the isolated Cartesian mind

As stated in the Call for Participation in this conference, Jung "tried to reconnect the isolated modern human psyche to the world soul". Despite this, his attitude towards the severance of mind from world was ambivalent and contradictory, reflecting the split in himself between Number 1 and Number 2 personalities. In his "Number 2" personality, Jung felt identified with "the spirit of the depths" (Jung 2009, p. 229). In this aspect, Jung experienced for himself the oneness of the world with the living soul and many of his major concepts reflect this, especially the self, the psyche, the unconscious and latterly the archetypes. All these concepts implicitly transcend the boundaries of the individual mind and include aspects that unite our personal lives with something far greater, for which the *anima mundi* and the *unus mundus* are both symbolic expressions. Yet the revolutionary transformations brought about by Jung's "confrontation with the unconscious" did not dispel the firmly held beliefs of his No. 1 personality, rooted in the "spirit of the times" (ibid.) Jung was not willing to give up his scientific convictions to become a mystic or prophet but, throughout his life, sought to reconcile the one with the other.

These opposing tendencies can be seen quite clearly in the quotation heading the Call for Participation:

> The development of Western philosophy during the last two centuries has succeeded in isolating the mind in its own sphere and in severing it from its primordial oneness with the universe. Man himself has ceased to be the microcosm and eidolon of the cosmos, and his "anima" is no longer the consubstantial scintilla, or spark of the *Anima mundi*, World Soul (Jung 1939/1954, para 759).

On the surface, it appears as if Jung is lamenting this trend and eulogising the lost union with the anima. Yet, if we read further, it becomes apparent that Jung not only accepts the Cartesian divide between mind and world but regards it as a positive progression. This is most apparent in his view that pre-Cartesian ways of being in the world were the result of "projections" that hark back to a more primitive condition that modern man has now left behind:

> If we accept the restrictions imposed upon the capacity of our mind ... we bid farewell to that miraculous world in which mind-created things and beings move and live. This is the world of the primitive, where even inanimate objects are endowed with a living, healing, magic power, through which they participate in us and we in them. Sooner or later we had to understand that their potency was really ours, and that their significance was our projection (ibid., para 761).

Elsewhere he writes "through the withdrawal of projections, conscious knowledge slowly developed" (Jung 1938/1940, para 140) and expresses the view "that there is, in a certain sense, nothing that is directly experienced except the mind itself" (Jung 1926, para. 623). Thus he accepts without question the view that "cognition is a mental faculty and, if carried beyond the human plane, a projection" (Jung 1939/1954, para. 765) and that man is therefore "shut up inside his mind and cannot step beyond it" (ibid.). Jung derived most of this from Kant's rejection of transcendent knowledge and his strictures on the fundamental unknowability of the "thing in itself". Yet the image of being "shut up inside his mind" is also a perfect representation for Descartes *"cogito ergo sum"* in which only the contents of his own thinking mind can be guaranteed as real. Jung's approach is therefore to render unto Kant and Descartes what is due to Kant and Descartes but then to seek a way of nevertheless rendering unto God what is due to God – and to the *anima mundi*.

His solution is an ingenious one: to the conflict between *esse in intellectu* (being in the mind) and *esse in re* (being in actuality), Jung proposes a third possibility, *esse in anima*, being in soul, and he makes this the overarching reality that incorporates the other two (Jung 1921, paras. 66, 77). Jung's ploy here is to take the notion of psyche as the primary datum, the only thing which we can directly know, and then suggest that since both the phenomenal and noumenal worlds are experienced psychically, they can be interpreted as functions of the psyche. Furthermore, since what is most important in the psyche is not mere consciousness but the vast untapped resources of the unconscious and especially the archetypes, it is the archetypes that become the real powerhouse, not only of psychic life but of the world as a whole. The entirety of world history and ultimately the cosmos itself can be seen as the manifestation of the archetypes. But rather than this being seen philosophically, as in Plato's Ideal Forms or religiously as in the Christian notion of God's will, it can now be demonstrated psychologically, and therefore scientifically.

The origins of this ingenious solution lie in Jung's encounter with the god Izdubar, reported in *The Red Book*. Izdubar, the old God of the East, cannot survive the encounter with modern science from the West which threatens to kill him off altogether in Neitzschian style. So Jung offers him a way out – he puts the god in his pocket and preserves him as a psychic image, a fantasy. Yet this fantasy, it turns out, is mightier than anything else because it is the psyche that *creates* reality. As he formulated it in *Psychological Types*:

> What indeed is reality if it is not a reality in ourselves, an *esse in anima*? Living reality is the product neither of the actual objective behaviour of things nor of the formulated idea exclusively, but rather of the combination of both in the living psychological process, through *esse in anima* … *The psyche creates reality every day*. The only expression I can use for this activity is *fantasy* (Jung 1921, para. 77-78).

By this means, Jung is able to use the reality of the psyche as a trump card with which to put not only Izdubar in his pocket but the science and philosophy that threatened to kill him off. Psychological explanations trump philosophical ones by revealing their underlying archetypal origins. Yet despite this ingenious solution, Jung was still unable to reconcile the divide between spirit and matter, body and soul that preoccupies his later work on synchronicity, the psychoid, and the attempt to find a common ground between atomic physics and archetypal psychology.

In my view, these difficulties were because Jung made the wrong call in accepting the Kantian/Cartesian limitations on the mind as "shut up in its own sphere", isolated from the living world in which we actually participate all the time. It is this disconnect in Jungian psychology itself that results in frequent attempts to interpret world events as the expression of archetypal forces, as if the real forces at work in our collective lives are not geography, climate, competition for resources and social and political conflict but "the great mother", "the trickster", "the shadow" or "the anima". To my mind, this not only fails to address the complex interrelation between states of mind and the state of the social world but reduces the latter to a kind of ghost-life as if it is merely a screen for psychic projections.

An example of this can be found in Jung's 1936 essay where he interprets events in Nazi Germany as the re-awakening of Wotan in the German psyche. It is not difficult to see that the catastrophic economic conditions in Weimar Germany, together with the humiliating shock of defeat in the First World War, would have evoked states of fear, confusion, rage and impotence to which Nazi ideology appeared to offer a radical solution. Wotan may be a very useful metaphor for this that roots the specific features of National Socialism in German history and the symbols of German culture. But Jung goes much further than this to suggest that Wotan is "a fundamental attribute of the German psyche" (para. 389) whose "unfathomable depths ... explain more of National Socialism than [economic, political and psychological factors] put together" (para. 385). Jung takes his own metaphor as a causal explanation, as if it is not the aftermath of the First World War that has created these social conditions, but that history itself is to be understood as the working out of archetypal forces, an argument pursued on a grand scale in *Aion*.

In my view, if we are to appreciate how the soul lives in the world, we need first to see how living in the world creates the soul. To do so, we need to tackle the Cartesian world-view at its roots, challenging the separation between mind and world in favour of an approach that relocates the mind in embodied action in the world.

## Embodiment, Practice and the Extended Mind

The roots of this alternative view go back to Aristotle's very different view of the relation between body and soul. For Aristotle, the soul cannot exist without the body so it makes no sense to think of them as separate entities.[1] Richard Swinburne explains:

> Aristotle thought of the soul simply as ... a way of behaving and thinking: a human having a soul just is the human behaving and thinking in certain characteristic human ways. And just as there

---

[1] 'The soul neither exists without a body nor is a body of some sort. For it is not a body, but it belongs to a body, and for this reason is present in a body, and in a body of such-and-such a sort' (De Anima 414a20ff). faculty.washington.edu/smcohen/320/psyche.htm

cannot be a dance without people dancing, so there cannot be ways of behaving without embodied humans to behave in those ways.
(Swinburne 2000, p. 851-852).

The soul is simply the actuality of a living being, it is what makes them the kind of thing they are. This leads to a strong emphasis on practical action and behaviour in Aristotle's thought – concepts like *phronesis*, the practical wisdom garnered by experience, and *techne*, the practical action of making and doing, as opposed to the disinterested understanding of *episteme*.

Aristotle's view of embodied souls engaged in practical action is the philosophical ancestor of modern phenomenological approaches that see cognition as inherently tied to the material world, arising in and through our engagement with things and other people. Cognition is therefore best understood, as "the exercise of skilful know-how in situated and embodied action" (Thompson 2007, p. 11). We learn about the world as it presents itself to us and acts upon us. This means that even the material world of supposedly inanimate matter has agency in the cognitive process.

Consider, for example, the making of stone tools. Almost two million years ago, an early hominin species known as *Homo erectus* began making stone tools in a characteristic teardrop shape known as Acheulean axes. These axes remained in use until a mere 60,000 years ago, which makes them arguably the most important technological advance of all time. Many of these tools are so pleasing to the eye (and hand) that it seems as if they must have been made with conscious intention by people with a well-developed aesthetic sensibility. Yet it is more likely that their shape and form were determined by the practical engagement of the knapping process – the striking of flakes from cores. Cognitive archaeologist, Lambros Malafouris, argues that knapping activity does not arise "within" the mind and is then enacted – it is the actual practice of knapping that shapes the knapper's intentions as he or she discovers what the stone itself requires.

> The best angles for flake removal are neither identified nor imagined in the knapper's head before the act ... they are embodied and therefore they must be discovered in action. ... The stone projects towards the knapper as much as the knapper projects toward the stone and together they delineate the cognitive map of what we may call an *extended intentional state*. The knapper first thinks *through* and *with* the stone before being able to think *about* the stone and hence about himself as a conscious and reflectively aware agent. (Malafouris 2013, p. 174; 176)

In this view, the stone itself is an active element in the cognitive process. This is an example of what philosopher, Andy Clark, has called the extended mind – the idea that the tools and technologies used by humans are not merely aids to cognition but are intrinsically part of the cognitive process (Clark and Chalmers 1998). This can be illustrated in relation to the alchemical *opus*. Jung interprets this almost entirely in terms of projection. He assumes that what the alchemists saw in their retorts and vats were projections of their own psyche and that what they were "really" engaged in transforming was themselves, a process of individuation. Yet this misses the point that the alchemical *opus* was essentially an embodied practice undertaken with material elements and objects. Their metaphorical accounts were inseparable from this practice just as soul is inseparable from the body in Aristotle's account. There is no way to sever the material activity with mercury, sulphur and lead from the symbolic meanings with which these materials were imbued; arguably, it may only have been through the practice that the symbolic meanings could be understood.

The mind is not, as Andy Clark puts it, bound by skin and skull but extends into the world. *A fortiori*, the mind is dependent on the world which it cognizes to exist at all and especially, of course, the human body. So the only way we could ever "build a human mind", the holy grail of artificial intelligence, would be to build a human body together with the species-specific environment in which the human body functions. Already, then, we are long way from being "shut up in the mind and unable to step beyond it". Nor are we shut up in our bodies since our bodies are open to the world at every pore.

What confuses us as we reflect upon our self-reflective minds is our capacity to create virtual worlds in the space of our own imagination. I suspect that this is often what we mean when we say "psyche"; it is certainly what is meant by terms such as the "internal world" and its characteristic mode of fantasy. Yet imagination would not be possible without the symbols we use to imagine with and these depend on our engagement with an environment, especially the cultural environment of symbols in which all humans live. Symbols are the tools we use to think with and because we are able to use these tools "in our minds" without apparent converse with the world of things and other people, we tend to believe that this activity is going on "in our heads" and that the mind is therefore a separate thing from the world we inhabit. I now want to show why I consider this to be a mistaken illusion.

## Shared language, distributed cognition and constitutive symbols

Let me start with language. Here I am using the term symbol in its wider meaning as a representation of one thing by another in a conventionally agreed system of meanings. Other animals communicate by means of indicative signs such as the vervet monkey whose cry warns the troupe of an approaching predator. Human symbolic language is quite different from this because the symbols of language are, we might say, self-standing – they continue to exist and have meaning even in the absence of the things to which they refer (Deacon 1997). "Fire" means "fire'" whether there's a fire in the hotel or not, whereas a dog will soon cease to respond to the sound "walk" if an actual walk fails to take place soon afterwards. For the dog, the word is only an indicator not a symbol. That is, the symbols of human language have a *virtual* existence and meaning, which enable us to imagine a fire or a walk independently of the actual events.

Now for this to be the case, these meanings have to be shared. That is, language and the use of symbols generally is primarily a form of communication and therefore can only develop in the context of shared communication *between* people. Language relies on a pre-existing context of social co-operation and common ground within which speakers are able to recognise each other's intention to communicate and what they are likely to be communicating about (Tomasello 2008). This kind of mutual co-operation is virtually unique amongst humans.[2] We also communicate not only for imperative reasons – what we want from others – but in order to share with each other and help each other. For example, young children spontaneously begin to point at around one year old, not only to ask for things but to declare their interest and pleasure and share that with others (ibid.) Declarative pointing is also used in conjunction with language learning: a child may point out an object of delight and the parent will add the word "Yes, it's a *bus!*" And on a later occasion the child will point and say to the parent "Bus!" (Colman 2016, p. 109).

Thus human language is a fundamentally social activity in which meanings are constructed and shared between people prior to their being a means of private thought. Without language, Descartes could never have formulated the thought that he was thinking. It is only through our communication with others that we come to know we exist at all. It would be more true to say "I think, therefore we are" but it is even more the case that "We are, therefore I think".

This is true not only for language but for cognition more generally. Far from being a faculty of isolated minds, human cognition is distributed between agents acting together in shared endeavours. This has been extensively demonstrated by Edwin Hutchins, initially in relation to ships' navigators but subsequently in many other fields as well. In a modern elaboration of Aristotle's *techne*, Hutchins showed that the reasoning processes of navigators involved an interaction between embodied gestures, material objects (tools) and shared communications with colleagues working on a shared task (Hutchins 1995).

---

2 Important though limited exceptions have been demonstrated in a few apes whom humans have taught to sign, notably Kanzi, the bonobo and Koko, the gorilla.

From a different perspective, philosopher Shaun Gallagher (2012) has shown how cognition is distributed amongst social groups so that the individual mind is extended through participation with others. Social and cultural institutions such as educational, scientific and professional institutions, the legal system and religious organizations, all act as repositories of previously established cognitive information. Learning to think within the rules and procedures of these established institutions greatly enhances the cognitive resources available to individual actors who do not have to rely on creating their own knowledge *ab novo*. For example, "legal judgments are not confined to individual brains, or even to the many brains that constitute a particular court. They emerge in the workings of a large and complex institution" (ibid. p. 62). Gallagher concludes that "human cognition relies not simply on localized brain processes in any particular individual ... but often on social processes that extend over long periods of time" (ibid. p. 64).

Distributed cognition is a key feature of the adaptations responsible for human evolutionary success, based in the development of social co-operation and common ground. By encoding information in symbolic form, humans became able to pass on their learning from one generation to another. The development of a brain capable of processing symbolic information is thus already sufficient to open up the possibility of social and psychological change without this requiring any further change to the genome, giving humans a unique adaptive capacity. As sociologist Norbert Elias says, "Human beings are biologically capable of changing their manner of social life. By virtue of their evolutionary endowment they can develop socially" (Elias 2011, p. 52). So, for example, there is no need to postulate some kind of genetic modification to account for the development of painting, sculpture and increasingly complex tools in the Upper Palaeolithic period of around 40,000 years ago: the necessary biological changes would have already been in place from the time of the first early modern humans some 200,000 years ago. Symbols also enable us to develop psychologically by creating symbolic form and meaning for inchoate thought and feeling, especially the symbols of dream, art and myth whose meanings rely on potentially infinite metaphorical associations, giving them the necessary fluidity to express the complex nuances of our intangible psychic life (the world of soul and spirit).

Crucially, many symbols do not merely *represent* meanings but *constitute* them, bringing into being the realities they represent (Searle 1995; Colman 2015, pp. 529-532; Colman 2016 pp. 151-168). Archaeologist Colin Renfrew provides a useful illustration of this point. The introduction of stone weights in Neolithic cultures created the *concept* of weight, which could not exist without material symbols to represent it. Weight as a symbol of weight, as Renfrew puts it. Such concepts do not come out of our minds but, as Renfrew says, must first have been apprehended through physical experience – you could not make it up if you had not experienced it (Renfrew 2007, p. 117). But the concept of weight only arises in a social context where measurement has become necessary. Thus the concept as idea comes after the fact of physical experience and the exigencies of embodied social living.

Now just as the physical property of heaviness exists prior to the concept of weight, there are certainly psychic qualities that exist prior to their symbolisation, mainly in the area of affect. Emotion is the way we register what is significant to us in our environment, primarily via attraction and avoidance. It is also a means of communication, which we share with other animals. But human emotion is far more extensive and differentiated than that of any other animal and this, I suggest, is also the result of its symbolisation in a social context. Ritual has a key role to play here in the evocation, containment and management of powerful affects in the context of creating social meanings (Colman 2016, pp. 251-257).

But by the same token this means that symbolic forms of culture such as ritual are as essential to knowing what we feel as language is essential to knowing what we think. Our specifically human emotional life has developed within a particular environment, the environment of human symbolic culture. Symbolic culture is the human *Umwelt*. So deeply is culture written into our emotional and psychological lives that we could not be human without it. Culture is our nature and our relation to the natural, "more than human world" is cultural through and through.[3] Take away symbolic culture and we become, in Clifford Geertz' evocative phrase, "formless monster[s] with neither sense of direction nor power of self-control, a chaos of spasmodic impulses and vague emotions" (Geertz 1973, p. 99).

Effectively this means that symbols create the psyche, rather than the psyche creating symbols, albeit this occurs, as I have shown, via the processes of social and bodily engagement with the material world. In this reversed view, the soul is not as Plato believed, the "senior partner" in the body/soul relationship and "the place where belief and knowledge arise" (*Timaeus*, 34c); rather the soul is a symbol that long post-dates our bodily engagement in the world and its existence depends on the systems of symbolic representation through which it could originally be conceived – please note the embodied metaphor here. This does not, of course, imply that the soul is 'not real', as if it is 'merely' a symbol. As I have explained, it is in the nature of constitutive symbols to create the realities they represent. In a sense, before we can have a soul (or a self) we have to be able to "think a soul" and

---

3 The phrase "more than human world" was coined by David Abram in 1996 and, according to Wikipedia, has become "a key phrase within the lingua franca of the ecological movement".

we can only do that within a socially generated system of collective representations.

## Collective Representations and *Participation Mystique*

Such systems are the means by which social groups formulate and pass on their accumulated knowledge and understanding of the world. Here again, we can see how Jung demoted social reality in favour of the psyche as the primary datum (Segal 2007). In Durkheim's original usage, collective representations referred to the symbolic systems by which a society represented itself, particularly in its ritual practices and beliefs. The term was taken up by Lévy-Bruhl (1910) to explain the quality of *participation mystique* that characterised what he thought of as "pre-logical thinking". Lévy-Bruhl argued that this was not simply an inferior version of modern rational thinking but something qualitatively different, due to the very different collective representations pertaining in "native" societies, as they were then called. This included beliefs in a mystical unity between objects, animals and humans as well as animistic beliefs about the agency of so-called "inanimate" elements of Nature. For Lévy-Bruhl, then, *participation mystique* refers to socially organized perceptions, practices and beliefs that are formulated and impressed on the mind in affectively charged conditions, notably ritual.

Jung took up these terms in a quite different way. In Jung's usage, both collective representations and *participation mystique* originate not in society but in the psyche. Collective representations become the archetypes of the collective unconscious and *participation mystique* becomes projection or, in more recent parlance, projective identification. Jung replaces the social group with "the collective psyche" and thereby loses the sense of human participation in the group which is then reduced to "unconsciousness". He desocialises collective representations so that they become merely "psychic contents" (Jung, 1921, para 692.) In this way, he severs the link between the psychic world and the social world and loses the most significant feature of Lévy-Bruhl's thought – the recognition that people think as they do not because they exist in a state of primitive unconsciousness but because they live in a different form of society in different environmental conditions and their thought is structured in different ways (Segal 2007, p. 636).

However, despite this important insight, Lévy-Bruhl nevertheless maintained the prevalent view that people who thought in this way were "primitive" and that participation mystique belonged to a "lower" form of society that had been superseded by the "higher type" of nineteenth century Europe. In this way he showed himself to be just a much a creature of collective representations as the so-called primitives. For the upshot of Durkheim's analysis is that we are all subject to our collective representations and it is extremely difficult to think outside them. These collective symbolic forms are the matrix that shape and constrain our psychic sensibilities. They are the lens through which we experience the world and, as such, we are usually unaware of them – they are what we take for granted. So while we no longer accept that indigenous peoples are "primitive", nor do we really understand how they think and why. Most of us find it exceedingly difficult to make sense of things like rain-making, spirit travel, shamanic practices or even, truth be told, synchronicity, which we prefer to re-interpret in more familiar psychological terms. Just as other cultures take for granted that dreams are a message from the ancestors or a journey into the realm of the spirits, we take for granted that they are psychological events that take place in our heads and are, at best, a message from the unconscious. We know that the mind exists in the head and is separate from the world around us, that the inorganic world is not a living world and that there is something called Nature from which we have become separated, a belief powerfully expressed in the ancient myth of our expulsion from the Garden of Eden, a collective representation *par excellence*. We also know that objects are made up of atoms, that the universe was created in a Big Bang 14 billion years ago and a whole host of other things we do not really understand in the slightest but accept virtually without question, like the Red Queen in Alice's Looking Glass who believed six impossible things before breakfast. Above all, we accept that the scientific method is the guarantor of truth and we must either prove things within its terms or create an alternative enclave called "religion" or "the psyche" or, in my own term a few years ago "the imaginal world of meaning" (Colman 2011)[4].

It rarely occurs to us that all these beliefs are just as much the expression of symbolic imagination as the beliefs of those once written off as "primitive". That is, the Cartesian world of post-Renaissance science is a particular way of imagining the world and the scientific method is a socially agreed practice for investigating it in terms of supposedly objective mechanisms. Even if this does occur to us, it is actually the devil's own job to think our way out of the Matrix, just as it was for Neo in the eponymous film that imagined our world as an illusion created for us by our own machines.

---

4 At that time, I had not yet grasped that mind is an emergent feature of being in the world and was still talking about an interaction *between* mind and world, thus implying an ontological separation I would no longer accept.

## *Participation Mystique* as Lived Experience

This, it seems to me, is the real lesson from the anthropological study of indigenous cultures – not what they can learn from us but what we can learn from them. For a start, we can learn that our own ways of seeing the world are relative and that there other ways of living and thinking than those we take for granted. There is nothing like the challenge of difference to make us aware of our own presuppositions. Perhaps more deeply, though, Lévy-Bruhl's insight into *participation mystique* serves to remind us that this way of thinking and experiencing the world is not so much lost as overlooked, often reduced to a remnant that is no longer collectively represented but nevertheless still extant. In the following four examples, we can still catch a glimpse of the *anima mundi*, not as an overarching symbol but as lived experience through which, often unnoticed, we are released from our Cartesian constraints.

1) Whenever we visit the theatre or the cinema we are likely to experience states of identification in which we temporarily merge with others whom we experience as "real people". Similar experiences may occur listening to music, contemplating works of art or being inspired by the landscape.

2) Football matches and music festivals closely match Lévy-Bruhl's criteria for *participation mystique* as something that arises from socially organized perceptions, practices and beliefs formulated and impressed on the mind in affectively charged conditions. The "beautiful game" expresses and reinforces ideas about competition, success and the democratic acceptance of losing that are typical of Western capitalist societies. Sporting events consist of an agreed set of social practices, rules and behaviours in which both players and spectators experience sanctioned states of high emotion that are contained and made meaningful within the context of the game.

3) Animistic beliefs persist in the tendency to impute personhood and agency to entities, which according to official modernist doctrine ought to be classified as objects (Hornborg 2006). If I had not been writing about *participation mystique* at the time, I would not have even noticed when a call-centre worker apologised for a delay, saying "my computer is not liking me today". Sometimes, the only explanation we can find for the way our complicated machines play up is that they must be in a bad mood[5] and we regularly experience the boundaries of our cars as coterminous with the boundaries of our own body.

---

5 John Cleese's portrayal of Basil Fawlty attacking his car with a branch provides an enduringly funny illustration of this only too common state of mind. (available to view on YouTube)

4) There are some people in modern Western society – and Jung was certainly one of them – who seem to have an unusual openness and sensitivity to "parapsychological experiences" or "being psychic", knowing and experiencing things that are not admissible in our Cartesian world since they abrogate rules about time, space and causality. There is usually a correlation between such openness and a lack of emotional containment in early childhood (Merchant 2012). It seems likely that this correlation indicates areas of the psyche that remain unsocialised and unsymbolised, that slip under the radar of our collective representations. That is why they are often associated with "borderline" states of mind, areas of experience that cannot be mentalized and express themselves in overwhelming states of unformulated affect expressed in action without thought. Like heaviness in a culture without weights, they remain unconceptualised and without apparent social usefulness. It is these states that are more successfully formulated and conceptualised within the collective representations of indigenous cultures. In such cultures people need to be able to use all the senses of their bodies to negotiate the world and so are much more attuned to aspects of the world that usually remain unsymbolised in our culture. Much of Jung's work was an attempt to provide such symbolic representations, which was why he drew on pre-Cartesian traditions such as ancient myths, Gnosticism and alchemy as well as developing conceptions such as synchronicity. Unfortunately, as I have demonstrated, his work in this area was stymied by attempting to shoe-horn his theories into Kantian and Cartesian categories, not realising that these were responsible for the pinching constraints he was attempting to ease.

## Conclusion

In this paper I have attempted to sketch out an alternative way forward that challenges these Cartesian constraints at their root, namely the depreciation of the body and elevation of the mind that began with Plato. I have argued that, in fact, our minds are wholly dependent on our bodies, indeed they are, as Aristotle said, merely the way our particular bodies with our very unusual brains behave in the world. Our cognition is extended and distributed and our psychic life is constituted by symbolic representations. In the final section, I have discussed the role of *participation mystique* as a way of relating to and experiencing the world that cannot be captured by the Cartesian notion of projection. It is here that we may find an opening to ways of being in the world that lead us out of the Cartesian matrix.

In conclusion, I would like to mention the work of cultural ecologist, David Abram whose book, *The Spell of the Sensuous* (1997) presents an animistic or participatory account of rationality. Abram reminds us that we are always in participation with the world in one way or another – the question is how. All too often, modern ways of being in the world keep us at one remove from the consequences of our own actions. Corporate executives in New York make decisions that decimate the lives of South American peasants; air force pilots in Texas fly drone planes that kill and maim people in the Middle East. The problem here is not commerce or warfare – the problem is the dislocation between action and embodiment, the lack of sensorial cues that feedback the consequences of action. In direct contrast to this, Abram argues for:

> [a] genuinely ecological approach .. [that] strives to enter, ever more deeply, into the sensorial present. It strives to become ever more awake to the other lives, the other forms of sentience and sensibility that surround us in the open field of the present moment. (Abram 1997, p. 272).

Although, in this paper, I have not referred to the practice of psychotherapy, I think this is also a very appropriate description for what, as psychotherapists, we strive to achieve in the daily activity of our working lives.

## References

Abram, D. (1997). *The Spell of the Sensuous: Perception and Language in a More-Than-Human World*. New York: Vintage Books.

Carpenter, A.D. (2008). 'Embodying intelligence. Animals and us in Plato's Timaeus'. In *Platonism and Forms of Intelligence*, ed. John Dillon and Marie-Élise Zovko. Berlin: Akademie Verlag.

Clark, A. and Chalmers, C. (1998) 'The extended mind', *Analysis* 58:1, 7-19.

Colman, W. (2011) 'Synchronicity and the meaning-making psyche'. *Journal of Analytical Psychology*, 56:4, 471-491.

— (2015) 'A revolution of the mind: some implications of George Hogenson's "The Baldwin Effect: a neglected influence on C.G. Jung's evolutionary thinking".' (2001). *Journal of Analytical Psychology*, 60:4, 520–539.

— (2016). *Act and Image. The Emergence of Symbolic Imagination*. New Orleans, LA: Spring Journal Books.

Deacon, T. (1997). *The Symbolic Species: The Co-Evolution of Language and the Brain*. New York: W. W. Norton & Co.

Descartes, R. (2009). 'Letter to Princess Elisabeth, May 21, 1643'. In *An Unconventional History of Western Philosophy: Conversations Between Men and Women Philosophers*, ed. K.J. Warren. Lanham, MD: Rowman and Littlefield.

Elias, N. (2011). *The Symbol Theory. Vol. 13, The Collected Works of Norbert Elias*, ed. Richard Kilminster. Dublin: University College Dublin Press.

Gallagher, S. (2012). 'The Over-Extended Mind', *Versus* 113, 57-68.

Geertz, C. (1973). *The Interpretation of Cultures. Selected Essays*. New York: Basic Books.

Hornborg, A. (2006). 'Animism, fetishism, and objectivism as strategies for knowing (or not knowing) the World'. *Ethnos: Journal of Anthropology* 71:1, 21-32.

Hutchins, E. (1995). *Cognition in the Wild.* Cambridge, MA: MIT Press, 1995.

Jung, C.G. (1921). *Psychological Types.* CW6. London: Routledge & Kegan Paul.

— (1926). 'Spirit and Life', *CW8.* London: Routledge & Kegan Paul, 2nd Edn. 1969.

— (1936). 'Wotan', *CW10.* London: Routledge & Kegan Paul, 2nd. Edn. 1969.

— (1938/1940). 'Psychology and Religion (The Terry Lectures)', *CW11.* London: Routledge & Kegan Paul, 2nd Edn. 1969.

— (1939/1954). 'Psychological Commentary on The Tibetan Book of the Great Liberation', *CW11*, para. 759-830. London: Routledge & Kegan Paul, 2nd Edn. 1969.

— (2009) *The Red Book.* Liber Novus, ed. S. Shamdasani, tr. M. Kyburz, J. Peck, and S. Shamdasani. London & New York: W. W. Norton.

Lévy-Bruhl, L. (1910). *How Natives Think*, trans. Lilian A. Clare. London: Allen & Unwin, 1926.

Malafouris, L. (2013). *How Things Shape the Mind: A Theory of Material Engagement.* Cambridge, MA: MIT Press.

Merchant, J. (2012). *Shamans and Analysts: New Insights on the Wounded Healer.* London: Routledge.

Plato (1951). *The Symposium*, trans. Water Hamilton. London: Penguin Books.

— (2008). *Timaeus and Critias*, trans. Robin Waterfield. Oxford: Oxford University Press.

Renfrew, C. (2008). *Prehistory. The Making of the Human Mind.* London: Phoenix.

Searle, J. (1995). *The Construction of Social Reality.* London and New York: Penguin Books.

Segal, R. (2007). 'Jung and Lévy-Bruhl', *Journal of Analytical Psychology*, 52:5, 635-658

Swinburne, R. (2000). 'Nature and immortality of the soul', *Concise Routledge Encyclopaedia of Philosophy.* London and New York: Routledge.

Thompson, E. (2007). *Mind in Life. Biology, Phenomenology and the Sciences of Mind.* Cambridge, MA. & London: Harvard University Press.

Tomasello, M. (2008). *Origins of Human Communication.* Cambridge, MA: MIT Press.

Winborn, M, (Ed.) (2014). *Shared Realities: Participation Mystique and Beyond.* Skiatook, OK: Fisher King Press.

# What is a Jungian Analyst Dreaming When Myth Comes to Mind?
## Thirdness as an Aspect of the Anima Media Natura

*August J. Cwik*
(USA, CSJA)

## Introduction

Listening analytically is not listening just to what is said, but listening to what is just below the surface waiting to be said – or as the alchemists so aptly phrased it, "the search for what not yet is" (Petrus Bonus, 1330). The royal road to apprehending this mercurial element is through the use of the imagination as informing one about the nature of the *third thing* that is being co-created in the analytic situation. Ghent (1989), of the relational school, suggested that all analysts need to find and express their own "Credo" – an expression of his or her own beliefs about how therapy works. This is my "credo" and orienting compass that guides me through the analytic day.

We are always seeking to reimagine the theory and practice of analytical psychology by putting forward newer ideas that assent to continuity while allowing revitalization of our understandings. This presentation will focus on imagining the analytic encounter through Jung's fundamental insight of a *third thing* being created in analysis. We will explore how the state of *thirdness* is created and accessed, how the material emerging from it is used, and the eventual fate of the *third* in a successful analysis by a reexamination of the Rosarium plates. We will look particularly at the awareness and possible meanings of mythological motifs appearing in the mind of the analyst while in session. We will also explore how *thirdness* can be viewed as the interpersonal aspect of the *anima media natura*.

## Jung's View of Thirdness

Here is a well-known image with which you may be familiar (Figure 1). It is comprised of two faces and a goblet-like space in-between them. Or is it a white goblet on a black background? As we reflect on this image it becomes immediately apparent that it is difficult, if not impossible, to focus on both images, both truths, simultaneously. Like looking at the interactive process of analysis – at one moment it falls into complementarities, at another, one can see the *third space* in-between the two. Trying to hold both is similar to the state of consciousness to which we aspire in analysis: to suppress nothing, to remain open to the paradox, to maintain the tension of opposites. It is this *third space* between the two that is the focus of this paper.

*Figure 1*

Jung's earliest writings on the *third* emphasized an introverted and intrapsychic perspective. In the "Transcendent Function" he states his most notable and clearest expression of the *third*, "The confrontation of the two positions generates a tension charged with energy and creates a living, *third* thing – not a logical still birth in accordance with the principle *tertium non datur* (the *third* is not given), but a movement out of the suspension between opposites, a living birth that leads to a new level of being, a new situation" (1916, par. 189).

He postulates that this *third thing* was the creation of a new symbol that had the possibility of uniting the opposites. Later he begins to link it to imagination and typology: "The *third* element, in which the opposites merge, is fantasy activity, which is creative and receptive at once. This is a function Schiller calls the play instinct..." (1921, par. 171). Jung also referred to a "higher *third*, as...the creative fantasy that creates the goal" that can be reached by neither intellect or feeling alone (1921, par. 85).

We could look at Jung's early theorizing on the nature of the *third* as actually a more inter-psychic rather than intrapsychic approach, as it involves a tension between two elements of psyche whether unconscious vs. conscious, or thinking vs. feeling. But even this being the case, he argued that the unconscious itself could best be under-stood, and related to, *as if* it were another person. Regarding active imagination he suggests that, "It is exactly as if a dialogue were taking place between two human beings with equal rights, each of whom gives the other credit for a valid argument and considers it worth while to modify the conflicting standpoints by means of thorough comparison and discussion or else to distinguish them clearly from one another" (1916, par. 186).

So when Jung was being pressed to comment on the value of transference, the unconscious itself had already assumed aspects of the other. With an actual other in the room it was a natural conclusion that a *third* would also be created between two participants, an inter-personal approach. He described it in the "Psychology of the Transference" as, "The elusive, deceptive, ever-changing content that possesses the patient like a demon flits about from patient to doctor and, as *the third party* in the alliance, continues its game… alchemists aptly personified it as the wily god of revelation, Hermes or Mercurius" (1946, par. 384, italics added). And also, "Psychological induction inevitably causes the two parties to get involved *in the transformation of the third* and to be themselves transformed in the process, and all the time the doctor's knowledge, like a flickering lamp, is the one dim light in the darkness" (1946, par. 399, italics added).

Out of this notion of *thirdness* comes Jung's many statements about the mutuality of the analytic process epitomized in his statement that

> For two personalities to meet is like mixing two different chemical substances: if there is any combination at all, both are transformed. In any effective psychological treatment the doctor is bound to influence the patient; but this influence can only take place if the patient has a reciprocal influence on the doctor. You can exert no influence if you are not susceptible to influence (1931, par. 163).

## Psychoanalytic Views of Thirdness

The relational and intersubjective schools focused on the clinical aspects of *thirdness* (see Baranger, 1993; Benjamin, 2004; Bollas, 1992; Green, 2004; and Ogden, 1997, 1999, 2007). This presentation focuses on integrating the work of Ogden and Benjamin into a Jungian model. Ogden states:

> I use the term *analytic third* to refer to a third subject, unconsciously co-created by analyst and analysand, which seems to take on a life of its own in the interpersonal field between analyst and patient. This third subject stands in dialectical tension with the separate, individual subjectivities of analyst and analysand in such a way that the individual subjectivities and the third create, negate, and preserve one another. In an analytic relationship, the notion of individual subjectivity and the idea of a co-created third subject

are devoid of meaning except in relation to one another, just as the idea of the conscious mind is meaningless except in relation to the unconscious. (Ogden, 1999, p. 1)

This is a very precise definition and it is my preference to use this wording of *analytic third* to describe this *third thing* as it arises in analysis. Benjamin's (2004) theorizing sees the *third* as a process, function or relationship, rather than as a thing in itself. Coleman (2007) and Kieffer (2007) express this aspect of *thirdness* as an emergent construct. For Benjamin the goal of analysis moves toward mutual recognition, with the analysand gradually becoming capable of recognizing his/her own subjectivity while acknowledging, and taking seriously, the subjectivity of others.

### Thirdness in the Rosarium

Due to time constraints we are only going to focus on plates 4 and 10 of the Rosarium. I am sure many of you are quite familiar with this series. Alchemical imagery has a unique way of capturing the interplay between interpersonal relatedness and imaginal, intrapsychic activity (Samuels 1985). But using this series also allows a right-brain imagistic understanding of the analytic process – a graphic novel, or even Manga-like, version of relational individuation (Figure 2).

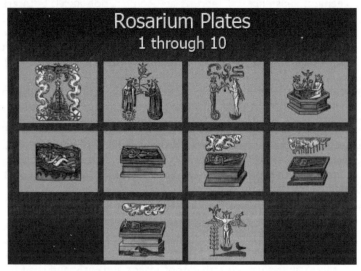

*Figure 2 (Colored Rosarium plates courtesy of Adam McLean,*
*The Alchemy Web Page, www.alchemywebsite.com)*

I see Plate 4 as portraying the establishment of a formal *analytic third* – formal only in that we now have spent enough time with the patient to know their history, dreams and defining images more intimately and, therefore, have more to draw on. Benjamin (2004) reminds us that the *third* is never quite a static achievement; it is always collapsing and being repaired throughout analysis.

*Figure 3: Plate 4 of the Rosarium Immersion in the Bath*

The six-sided star initially presiding over the encounter might be thought of as an image of the top down energy of a self-organizing system that orders the dyad into a level of complexity beyond what normally could be understood by the complementarities of the individuals (Cambray, 2006). That star can be thought of as an image of celestial, archetypal energies, enveloping the relational aspects of the couple in the moment and over time. This notion of an over-riding organizing force tends to be neglected in interpersonal and intersubjective theories that focus purely on the subjectivities of the participants. This energy first "moved down" into the communication system itself, symbolized by the six points of the branches bridging the two individuals. In Plate 4 this six-ness, representing the marriage of the elements, actually has reached the level of the container itself, as seen in the hexagonal shape of the bath – "For it is both the container and that which is contained, in that it holds the contents worked upon, while, at the same time, it is also that which is worked on. It contains the process as well as being the process" (Newman, 1981, p. 230).

The dove is the embodiment of this energy constellating through the bifurcating action of attraction, related to Aphrodite, and annunciation, or assignment of a great task, as related to the Holy Ghost – one is held by attraction into a path of individuation (Edinger, 1994, p. 48). Note that Jung described this function of the Holy Ghost as related to the *anima mundi* – "The world-soul is a natural force which is responsible for all the phenomena of life and the psyche" (Jung, 1954a, par. 393) – something larger is changing the path of one's life.

Our familiar quaternio diagram (Jacoby, 1984) of all the possible conscious and unconscious connections between two individuals arose from this plate (Figure 4).

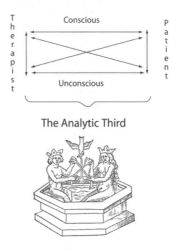

*Figure 4*

I am equating the *analytic third* to the unconscious-to-unconscious connection between the two individuals; by definition we cannot know the exact nature of this co-created interaction, but we can access indicators of what might be occurring. It can be considered the relational unconscious as it wraps the relationship, infusing the expression and constriction of each partner's subjectivity and individual unconscious. (Gerson, 2004).

The half-submerged figures can be seen as relating to a state-of-consciousness with attentiveness to the outer, while also demonstrating a type of ego receptivity (Cwik, 1995) to what is emerging from the inner world and body. The state-of-mind of the analyst can be thought of as a type of *analytic mindfulness*, which observes what arises, but also engages that material, to yield some useful understanding of what is happening at the unconscious level. This engagement can be likened to a type of in-session active imagination with countertransference experiences (Cwik, 2006a, 2006b, 2011; Schaverien, 2007; Wiener, 2009).

Active imagination becomes the paradigm for a way of approaching and interacting with material arising from one's own unconscious while in session.

Ogden (2007) prefers to use the metaphor of dreaming to describe this sate: if the patient is unable to dream his emotional experience, that individual cannot change, grow, or become anything other than who he has been. The analyst is then thought of as needing to dream the undreamt and undreamable dreams of the analysand. He used reverie to enter this state; it is comprised of mundane, unobtrusive thoughts, feelings, fantasies, ruminations, daydreams and bodily sensations that usually feel utterly disconnected from what the patient is saying and doing at the moment (Ogden, 1997). Dreaming as described by Ogden, draws on Bion's notion that both reverie and dreaming were thought to be alpha functions used in metabolizing raw beta sense impressions (Bion, 1962).

I (Cwik, 2011) suggest we view the inner experiences coming into the mind of the analyst on a continuum from: traditional Ogden-like reverie; to more general material, i.e., images, books, movies, feelings; into more organized forms like myth and fairytale; and finally to more active cognition like theoretical formulations. To differentiate common reverie from more organized forms of mental activity where the association to the ongoing process can be more easily identified, I used the term associative dreaming. While most psychoanalysts speak *from* this material (Ogden, 1999), we could also speak *about* it directly, with individuals who are considered capable of having, and being responsive to, symbolic activity – those that maintain some capacity to "dream" as Ogden would say.

For the purpose of this presentation I am particularly focusing on when some form of myth enters the mind of the analyst. This type of "mythological reverie", or associative dream, is not all that uncommon amongst Jungian analysts as most training institutes have numerous classes on mythology and fairytales. Myth becomes a type of diagnostic manual potentially illuminating the patterns of behavior in which the analysand is caught. Speaking at the *about* level when myth comes to mind during a session is considered amplification. But just because a myth comes to mind does not mean we have to say it to the analysand.

Drawing our attention to the 4th plate we might notice that one particular pole has been left out of our familiar diagram – the one descending from above depicting the influence of archetypal and/or synchronistic energies. A more comprehensive diagram might look something like this (Figure 5)

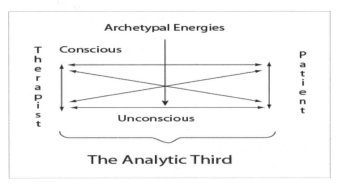

Figure 5

Cambray (2001), in an article entitled, *Enactments and Amplification*, suggests that the impulse to amplify is itself an indication of emergent phenomenon arising out of the *analytic third*. Given the new diagram noted above, I am suggesting that when myth comes to mind the analyst may be dreaming the form of the archetypal energies enveloping and shaping the relationship. As Cambray states we are "in" myth not that the myth somehow belongs only to the analysand. This is often enacted in spontaneous moments during an analysis, but is also the shape the analysis will take over time. The art of Jungian analysis is when to speak directly *about* the myth, and when to speak *from* the affective foundations of the myth using language comprehensible to the particular analysand. Fordham (1957) thought that speaking from the *about* level when myth was present tended to bring in extraneous intellectual material obscuring the nature of the transference.

The next four plates (Figure 2) can be thought of as moving from a fully interpenetrating *analytic third*, through the death and mourning of that experience, to a final internalization of *thirdness* into intrapsychic structure. I have come to see that process as, what Stark (2015) would call, the dying of "relentless hope" that there exists a real person who can meet all of our needs exactly when we need them – in perfect *thirdness*. Schwartz-Salant (1995) notes that if indeed the Rosarium is a template for the pattern of powerful relationships, union states and the death of structure are always encountered in succession. This loss and mourning can be seen as the soul realigning with a new set of archetypal energies and returning to bring forth a rebirth. As Jung states, "The 'soul' which is reunited with the body is the One born of the two, the *vinculum* common to both. It is therefore the very essence of relationship" (1946, par. 504).

*Figure 6*

The last plate (Figure 6) can be imagined as the formation of this new internal structure resulting from the successful grieving of the actual relationship. Although very rich in symbolism, we will focus on the opposites having been reconciled into a merged new image – the two have become a totally new One. Though Jung in his day thought it a monstrosity – "the monster is a hideous abortion and a perversion of nature" (1946, par. 533) – today we might wonder whether this hermaphroditic symbol is closer to consciousness as gender itself is undergoing a *thirdness* process. Firmly standing on the lunar symbol, this emblem demonstrates a certain objective stance rooted in reflectiveness and stability – an observing or objective ego. We might imagine that it holds a capacity to: regulate the body, attune to others, balance emotions, be flexible, extinguish or modify fear, utilize insight, empathize with others, and have a moral compass – all components of an affect-regulated and potentially balanced psyche (Kornfield and Siegel, 2010). I want to focus on the image of the three snakes in the goblet held in the right hand and the one snake in the left. This tension portrayed between the *one* and the *three* might be best amplified by Benjamin's work on *thirdness*.

Using an interesting terminology, Benjamin (2004, pp. 13-18) discussed the dynamics of *thirdness* through what she called the *one in the third* and the *third in the one*, which can be understood as an additional amplification of the 10th plate. For her true *thirdness* requires affective resonance or union requiring a capacity for accommodation to a mutually created set of expectations and a certain rhythmicity of attuning to the other – she called this *the one in the third*. This aspect of *thirdness* emphasizes that one person in the dyad empathizes and accommodates to the other, and may even sacrifice their own needs so that the oneness can be experienced and be reparative for the other.

The *third in the one*, on the other hand, is the ability to have internal awareness and to sustain the tension of difference between my needs and yours while still being attuned to, and caring for, you. This occurs when the limits of the analyst have been reached and it may signify that the *relentless hope* mentioned above has to begin to be mourned. The *one in the third* and *third in the one* must be held in balance for analysis to proceed satisfactorily. This may best be understood in the clinical situation.

## Clinical Material

*Fred*

I had seen Fred earlier in an analysis that lasted for 15 years. A colleague who specialized in working with torture victims had referred him. He called himself "white trash" and as a child lived in a chaotic household of physical abuse, shaming, and even shootings. He demonstrated aspects of Kalsched's (1996) self-care system, but the predominant energy of this 6 foot tall man was that of the hero archetype (Campbell, 2008): he was an anesthesiologist, pilot, men's group leader, and once when confronting a spider phobia purchased a tarantula to roam over his naked body. He, like no other patient, constellated my own trauma history and body memories, even though our traumas were not at all similar. I often wondered if my own envy of his heroic attributes made me hesitant to analyze them as defenses against the chaotic madness of his childhood experience. The *third* as enacted between us entailed my being fearful and afraid to show him my fear, as he would think me weak. This dynamic came to the fore when I felt I had to confront his crazed movements around the office in various emotional and often rageful states. The *one in the third* had allowed me stay in rhythm with, and accept, his anger, but finally the *third in the one* became more prominent as I had to express my own needs to protect myself. Having the associative dream of the "bull in the china shop" and working with it internally I noted the presence of powerful instincts and I realized that I could be hurt accidently. I finally shared that his behavior was frightening me. He immediately calmed down and assured me that he would/could not hurt me. We named the enactment we were in, but in my relief I missed that the fear I was experiencing might also be reflecting his own inner persecution and terror. I realized that my trauma was being evoked because I unconsciously thought that being heroic was a way out of my own trauma, and soon became aware through our work together, that this, sadly, was not the case. We ended the analysis when he was able to marry, and we noted that he probably would not do well with the aging process due to remnants of the heroic process.

He reentered analysis 5 years later when he was having sexual difficulties and turning 60. We picked up as though he had never left and he proceeded to have the following dream:

> I'm outside somewhere and it is the evening. There are two large similar structures maybe 20 feet tall and roundish shape, like two half's of something with a little space between them – reminded me of 2 cerebral hemispheres. I work my way in between the two half's and with difficulty take a copper band and find a way to hook the two things together and work my way back out – it was in the bag and couldn't be undone.

My contribution to the co-creation of this image was that I was working on this paper using the right brain imagery noted earlier. My reverie at the time was of this conference and the anxiety of presenting. Engaging the reverie I spoke to him *from* the experience saying that perhaps we both were needing to make inner wholeness connections to confront our fears through striving for more love and caring for ourselves (the copper related to the metal associated with Aphrodite). In the next session he was extremely agitated, knelt down before me, said that I would be safe, and proceeded to express rage at a level I had never experienced: he pounded the walls and door and screamed, yelled, and cursed – but this time clearly giving voice and action to the persecutor/protector that attacked him on a daily basis. I was better able to stay in the *one in the third*, especially because of his assurance at the beginning, although at one point he came right up to my face and I could see the demonic, seething energy in his eyes. As we discussed the session afterwards, he did not remember our encounter of years ago, but felt that something inside had changed, permanently.

### Thomas

Thomas was a lawyer who did *pro bono* work for the wrongly accused and was very successful at it. He worked tirelessly and wrote volumes in their defense leading to the release of a number of incarcerated individuals. He came to analysis after trying hypnotherapy to free himself of near debilitating phobias: claustrophobia, fear of heights, and a fear of cataract surgery – because the surgeon would see the evilness in his eyes their being "the window to the soul." His childhood memories were of a terrifying father who shamed him mercilessly, particularly when he was sick. When ill, he would be locked in his room or even a closet – so as not to "infect" the rest of the family. Here is another man who demonstrated Kalsched's (1996) self care system to an extreme degree and attempted to repair himself through his work.

One day he talked about how literally paralyzed he felt while walking through an atrium "in the shadow of" one of Chicago's tallest building. During this session I *dreamt* the Hephaestus myth (Graves, 1955), thinking him the crippled craftsman who wrote and created beautiful and moving arguments, yet was so impaired by his anxieties. Thinking that speaking at the *about* level and sharing the myth with him would take us far afield from the affect, I actively engaged the myth. What came to mind was the image of the child with braces and crutches from the *March of Dimes* poster – an organization dedicated to those children who had caught polio. This image emerged from our mutual history, but a more powerful co-created element was that at the time I was facing a major life decision and felt stuck and paralyzed myself. Kohut (1977, p. 109) described certain dreams as being "self-state" dreams in that they capture the patient's current inner world in concise imagery. I think this associative dream could be considered a type of "third-state" dream, reflecting the current state of our *analytic third*. I spoke at the *about* level and shared the image with Thomas. He immediately responded saying that it gave some shape to his somatic experience – a naming of something that was just trying to be said in the moment, an undreamt dream. He left the session and later was watching a sports game when a commercial came on for – the *March of Dimes* – which was highly unusual in present day. The next day while walking through the atrium he began to experience the body paralysis, he spontaneously tightened his leg muscles and when he released the tension he imagined that he was that crippled child and felt the braces breaking from his legs. He walked unimpeded through the atrium for the first time in his life. As he said this, the solution to my personal problem became clearer and I also was able to move forward in my life. The synchronicity of the image coming to him from the outer world was an archetypal activation motivating him, and me, to a co-created solution of our mutual problems.

*Judy*

I began my relationship with Judy as a supervisor. As we repeatedly encountered difficulties with her countertransference reactions with sexually abused patients, her own trauma became silhouetted in the work. She eventually decided to enter analysis with me with an understanding that she needed to experience a working through of her own trauma history before she could be of use to her patients. She remembered one static image from age five of performing oral sex on her older brother in the family bathroom. The myth of Persephone (Graves, 1955) came to mind – the naive maiden who is pulled down into the underworld by Hades, although in her situation there was no remembered overt force, but perhaps more one of seduction. The little girl was seeking something from her brother, just not what she received (Ferenczi, 1951). I never mentioned the myth to her. While I was working on the section of this paper related to the *third in the one* and the *one in the third* she dreamed:

> I am in a room and at a window where there is a fish caught between the screen and the window with a fishing lure in its mouth that it is spitting out. Across the room there is another window in which there are three fishes. They all seem to be dying unless I can save them in time.

She associated the spitting out of the lure to the childhood trauma of the oral sex. But the "lure" aspect also brought us directly into our relationship in which she unconsciously felt that I had 'lured' her into analysis, thus recapitulating aspects of her relationship with her brother. She was having difficulties in her relationship with her husband and was reluctant to say anything – her *third in the one* needing to come forth, but our clinical *one in the third* was impeding her, and it all threatening to die. In this situation I believe the *analytic third* utilized my own imaginal language in an attempt to communicate what was just below the surface trying to be said. Again, the immediate co-created elements, which I brought into the encounter, seemed apparent.

### Thirdness as an Aspect of the Anima Media Natura

There is no doubt that Jung held the practice of analytical psychology, and especially work in, and with, the transference (Wiener, 2009) to be of the utmost importance, as best reflected in his statement:

> So, when the psychotherapist has to struggle with difficult transference problems, he can at least take comfort in these reflections. He is not just working for this particular patient…but for himself as well and his own soul…Small and invisible as this contribution may be, it is yet an *opus magnum*, for it is accomplished in a sphere but lately visited by the numen, where the whole weight of mankind's problems has settled. The ultimate questions of psychotherapy are not a private matter – they represent a supreme responsibility (1946, par. 449).

Clearly Jung connected analytic work not just with changes and transformation of the two participants, but also with changes to collective consciousness. Here we already see that he was expanding the impact of analytic work to realms clearly beyond the immediacy of the analysis itself.

But more importantly to the theme of this presentation, analysis may be one of only a few places where every thing that happens once the vessel is sealed, is drawn into and seen as informing, the *analytic third*. This interconnectedness of all things brings us right into an experience of the *anima media natura* – the notion that the medium itself in which we operate is indeed a real space and carrier of meaning, affect, and depth – the container is both that which is contained and that which is worked on.

In his philosophical book, "Anima Mundi: The Rise of the World Soul...Examined in the Perspective of the Relation of the Finite with the Infinite", Vassanyi states

> The *function* of the soul of world is to recognize the identity and difference, the proper place and function of each individual substance in relation to the things that come to be, *and* that are, respectively, eternal and unchangeable. It carries on a constant internal inaudible discourse inside itself as it imperceptibly moves around itself and comes into contact with every single thing, dissoluble or partless that constitutes the universe (Vassanyi, 2007, p. 2).

As we have seen, it is this "identity and difference" that is the hallmark of the dynamics of the *analytic third* and the relational unconscious – what belongs to whom, and more importantly, what is being said about us, who and where we are, where do we need to go, and by what archetypal form are we being carried in the process? The *analytic third* functions in a way that informs us that there is a permeability in and between individuals, while the operation of the *anima mundi* means that there is always an inseparability of the individual with the world.

The microcosm of analytic space reflects the macrocosm of world: so as above, so as below. So, if we wanted to envisage a right brain approach to our discussion while also locating it in deeper religious tradition we might look to the image of Indra's Net (de Barry and Bloom, 1999). It is an extraordinary metaphor for a vision of the interrelationship of all things without their necessarily being blended into one homogeneous entity.

Indra's Net (Figure 7) is made up of jewels that are faceted and reflect each other successively with their images permeating each other over and over again. Within each single jewel are contained the unbounded repetition and profusion of the images of all the other jewels. If you sit in one jewel you are sitting simultaneously in all of them.

This image from an ancient tradition glimpses a quite holographic vision of the universe. *Thirdness* might prove to be a "fractal attractor" operating through archetypal forms. Fractals repeat themselves at different scales of observation underlying chaotic dynamics (Van Eenwyk, 1997). One might imagine that all consulting rooms that honor the knowledge that all things are related to the one thing, are linked by an imaginal *viniculum*, invisible linking fibers. This *pneuma* forms a vast network of pathways by which information and experience can be carried and potentially influence one another. This is one way to imagine the *anima media natura*.

*Figure 7: Indra's Net*

But lest we get too carried away with our celestial theoretical reveries, we should be reminded of Jung's (1954b, par. 335) statement that, "One does not become enlightened by imagining figures of light, but by making the darkness conscious." Here, pondering the infinite possibilities of the world soul really does not take us any closer to the experience of immediate difficulties inherent in finite interactions with the other. Or as Hillman states

Let us imagine the *anima mundi* neither above the world encircling it as a divine and remote emanation of spirit, a world of powers, archetypes and principles transcendent to things, nor within the material world as its unifying panpsychic life-principle. Rather let us imagine the *anima mundi* as that particular soul-spark, that seminal image, which offers itself through each thing in its visible form. Then *anima mundi* indicates the animated possibilities presented by each event as it is, its sensuous presentation as a face bespeaking its interior image – in short, its availability to imagination, its presence as a *psychic* reality (Hillman, 1982, p. 77).

I am reminded of a clinical interaction with the patient discussed earlier that suffered from the severe phobias. While he was discussing his consuming experience of actually becoming smaller and smaller when in proximity to large towering buildings, I had an associative dream about a 50's movie entitled, "The Incredible Shrinking Man" (1957) – particularly its ending. Through certain mishaps common to many themes and fears of that period, and common to us both, the main character begins to shrink uncontrollably. He has to face challenges with ordinary things, such as the house cat and a spider, that become demonic and threaten to destroy him. Then he finally realizes that he will eventually shrink until he reaches the atomic level. By finally moving through his ever-present fears and anxieties, he concluded that he would still matter in the universe because, to God, "there is no zero."

*Thirdness* represents a type of psychological intimacy with an other; we might even consider thirdness as one facet of the archetype of intimacy – one that illuminates the dynamics of the relational unconscious noted earlier. Jung's insight here is that

> ... the underlying idea of the psyche proves it to be a half bodily, half spiritual substance, an *anima media natura,* as the alchemists call it, an hermaphroditic being capable of uniting the opposites, but who is never complete in the individual unless related to another individual. The unrelated human being lacks wholeness, for he can achieve wholeness only through the soul, and the soul cannot exist without its other side, which is always found in a "You" (1946, par. 454).

Ghent (1990, p.108) suggests "an underlying theme in human nature is a quality of liberation and expansion of the self as a corollary to the letting down of defensive barriers." He hypothesizes that there is passionate longing for a need to surrender as a basic human desire – not, as typically understood as defeat, but as one of letting go. Only in this way might we find true otherness in the other rather than "nothing but" our projections of what we need or fear them to be. Benjamin (2004, p. 8) expresses the notion that it is precisely the *third* to which we must surrender, "surrender refers us to recognition – being able to sustain connectedness to the other's mind while accepting his separateness and difference. Surrender implies freedom from any intent to control or coerce." Doi (1989) discusses a similar notion using the Japanese word *amae*. What distinguishes *amae* from the ordinary meanings of love, and relates it to surrender, is that it presupposes a passive stance toward one's partner, as it invariably involves a kind of dependence on a receptive partner for fulfillment.

The psychological problem has been that this need often falls into its more pathological counterparts, as seen in the case material presented earlier, as compliance, submission, or outright sadomasochism. Schwartz-Salant (1998, p. 222) expresses, "Finding... this *third area* between the two partners requires the surrendering of ego control and the establishment of trust in a mutual process that is both frightening and exhilarating." *Thirdness* transcends individual subjectivities and becomes a space unto itself. To reach such a space Benjamin (2005) argues that the responsibility for feelings of shame, inadequacy, and guilt aroused by falling into enactments usually must be borne – by the analyst. Only in this way may the empathic connection adequately be restored. I think of this as a required ethical attitude if one is going to work and live from a *thirdness* model. She asserts that clinical practice might require moral or ethical values that insist on the acceptance of "uncertainty, humility, and compassion that form the basis of a democratic or egalitarian view of psychoanalytic process."

I am suggesting that in the singularity of this finite moment of surrender the *anima mundi*, world soul, can be experienced in a deeply profound and meaningful way, carrying its own numinosity. Earlier, we saw that Jung suggested we approach the unconscious as *other* when attempting to encounter and engage it; here, the *other* actually functions exactly as the unconscious by providing us with both positive and negative compensatory material necessary for our own individuation.

## Conclusion

As the alchemist Maria Prophetissa expounded: "One becomes two, two becomes three, and out of the third comes the one as the fourth. (1953, par. 26). We have discussed the role of *thirdness* at length, but what about that *fourth* waiting to be born as the One from the *third*. I (Cwik, 2011) have suggested that we could think of the contents emerging from the *third* as micro-activations of the transcendent function resulting in new images, thoughts, feelings, and body sensations. The analyst then uses these to speak *from* and *about* them to the patient. This is the transcendent function of everyday analytic life rather than the "big" creation of a new and grand uniting symbol as can happen in formal active imaginations or profound numinous experiences. These could be thought of as "lesser" fourths, just slightly moving the analytic couple forward into the next moment providing a sort of analytic compass for the work. But what of the larger arc that even brought these two particular individuals together in the first place.

Ulanov (2007) addresses this issue in her paper, "The Third in the Shadow of the Fourth." She suggests that the *fourth* is something prompting and yet arising out of the *third* and is the result of more than the individual subjectivities of the participants – it bridges to transpsychic reality. She says:

> The fourth that sponsors the generative third leads back to the mundane, to our livingness in the world. The fourth, however shadowy, engineers our living in the third. The fourth gets in directly through what each of us leaves out, through what the analytical couple leaves out – the wild animal, the formless pleroma, the God who wants to step over into visible life (Ulanov, 2007, p. 594).

Figure 8

This larger view is imaged in the World card from the tarot (Figure 8). We see the *anima mundi* accenting our numerical sequence of the 1 to the 4. One is represented by her figure and larger circle, two by the right and left wands or scrolls she is holding, three in the shape of the scarf and four by the position of her body and the four fixed signs of the zodiac represented at the corners. *Anima mundi,* means that there is always an inseparability of the individual with the world, it truly is "the motor of the heavens" (Jung, 1959, par. 212). Our ultimate goal is not just to realize the soul of the world, but also actually to create it by giving out soul into the world. As Benjamin (2005, p. 189) states, "… the sense of one's own wholeness is enhanced, not diminished, by the sense of unity with other living beings." Jung (1934, p. 172, italics added) says, "In the deepest sense we all dream *not out of ourselves* but out of what lies *between us and the other.*" Then our *analytic mindfulness* begins to be a natural way of being in the world that engages all experience both inner and outer – truly to live and embrace the symbolic life through *thirdness.*

## References:

Baranger, M. (1993). The mind of the analyst: From listening to interpretation. *International Journal of Psycho-Analysis*, 74, 15-24.

Benjamin, J. (2004). Beyond doer and being done to: An intersubjective view of thirdness. *Psychoanalytic Quarterly*, 73(1), 5-46.

Benjamin, J. (2005). From many into one: attention, energy, and the containing multitudes. Psychoanalytic Dialogues, 15, 181-201.

Bion, W. R. (1962). A theory of thinking. In *Second thoughts*. New York: Karnac Books, 110 – 19.

Bollas, C. (1992). *Being a character. New York: Hill & Wang.*

Cambray, J. (2001). Enactments and amplification. *Journal of Analytical Psychology*, 46, 275-303.

Cambray, J. (2006). Towards the feeling of emergence. *Journal of Analytical Psychology*, 51, 1-20.

Campbell, Joseph. (2008). *The Hero with a Thousand Faces.* New World Library

Colman, W. (2007). Symbolic conceptions: The idea of the third. *Journal of Analytical Psychology*, 52, 565-583.

Cwik, A. (995). Active imagination: Synthesis in analysis. In Murray Stein (Ed.), *Jungian Analysis (2nd Edition).* Chicago: Open Court.

Cwik, A. (2006a). Rosarium revisited. *Spring*, 74, 189-232.

Cwik, A. (2006b). The art of the tincture: Analytical supervision. *Journal of Analytical Psychology*, 51, 209-225.

Cwik, A. (2011). Associative dreaming: Reverie and active imagination. *Journal of Analytical Psychology*, 56, 14-36.

de Barry, W.T. and Bloom, I. (eds.) (1999). *Sources of Chinese Tradition: Volume 1: From Earliest Times to 1600*, second edition. New York: Columbia University Press.

Doi, T. (1989). The concept of amae and its psychoanalytic implications. *International Review of Psycho-analysis* 16(3), 349-354.

Edinger, E. 1994. *The Mystery of the Coniunctio: Alchemical Image of Individuation.* Toronto: Inner City.

Ferenczi, S. (1951). Confusion of Tongues Between the Adult and the Child. *Psychoanalytic Quarterly,* 20, 641-642.

Forham, M. (1957/1996). Notes on transference. In Sonu Shamdasani (Ed.) *Analyst-patient interaction: Collected papers on technique.* London: Routledge.

Gerson, S. (2004). The relational unconscious: A core element of intersubjectivity, thirdness, and clinical process. *Psychoanalytic Quarterly,* 73(1), 63-98.

Ghent, E. (1989). Credo – The dialectics of one-Person and two-person psychologies. *Contemporary Psychoanalysis,* 25,169-211.

Ghent, E. (1990). Masochism, submission, surrender: Masochism as a perversion of surrender. *Contemporary Psychoanalysis,* 26(1), 108-136.

Graves, R. (1955). *The Greek myths:* Volume one. New York: Braziller.

Green, A. (2004). Thirdness and psychoanalytic concepts. *Psychoanalytic Quaterly,* 73(1), 99-135.

Hillman, J. 1982. *Anima mundi: The return of the soul to the world.* New Orleans: Spring.

Jacoby, M. (1984). *The Analytic Encounter: Transference and Human Relationship.* Toronto: Inner City.

Jung, C.G. (1916). The transcendent function. CW 8, 67-91.

Jung, C.G. (1921). CW 6, *Psychological types.*

Jung, C.G. (1931). Problems of modern psychotherapy. CW 16, *The practice of psychotherapy,* 53-75.

Jung, C.G. (1946). The psychology of the transference. In CW 16, *The practice of psychotherapy,* 163-320.

Jung, C.G. (1953). CW 12, *Psychology and alchemy.*

Jung, C.G. (1954a). On the nature of the psyche. CW 8, *The structure and dynamics of the psyche,* 159-234.

Jung, C.G. (1954b). The philosophical tree. CW 13, *Alchemical studies.*

Jung, C.G. (1959). CW 9(II), *Aion.*

Jung, C G. (1973). *Letters,* Vol. I. Princeton: Princeton University Press.

Kohut, H. (1977). *The restoration of the self.* New York: International University Press.

Kalsched, D. (1996). *The Inner World of Trauma: Archetypal Defenses of the Human Spirit.* London: Routledge.

Kieffer, C. (2007). Emergence and the analytic third: Working at the edge of chaos. *Psychoanalytic Dialogues,* 17(5), 683-703.

Kornfield, J. and Siegel, D. (2010). *Mindfulness and the Brain: A Professional Training in the Science and Practice of Meditative Awareness.* Louisville, CO: Sounds True.

Newman, K D. 1981. The riddle of the vas bene clausum. *Journal of Analytical Psychology,* 26, 229-341.

Ogden, T. (1997). Reverie and metaphor: Some thoughts on how I work as a psychoanalyst. *International Journal of Psycho-Analysis,* 78, 719 – 732.

Ogden, T. (1999). The analytic third: an overview. *fort da, 5,* 1. Also in *Relational Perspectives in Psychoanalysis: The Emergence of a Tradition,* S. Mitchell & L. Aron (Eds.). Hillsdale, NJ: Analytic Press, 487 – 92.

Ogden, T. (2007). *This Art of Psychoanalysis: Dreaming Undreamt Dreams and Interrupted Cries.* London: Routledge.

Petrus Bonus. (1330). www.ritmanlibrary.com/collection/alchemy.

Samuels, A. (1985). Symbolic dimensions of eros in transference-countertransference: Some clinical uses of Jung's alchemical metaphor. *International Review of Psycho-Analysis,* 12, 199-214.

Schaverien, Joy. (2007). Countertransference as active imagination: Imaginative experiences of the analyst. *Journal of Analytical Psychology,* 52, 413-431.

Schwartz-Salant, N. (1995). On the interactive field as the analytic object. In *The Interactive Field in Analysis,* 1, 1-36.

Schwartz-Salant, N. (1998). *The Mystery of Human Relationship: Alchemy and the Transformation of the Self.* London: Routledge.

Stark, M. (2015). Relentless hope: the refusal to grieve. E-book 2015 International Psychotherapy Institute.

The incredible shrinking man. (1957). Universal-International.

Ulanov, A. (2007). The third in the shadow of the fourth. *Journal of Analytical Psychology,* 52, 585-605.

Van Eenwyk, J. (1997). *Archetypes & strange attractors: The chaotic world of symbols.* Toronto: Inner City.

Vassanyi, Miklos. (2007). *Anima mundi: The rise of the world soul theory in German enlightenment and early romanticism, examined in the perspective of the relation of the finite with the infinite.* New York: Springer.

Wiener, Jan. (2009). *The Therapeutic Relationship: Transference, Countertransference, and the Making of Meaning.* College Station: Texas A&M University Press.

*Friday, 2 September*

# The Dao of Anima Mundi: I Ching and Jungian Analysis, the Way and the Meaning[1]

*Heyong Shen*
(China, IAAP IM)

Certain Chinese philosophical ideas inform this presentation. I am going to discuss the ancient ineffable notion of "Dao" as an archetype, with emphasis on the goal of embracing "the Heart of Dao", together with the meaning pointed to by Confucius in introducing the term "Zhong" ("Equilibrium") as the psychological path to the state of harmony implied by the word Dao. I will also mention "Shi" ("Timing", which in a parallel way spans both the Greek notion of Kairos and the Jungian notion synchronicity) and will link Zhong to Shi to discuss "Shi-Zhong" (an "equilibrium with time" achieved through a heartfelt influence often best achieved through wu-wei/acting without acting) as we often must as analysts. I need such ideas to speak in a Chinese way to the theme of this Conference, which has been stated in Jungian Latin: "Anima Mundi in Transition: Cultural, Clinical and Professional Challenges".

## The Mysterious Heart of Dao, the Subtle Words with Great Meaning

Let us start with the Dao. This is not only the Great Watercourse Way of Taoism. It is also the goal of the rational Confucian path of "Faithfulness and Forbearance"(which never forgets that we all have the "same Heart") and the intuitive genius of the Buddhist focus on the "Middle Way (madhyamā-pratipad)" and of Buddhism's profound respect for "Suchness (Tathātā)." Even more, Dao is the reality whose manifold Meanings are contained within and conveyed by *I Ching* to the psyches of those who consult this wise Chinese oracle. This is the image of "Dao" in Chinese bronze inscriptions (as shown below):

1 Acknowledgments: The paper is based on the research project supported by Chinese National Social Science Foundation (16ASH009). My thanks to John Beebe, who edited the paper with his profound understanding of Chinese philosophy and I Ching.

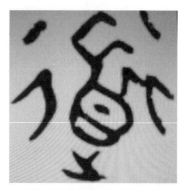

*Fig. 1: San Family Plate, late Zhou Dynasty*

For me, however, *I Ching* itself, the book that, thanks to Jung, sits on so many bookshelves, is the embodiment of Dao. As is said in the commentary, Jung was sure that Confucius himself had written in the *I Ching – Xi Ci*, ("The Great Commentary): "*I Ching* is made on the principles of heaven and earth, therefore it contains all the rules and ways from heaven to earth… to have the knowledge of all, and serve the world with Dao".

Jung thus did not overstate when he observed, "In Chinese philosophy one of the oldest and most central ideas is that of Tao, which the Jesuits translated as 'God.'" But this is correct only for the Western way of thinking. Other translations of Tao (or Dao), such as "Providence" and the like, are mere makeshifts. Richard Wilhelm brilliantly interprets Tao as "meaning." "The concept of Tao pervades the whole philosophical thought of China" (CW8. par. 917).

Jung points out that: "Lao Tzu described "Dao" as such in the famous *Tao Te Ching*:

> There is something formless yet complete
> That existed before heaven and earth.
> How still! How empty!
> Dependent on nothing, unchanging,
> All pervading, unfailing.

One may think of it as the mother of all things under heaven.
I do not know its name, but I call it 'Meaning.' (Dao)
If I had to give it a name, I should call it 'The Great.' [Ch. XXV.] (CW8. par. 918)

The word "name" as used here in Wilhelm's rendering of the Chinese text is often formed by two characters, only one of which really means "name" in the secular Western sense of "signifier." The other character means the more ambiguous term "word", as it used in the last sentence by Lao Tzu used here. For example, Lao Tzu, whose common name is "Er" (ear), has the styled word "Dan" (big ears). Similarly, the styled word of "Dao" is the beautifully symbolic "Meaning", which includes the idea of finding the Mean, but the common name of it, the "Great" (Da) points to its value, and why we should want to revere it. The basis of this evaluation is unpacked more fully if you look more closely at the word Da.

The Chinese character "Da" (Great), from its image on the Oracle Bone Inscriptions in which it was first found, in the image a man – a person standing tall and stretching out, thus called "Da-Ren" (Great man).

*Fig. 2*

The image of "great" (Da) in Chinese looks simple, but it conveys the symbolic meaning of transforming and attaining what is beyond man. And in such an image, just as Lao Tzu said: "The great square shows no corner", and "the great imagery has no form"(*Tao Te Ching*, Chapter 41). From great and (moving or transforming) "nothingness" (such as "wu wei"/no-action, and "wu wo"/"no self"/Anatta), we reach the transcendent function and transformation.

In *I Ching,* we can read another meaning to the word "great", especially the "Great Man" (Da-Ren), an idea which both Richard Wilhelm and C.G. Jung appreciate very much: "A great man is he whose virtues are in accord with heaven and earth, whose brightness is in accord to the sun and the moon, whose order matches the four seasons, and who listens to the spirits for the fortune and misfortune." (*I Ching – Xi Ci* /the Great Commentaries). I must say, I have always viewed this passage from the I Ching as Chinese philosophy's description of the Individuation process.

But there is as much differentiation of this idea in the rest of Chinese philosophy as we find within our own psychology in the works of von Franz, Neumann, or Edinger. For instance, the aforementioned quote from Lao Tzu by Jung is in the first half of *Tao Te Ching*'s Chapter 25. The second half goes thus:

Great (Da) is also called Shi (i.e. constantly on the move). Shi is also called Yuan (i.e. far-reaching), and Yuan is also called Fan (i.e. returning to the very beginning). Therefore, the Dao (the Meaning and the Way) is great, the Heaven is great, the Earth is great, the Man is also great. In the universe there are four greats, and the Man is one of the four. The Man copies the Earth as example, the Earth copies the Heaven as example, the Heaven copies the Dao as example, and the Dao just copies the Great Nature (*Tao Te Ching.* Chapter 25).

If I were to try to put this in the language of Analytical Psychology, then I would want to say, Dao is great because, like the Self, it is a container of everything. Indeed, a Chines proverb says: "The capacity of containing makes greatness." But of course Lao Tzu has added the thought that only through greatness may things transform. This has profound implications for our understanding of individuation, including the individuation that sometimes will not happen because the patient cannot embrace his or her capacity to take their place among the Greats in life.

In the future, though, when I see texts related to Dao, *I Ching* and Jung's interpretation of them, I know I will want to recall the theme of this Conference, "Anima Mundi in transition: Cultural, Clinical and Professional Challenges." It is these very challenges that require us to be the Great men and women, to serve those forces in the universe that are driving Anima Mundi's transition into Tao, if only we will allow them to speak to us. We ourselves came to Kyoto, Japan, in a similar way that Obama recently went to Hiroshima to strive to foster the relationship between the East, the West and Nature. We do this too when we explore together the clinical and professional challenges of our field in today's rapidly changing, and increasingly dangerous world.

I use "Dao Xin Wei Wei" (the Mysterious Heart of Dao) in Chinese to express my understanding of "the World Soul" – Anima Mundi, really the Soul of the Universe, and I mention both the Soul's mystery and it's reach to get to the heart of this Conference.

"Dao Xin Wei Wei" (the Mysterious Heart of Dao), comes from a "16-characters scripture" recorded in *Shang Shu* (on of the five Classic books of ancient Chinese literature). The full text goes as follows:

> The heart of man is perilous,
> the heart of Dao is mysterious;
> be refined and be focused,
> and to hold the honest Mean.
>
> (*Shang Shu*/the Book of History,
> chapter: Counsels of the Great Yu).

It is said that this scripture has been passed on from the ancient Emperors Yao (about 2350 BC.), Shun and Yu generation after generation.[2]

"The Mysterious Heart of Dao", may also be known as "the obscure and vague way" or "the formless and soundless great path". This is exactly the connotation of Dao used by Jung – its wonderful evocation of the not-knowing which is known so well by analysts, in their way of helping patients gain an insight into the collective unconscious and thus into their place within the archetypal image of Anima Mundi in its present moment of transition.

Within this quatrain of four lines, each composed of four characters, beginning with "The heart of man is perilous" we are given a 16-characters scripture that expresses the fundamental idea of "holding the two extremes while employing the middle course or unity", the method of clinical practice utilized by C.G. Jung which may be referred to as the "transcendent function" but is really an invitation to "active imagination"—a journey that is in Dao to realize the Self that has always, mysteriously, been there.

In Jung's opinion, the archetypal image of Dao contains the integration of the conscious and unconscious, the wholeness of Yin and Yang. Jung says that

> Out of this union emerge new situations and new conscious attitudes. I have therefore called the union of opposites the 'transcendent function.' This rounding out of the personality into a whole may well be the goal of any psychotherapy that claims to be more than a mere cure of symptoms (CW9i. par. 524).

*The Metaphor of He-Tu, The Image of I Ching*

In his 1935 *Tavistock Lectures* Jung stated (on ancient Chinese philosophy),

> The ideal condition is named Tao, and it consists of the complete harmony between heaven and earth. Figure 13 represents the symbol for Tao. The condition of Tao is the beginning of the world where nothing has yet begun—and it is also the condition to be achieved by the attitude of superior wisdom. The idea of the union of the two opposite principles, of male and female, is an archetypal image (CW18. par. 262).

This is the Chinese Tai Chi Diagram used by Jung.

---

2 Although there have been doubts regarding when was Shang Shu written, the ancient texts recently presented in the bamboo manuscript at Tsinghua University give sufficient support to the 16-character scripture we quoted.

*Fig. 3*

As stated in *I Ching* – *Xi Ci*, "equal parts of Yin and Yang is called Dao".

So, too, is as Chuang Tzu's comments on *I Ching*: "*I Ching* is about the way of Yin and Yang." (*Chuang Tzu*. Chapter Tian Xia/ the Land under Heaven)

As some of you know, Jung met Richard Wilhelm at the opening ceremony of Count Keyserling's School of Wisdom in Darmstadt, Germany. This was in November, 1920. The two men must have "clicked," because Jung then invited Wilhelm to give a seminar on *I Ching* at the Psychology Club in Zurich in December 1921.[3] Already, Jung had grasped that Richard Wilhelm's great contribution was bringing the meaning of *I Ching* and, through it, passing on the flame of Chinese culture (the living germ of the Chinese spirit) to the West.

Jung is quite clear about this: explaining "blocking of libido" in *Symbols of Transformation* (1912), he writes: "The ancient Chinese philosophy of the *I Ching* devised some brilliant images for this state of affairs" (CW5. par. 250). Also in Part VI "the battle for Deliverance form the mother" in Vol. 2 of *Symbols of Transformation*, Jung used the legend of the dragon-headed horse, He Tu (River Map) and *I Ching* to analyze the symbol of the horse. He describes it thus: "The *I Ching* is supposed to have been brought to China by a horse that had the magic signs/the 'river map' on his coat" (CW5. par. 423).

"He Tu" (River Map) and "Luo Shu" (Luo Script) are the origins and the first images of *I Ching*. Legend has it that in the ancient days during Fuxi's time, a dragon-headed horse emerged from the Yellow River near Luoyang with "He Tu"; and a turtle spirit emerged from the Luo Shui River with "Luo Shu" on its back. Fuxi then evolved Bagua (the Eight Trigrams) and the rules of Wuxing (the Five Elements) from them, thus originating *I Ching*.

---

3 In *Memories, Dreams, Reflections*, we read that Jung first invited Richard Wilhelm to the Psychology Club in Zürich in 1923. Thanks to Tom Kirsch, Ulrich Hoerni and Thomas Fisher, we know that the exact date is 15 December 1921. "This is confirmed by the existing lists of talks held at the Club since its beginning" (letter from Thomas Fisher to Heyong Shen).

In the classic scriptures from the Pre-Qin Period[4], there are many records of "He Tu" and "Luo Shu". As written in *I Ching – Xi Ci*: "Map from the River, Script from Lou Shui, the saints follow them".

This is China's "He Tu" and "Luo Shu" (see images below):

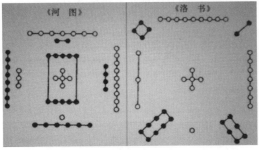

*Fig. 4*

However, "He Tu" and "Luo Shu" are not just legends, for their ancient history and actual existence have been repeatedly confirmed by modern archaeological discoveries. In 1987, a jade turtle with carved jade piece was unearthed at the Ling-jia-tan site at Hanshan, Anhui Province; it has been dated back to the Neolithic Age 5000 years ago. The jade piece was carved with primordial Bagua charts and placed in between the ventral and dorsal of the jade turtle, as if reenacting the legend of "He Tu" and "Luo Shu" being carried by spirits.

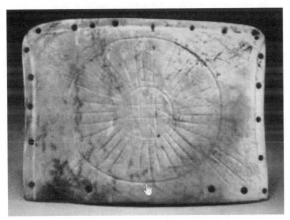

*Fig. 5: The jade turtle from Ling-jia-tan*

---

4 Pre-Qin Period usually means the history before 221 BC in China, particularly the Spring-Autumn and the Warring States period (770-221 BC).

In 1930, Jung gave a more detailed analysis of the "He Tu" images and *I Ching* in a seminar about Mandala. He said: "The 'River Map' is one of the legendary foundations of the I Ching, which in its present form derives partly from the twelfth century B.C. According to the legend, a dragon dredged the magical signs of the "River Map" from a river. On it the sages discovered the drawing, and in the drawing the laws of the world-order. This drawing, in accordance with its extreme age, shows the knotted cords that signify numbers. These numbers have the usual primitive character of qualities, chiefly masculine and feminine. All uneven numbers are masculine, even numbers are feminine (CW9i. par. 642).

This is the "He Tu" Jung used in his book:

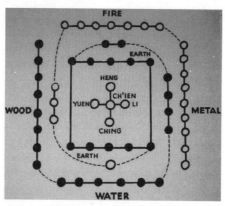

*Fig. 6: The "He Tu" used by Jung in "Concerning Mandala Symbolism"*

About "*He Tu*", Jung commented as follows, using the Qian Hexagram: "Qian in the middle is the heaven, which then originates the four virtues, such as the movement of heaven is full of power. So now we have:

> *Qian* : self-generated creative energy.
> *Heng*: all-pervading power.
> *Yuan*: generative power.
> *Li*: beneficent power.
> *Zhen*: unchangeable, determinative power
> (CW9i. par. 640).

"He Tu" is presented in the form of image which holds logic and is formed by numbers. Image, logic and number are crucial to *I Ching*. But of equal importance is the "*Chi*" in *I Ching* described by Jung although the English expression he used was "power" or "energy". "He Tu" tells us that numbers are based on *Chi. Chi* channels Dao and touches the Heart of Dao. Here is the connection to the mysterious heart of Dao and Anima Mundi. "*He Tu*" and "*Luo Shu*" are both the primal archetypal images and the inspirations contained therein. Ancient minds and their archetypal images are held in "*He Tu*" and "*Luo Shu*"'s circles, dots and the linking in between.

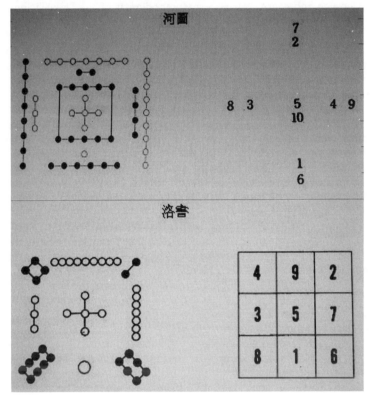

*Fig. 7*

As shown above: In the middle of "He *Tu*" is number 5 and 10, each group of numbers on the four sides subtract to 5, and the middle numbers also give 5 and 15. The middle of "Luo Shu" is also 5, and the horizontal, vertical, diagonal sums are all 15. Thus, in the archetypal images of "He Tu" and "Luo Shu", "wu" ("5") is the center. The Chinese character of "5"("*wu*"), it's oracle bone inscription like this:

*Fig. 8*

The image conveys the symbolic meaning of "crossing noon", and the "knotted point", the core and the middle number. It not only contains all of both Yin and Yang, but is also the foundation of the Five Elements (Wu-Xing); its logic holds the wonders of the numbers of heaven and earth. It is also the embodiment of the "equilibrium" (*Zhong*) within "to hold the honest Mean", the upmost Dao.

Therefore, the *"wu"* ("5") and "center" of *"He Tu"* is also referred to as "where the heart of Dao is", representing "the heart of heaven and earth". In Chinese context, the heart of heaven and earth is the heart of the universe; e.g. Lu Jiuyuan (1139—1193, idealist neo-Confucian philosopher) once said "my heart is the universe".

I see the "wu" ("5") in the middle of "He Tu" as part of "wu" ("I"/"self") in Chinese. "Wu"("I"/"self") may be taken as "Self", as Jung once quoted Chuang-tzu's "I (wu) lost myself" (or I lost my ego) in the *Secret of the Golden Flower.* When the ego of consciousness surrenders, the self from the heart begins to emerge; so when "wu" ("I"/"self") meets the heart, the "enlightenment"[5] comes. As a result, we have the "Psychology of the Heart", based on Chinese culture, and combined with analytical psychology.

Hence, from "wu" ("5") to "wu"("I"/"self"), from "wu" ("I"/"self") to "wu" ("enlightenment")[6]; only by the heart can we receive the meaning of the images. The mysterious heart of Dao shall bring us the heart of the universe (Anima Mundi).

In *Psychology and Alchemy*, Jung wrote: "The idea of the *anima mundi* coincides with that of the collective unconscious whose centre is the self" (CW12. par. 265).

Based on the archetypal images of "He Tu" and "Luo Shu", Chinese sages had inferred the Fuxi Primordial Hexagrams of *I Ching*, and the King Wen Manifested Hexagrams. The mystery of these diagrams, and the structure and pattern within *I Ching*, are all from the archetypal images of "He Tu" and "Luo Shu" – from them, we have "equilibrium" (zhong) and "to hold the equilibrium", movements of the "heart of the universe", the Chi it contains, as well as "time" and "equilibrium with time".

We can read on the back cover of the English translation of I Ching: "The I Ching, or Book of Changes, represents one of the first efforts of the human mind to place itself in the universe." "Its central themes, set forth in imagery of singular force and originality, is the continuous change and transformation underlying all existence" (Richard Wilhelm, 1950).

For Chinese philosophers, especially Taoists, these archetypal

---

5 The image of the Chinese character for "enlightenment" is the image of the Heart, and the image of "wu" ("self/I") together.

6 In Chinese, the characters of "I" or "self", and the enlightenment, are based on the number five (wu), and have similar pronunciation.

images contain the "returning to one's true nature" and the "unity of heaven and man" they pursue, and hold the way, the method and meaning of returning from "acquired" to "innate".

In *Memories, Dreams, Reflections* Jung writes:

> This raised the question of the unity which must compensate this diversity, and it led me directly to the Chinese concept of Tao.... It was only after I had reached the central point in my thinking and in my researches, namely, the concept of the self, that I once more found my way back to the world (MDR. p. 208).

### Shi-Zhong and Gan-Ying, Equilibrium with Time and Synchronicity

What *I Ching* brings to Jung, or what Jung brings to *I Ching*, has another crucial meaning relevant to this "equilibrium" and "to hold the equilibrium", which is "time" – the "synchronicity" developed by Jung.

For Jung, "synchronicity" is at once the embodiment of the Way and the Meaning of *I Ching* as a guide to knowing how to proceed to walk on this Way. As Jung said, "The method [of *I Ching*], like all divinatory or intuitive techniques, is based on an acausal or synchronistic connective principle" (CW8. par. 866). He further explains:

> I first used this term in my memorial address for Richard Wilhelm (delivered May 10, 1930, in Munich). The address later appeared as an appendix to *The Secret of the Golden Flower*, where I said: 'The science of the *I Ching* is not based on the causality principle, but on a principle (hitherto unnamed because not met with among us) which I have tentatively called the synchronistic principle' (CW15. par. 81).

When Jung expressed his understanding of synchronicity and explained its meaning, he not only quoted *I Ching*, but also used the Chinese "Dao", citing Chapter 25, Chapter 24, 11, 14, 21, 37, Chapter 73 etc. from *Tao Te Ching* in sequence. For example, Jung said:

> 'Nothing' is evidently 'meaning' or 'purpose', and it is only called Nothing because it does not appear in the world of the senses, but is only its organizer. Lao-tzu says:
>
> 'Because the eye gazes but can catch no glimpse of it,
> It is called elusive.
> Because the ear listens but cannot hear it,
> It is called the rarefied.
>
> Because the hand feels for it but cannot find it. It is called the infinitesimal. ...
> These are called the shapeless shapes,

Forms without form, Vague semblances' (CW8. par. 920).

Thus, the heart of Dao is mysterious. The way and the meaning of the Dao, is not for eye and ear, but for the Heart.

Jung stated that: "the development of Chinese philosophy produced from the significance of the magical the 'concept' of Tao, of meaningful coincidence, but no causality based science" (CW8. par. 941).

After quoting Lao Tzu's *Tao Te Ching* in explanation of synchronicity, Jung refers to Chuang Tzu:

> Chuang-tzu (a contemporary of Plato's) says of the psychological premises on which Tao is based: 'The state in which ego and non-ego are no longer opposed is called the pivot of Tao.' If you have insight, says Chuang-tzu, 'you use your inner eye, your inner ear, to pierce to the heart of things, and have no need of intellectual knowledge.' This is obviously an allusion to the absolute knowledge of the unconscious, and to the presence in the microcosm of macrocosmic events (CW8. par. 923).

"The Fasting of the Heart" by Chuang Tzu has a resonance for me that the words of Mountain Lake about "thinking with one's heart" might have had for Jung[7]; these were the keywords that inspired me and planted the seed in a dream I had back in 1993, which later grew to become the "Psychology of the Heart." What Chuang Tzu called "The Fasting of the Heart", echoes in Jung's writing on Synchronicity, that "the intellect should not seek to lead a separate existence, thus the soul (the Heart) can become empty and absorb the whole world. It is Tao that fills this emptiness" (CW8 par. 923). What Jung describes here is exactly the meaning of "The Fasting of the Heart" (Chuang Tzu. The Four Chapter: Ways of the Human World).

On Dr. Henderson's desk, there was a card. There were two Chinese characters on the card: "Timing and Chance". All around these two characters was handwriting in fine print; these were notes of understanding and insights on "timing" by Dr. Henderson. I asked him where did he learn of *I Ching*. Dr. Henderson said that he learned about it from Jung. He was inspired by Jung and went on to study *I Ching*. I then asked Dr. Henderson what was the meaning of *I Ching* for him. He answered that for him, the most important meaning of *I Ching* was "timing" (to investigate it in depth and in minute detail, to follow the flow and gain equilibrium with time).

That is very true. The three basic meanings of I Ching – what is changing, what is unchanging, and what is simple – are all related to "time". Only with the right timing can we attain the equilibrium and be

---

7 See Jung's conversation with the Native American elder, Mountain Lake, in 1924, recorded in *Memories, Dreams, Reflections*. Jung (1989 p.247). New York: Vintage Books

simple in the face of change, and therefore able to feel securely held in what cannot change, the Self.

The Dao in *I Ching* is profound. To sum it up, we may call it "equilibrium with time." For many traditional Chinese philosophers, this is the core spirit of *I Ching*. All of the Hexagrams are reflections of time, and all of the 384 Yao lines are how things change in accord with time. What "equilibrium with time" reflects is changing with time to follow Dao. In this way, we accept time, of which so many of us are usually terrified.

In recent years, I have been drawing upon a notion of heartfelt gratitude as a key to my increasing acceptance of time. I have been using "Gan" ("heartfelt influence") and "Gan Ying" ("heartfelt influence" and "responding from the Heart") to understand and interpret "synchronicity", as the images and meaning expressed by the Xian Hexagram (31, The Influence) and the Zhongfu Hexagram (61, The Inner Truth). Just as the I Ching says: "Yi, no thinking, no action, heartfelt influence that connects the world. If not for Yi being the greatest spirit in the world, it could not be so."(*I Ching. Xi-Ci* /The Great Commentaries).

To Jung, *I Ching* is a book that has its own life. Perhaps this life of Yi can also allow us to feel the aliveness of Anima Mundi in the face of its transitions.

*The Soul Flower, Images of I Ching, and Meaning*

One thing of particular importance is that Jung has integrated *I Ching* into the expression and the practice of Analytical Psychology – we see it in his clinical cases, his active imagination and the process of individuation.

In "A Study in the Process of Individuation", Jung began with a quote from Chapter 21 of *Tao Te Ching*:

> Tao's working of things is vague and obscure.
> Obscure! Oh vague!
> In it are images.
> Vague! Oh obscure!
> In it are things.
> Profound! Oh dark indeed!
> In it is seed.
> Its seed is very truth.
> In it is trustworthiness.
> From the earliest Beginning until today
> Its name is not lacking
> By which to fathom the Beginning of all things.
> How do I know it is the Beginning of all things?

Through *it!* (CW9i. par. 525)

However, there is one more sentence of 8 characters (in Chinese) before Jung's quote in this chapter: "The form of the grandest virtue follows only Dao" (Kong De Zhi Rong, Wei Dao Shi Cong).

If we look at this from the perspective of Analytical Psychology, and according to the images of the 8 Chinese characters, then "the form of the grandest virtue follows only Dao" may be explained as such: the grandest virtue is a great container, the capacity of containing makes greatness, only through greatness may things be contained, from Dao, the Way and the Meaning, will individuation be reached. Thus, this Chapter 21 of *Tao Te Ching*, and its description of "Dao" – the things, the seed, the truth and the trustworthiness – is it not an inspiration to feel and to reflect on Anima Mundi?

Jung provided 24 paintings by his patient Miss X in "A study in the process of individuation". The "soul flower" first appeared in the 9th painting. On this Jung wrote: "In Picture 9 we see for the first time the blue "soul-flower," on a red background, also described as such by Miss X." (CW9i. par. 596)

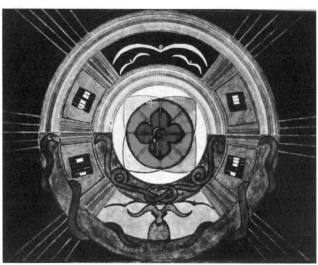

*Fig. 9*

For me, as I came to face this "soul flower" many times while working on this paper, I seemed to see – or feel – the "Magnolia" from Jung's Liverpool dream in 1927, and the *Secret of the Golden Flower* by Jung and Wilhelm ( 1928). So this "soul flower" is like the "suchness" (Jung would have said "just-so ness") of the Flower Garland World (the Jewel Net of Indras of the Huayen World) which displays the "equilibrium with time" we are urged toward by the *I Ching*. Surely this image is also a vivid manifestation of "the Mysterious Heart of Dao" one that allows us to feel its extraordinarily open connection to Anima Mundi.

We can see how Jung expressed his feeling for the living reality imaged in this painting within the unusual passion he summoned to describe the person who had created this image within "A study in the process of individuation": "Her heart overflowing with loving kindness … with compassion … with joyfulness … with equanimity…" (CW9i par. 596). Jung added, lest we mistake his patient's arrival at the core of her introverted feeling as merely the achievement of a sentimental view of life, that: "The underlying thought is clear: no white without black, and no holiness without the devil. Opposites are brothers, and the Oriental [person] seeks to liberate himself from them by his nirdvandva ("free from the two") and his neti neti ("not this, not that"), or else he puts up with them in some mysterious fashion, as in Taoism" (CW9i. par. 597).

In this painting, Miss X, though not herself an oriental person, used 4 Hexagrams from *I Ching* around the "soul flower": (upper left) Yu (Enthusiasm, Hexagram 16, thunder earth providing-for), (upper right) Sun (Decrease, Hexagram 41, mountain swamp diminishing), (down right) Sheng (Pushing Upward, Hexagram 46, earth wind ascending), (down left) Ding (Caldron, Hexagram 50, fire wind holding). Jung described: "The connection with the East is deliberately stressed by the patient, through her painting into the mandala four hexagrams from the *I Ching*" (CW9i par. 597).

Jung interpreted and analyzed the hexagrams one by one, in his *A study in the Process of Individuation*. The key in which, and the meaning contained in all the Hexagrams, is also the images and inspiration they draw from the old Chinese notions of "equilibrium", "timing" and "equilibrium with time" that eventually entered philosophy in a more codified way with Confucius.

The essence of the thought embodied in the I Ching is such: To act in undue time is excessive, to act in due time is equilibrium. Diminishing and increasing depends on time, so too is providing-for and ascending. Grand success holding in the cauldron, will respond when gain equilibrium.

Jung wrote: "The phases and aspects of my patient's inner process of development can therefore express themselves easily in the language of the *I Ching*, because it too is based on the psychology of the individuation process that forms one of the main interests of Taoism and of Zen Buddhism " (CW9i par. 602).

Jung discussed the case with the following analysis:

> Miss X's mandala, on the other hand, comprises and contains the opposites, as a result, we may suppose, of the support afforded

by the Chinese doctrine of Yang and Yin, the two metaphysical principles whose co-operation makes the world go round. The hexagrams, with their firm (yang) and yielding (yin) lines, illustrate certain phases of this process...Thus the Oriental truth insinuates itself and makes possible—at least by symbolic anticipation—a union of opposites within the irrational life process formulated by the I Ching (CW9i. par. 603).

As Jung was working on the Foreword for the English-language version of Wilhelm's translation of the I Ching, which finally appeared in 1950, he decided to invite the I Ching to describe how it felt about being thus translated, and drew the Ding Hexagram (Caldron). It was as though I Ching, already embodied in the image of "Ding", decided to identify itself to Jung as a way of entering into a conversation with him. For Jung, on the other hand, conversing with I Ching was like a kind of linking himself up with "spiritual agencies" in a particularly lively active imagination. He saw I Ching as having its own life and respected it as he would a god. As many religions teach, when supplicants place god in their heart, god will respond to them. As Confucius said: "Make sacrifices to the dead as if they were present, make sacrifices to the spirits as if the spirits were present." Or as the inscription on the lintel of Jung's house says: "Summoned and unsummoned, God will be present."

I call this "Gan-Ying"("heartfelt influence" and "responding from the Heart") and see it as the first principle of Psychology of the Heart. And of course it is also the embodiment of "the Mysterious Heart of Dao", and related to the "faithfulness and forbearance" by Confucius and "with all of one's heart" by Mencius, to "emptying one's heart-mind" by Lao Tzu, "the art of heart" by Guan Zhong, the "fasting of heart" by Chuang Tzu, and to the Heart tradition of Zen Buddhism and Huineng's nature of self.

## The Mysterious Heart of Dao, Heartfelt Influence and Response

The archetypal images of I Ching, such as the hexagrams Xian (Influence) and Ding (Caldron) are also closely related to the development of Analytical Psychology in China. We received the hexagram Xian (31), Influence, for the first international conference of Analytical Psychology and Chinese Culture in 1998. The archetypal image of Xian became the theme and initiation. Just as the Tuan commentary of Xian says: "Xian means gan (heartfelt influence, stimulate), heaven and earth stimulate each other, and all things take shape and come into being. The holy man stimulates the hearts of men, and the world attains peace and rest. If we contemplate the out-going stimulating influences, we can know the nature of heaven and earth and all beings" ( Wilhelm: I Ching. P. 541).

In 2006, after the Third International Conference of Analytical Psychology and Chinese Culture, we (with Murray Stein, John Beebe, Joe Cambray, Linda Carter and others) visited Wilhelm's former residence. We also visited Quindao, the homeland of Lao Nai Xuan, Wilhelm's teacher of I Ching. Under the thousand-year-old elm tree in the Temple of Supreme Purity on Mount Lao, we divined an answer to the question: "What is the future of Analytical Psychology in China?" The response from *I Ching* was the hexagram Ding, The Caldron (50), with the third line changing it into hexagram Weiji, Before Completion (64). There was much to consider in that change, but I would like to focus here on what in it was unchanging. This was that we start with a container that is itself in flow, and undergoing vicissitudes.

In the image of the Ding hexagram is fire over wood, thus the superior man consolidates his fate by making his position correct. The caldron is standing, so it settles the heart and puts it at ease. The seed is refined to consolidate the fate. The Chinese alchemy has long held the way of "Refinement of Essential Matter into Vital Breath".

Thus we were told, once again, as we incubated one part of the future of analytical psychology in Asia, that making one's position correct is the way to reach equilibrium with what we must work on at a particular time, that consolidating one's fate in the same process is the way to reach harmony. That means realizing that even when the state of equilibrium and harmony are truly understood, and in this way brought to conscious realization, only with time will they lead to any lasting equilibrium. In 2008, a powerful earthquake (8.0) hit the southwest of China. Like "The Tong (copper) Mountain shaking at the West, and the Ling (spiritual) bell resonating at East."[8] Members of our Chinese Federation of Analytical Psychology went to the earthquake zone and set up the "Garden of the Heart & Soul", for the psychological relief. Now, we have 76 work-stations with thousands of volunteers at the orphanages of China.

In 2013, the Sixth International Conference of Analytical Psychology and Chinese Culture was held in Qingdao, with the theme: "Wilhelm and *I Ching*, Jung and *Red Book*". Murray Stein and the *Red Book* drama group came and performed their enactment of Jung's confrontation with the unconscious as recorded in Liber Novus. Again, we visited Wilhelm's former residence, and Lao Nai Xuan's homeland at Mount Lao. Again, under that same thousand-year-old elm tree, when Paul

---

8  From *A New Account of Talks of the World*. Joseph Needham quoted the story in his *Science and Civilization in China*. Mr. Yin from Chinchow, who is reported to have asked a Monk (Hui Yuan), "What is really the fundamental idea of the I Ching?" To which the monk is said to have replied: "The fundamental idea of the I Ching can be expressed in one single word, Gan, Heartfelt Influence." Just like "The Tong (copper) Mountain shaking at the West, and the Ling (spiritual) bell resonating at East."

Brutsche spoke, it was as though he spoke with the voice of Jung, as though he felt that this second home of Richard Wilhelm had an atmosphere of "another Bollingen"... At that moment, the elm tree responded; the sound of the falling leaves was like music from nature and heaven.

That moment brought what we feel about *I Ching*'s "equilibrium with time"; from this, we seemed to have had the experience of "the Mysterious Heart of Dao".

I am not superstitious, but I knew in the presence of Murray Stein, Paul Brutsche, John Hill and others, that the moment we shared, the experience of being so near to the actual standpoint of Richard Wilhelm, and that feeling of being together in the same spirit, with the same heart, is what Jung really means by "synchronicity", which for me is "Gan-Ying"( "heartfelt influence" and "responding from the Heart"), literally entering "the Mysterious Heart of Dao".

Now, for closing, I think it would be good to hear Jung's words:

> Anyone who, like myself, has had the rare good fortune to experience in association with Wilhelm the divinatory power of the *I Ching* cannot remain ignorant of the fact that we have here an Archimedean point from which our Western attitude of mind could be lifted off its foundations (CW15. par. 78).

He continues:

> What is even more important is that he has inoculated us with the living germ of the Chinese spirit, capable of working a fundamental change in our view of the world. We are no longer reduced to being admiring or critical observers, but find ourselves partaking of the spirit of the East to the extent that we succeed in experiencing the living power of the *I Ching* (CW15. par. 78).

And then Jung says:

> We must continue Wilhelm's work of translation in a wider sense if we wish to show ourselves worthy pupils of the master. The central concept of Chinese philosophy is *tao*, which Wilhelm translated as 'meaning.' Just as Wilhelm gave the spiritual treasure of the East a European meaning, so we should translate this meaning into life. To do this—that is, to realize *tao*—would be the true task of the pupil (CW15. par. 89).

And now my own words: The Dao of Anima Mundi: *I Ching* and Jungian Analysis, the Way and the Meaning. I can only hope that we, here at this conference, can find it in us to feel "The Dao of Anima Mundi"—if so, then *I Ching* and Jungian Analysis will have come together, in a Chinese way, to understand how at this time of transition we can still find the Way and the Meaning that puts us in harmony with time.

## References

Confucius. *The Confucian Analects* (James Legge Trans.). Changsha: Hunan Publication. 1992

C.G. Jung (1965). *Memories, Dreams, Reflections.* New York: Vintage Books.

Lao Zi. *Tao Te Ching* (Arthur Waley Trans.). Changsha: Hunan Publication. 1994

*Shan Shu, The Book of History.* (Luo Zhiye Trans.). Changsha: Hunan Publication. 1997

Wilhelm, R. (1950). *I Ching or Book of Changes* (Cary F. Baynes, Trans.). New York: Princeton University Press.

Zhuang Zi. *Chuang Tzu* (Wang Yongpei Trans.). Changsha: Hunan Publication. 1997

# Paranoia as a Moral Problem: Archetype and History

*Luigi Zoja*
(Italy, CIPA)

"Madness is a rare thing in individuals, but in groups,
parties, peoples and ages it is the rule"
Friedriech Nietzsche, *Jenseits von Gut und Böse*

## Part I: Paranoia, Analytical Psychology, History

I first began to take an interest in paranoia when I lived in New York, at the beginning of the century. On September 11, 2001, the attack on the Twin Towers took place. That a paranoid Islamic fundamentalism existed, we already knew: the proclamations of Osama Bin Laden could be read on the Internet. I began to feel that I was a citizen of collective paranoia not on September 11, but on September 12. I was struck by the content of the mass media coverage and private conversations over the next few days. Certain patients who already "felt" the presence of too many "enemies" around them rounded on their therapists. They said "It's not right that analysis should always be discussing an 'inner enemy'. The external, real world is full of real enemies."

That is true. The "enemy" can be two things at the same time: an objective reality and an inner image of evil projected outwards. I remember one of the first lectures I heard at the Jung Institute in Zurich, almost half a century ago: "Where there is a projection, there is always a hook [where you can hang it]" ( von Franz 1980 Letters II)). The inner world, however, often seems the more powerful of the two; and it is certainly the one that interests our profession. In extreme words: "There may not actually be an enemy [...]. What is indispensable for war and a cause of war is not the enemy, but the imagination" (Hillman, 2004, p. 25)

### The Archetype of Suspicion

Jungian psychology studies every psychological dynamic as a potential universal. Even psychopathology is not something separate, but a process of the normal mind that has lost its way. The same is true of paranoia: in origin it corresponds to a necessary function. By instinct, man is a social animal. But instinct also tells him that he can't trust everyone. Cooperation is a universal need. But so is suspicion.

From this point of view, paranoia has archetypal roots. It can be found in ancient myth. In Hebraeo-Christian myth it already appears in Cain, who projects his suspicion on to his brother, laying the foundations for his murder. In Greek myth, its most tragic figure is Ajax, who is convinced that Ulysses, Menelaus and Agamemnon are plotting against him. He thinks that killing them all is the only option left to him.

The ritual of the scapegoat

Anthropology, too, informs us about the historical dimension of our theme. In pre-modern societies scapegoat rituals are practised. Where magic prevails over science, an epidemic or a scarcity of crops or fish may be blamed on a spell. Someone responsible for this invisible presence is sought (the hook). In ancient times the carrier of evil who had to be sacrificed might be a person, but often an animal was used: typically a goat, which shares some symbolic elements with the devil (horns, hooves, etc). In part, the killing would be replaced by an expulsion. Two aims were achieved by a single act. The pressure of the collective was alleviated, removing the shadow. At the same time cohesion in the collectivity was reconstructed: an essential step, for with the suspicion that a member was responsible for the evil eye, the mistrust had become internal to the group. By his expulsion, the evil was unanimously projected: it became external again. There was no need to prove that the negative event had been "caused" by the scapegoat: as happens with rituals, the catharsis can be true even if the explanation is false. That remains true in the modern world. Hitler's theory of a Jewish conspiracy was so false that he didn't even try to prove it; but he used it as a collective scapegoat ritual.

In short, the core of paranoia is a projective relationship with evil: and evil concerns everyone. Long before it is "reduced" to a clinical problem, paranoia is a moral problem. Long before it is "reducible" to an individual problem, paranoia is a collective problem.

*Two Preliminary Questions*

1. When does functional mistrust degenerate into pathological suspicion?

   Even if real enemies exist in the external world, it is for the most part our inner world, which magnifies mistrust: to the point where, instead of being controlled by the ego, it becomes its master. In this way a function, which is useful in nature ends up making us lose its functional relationship with the world.

   Unfortunately, our instincts basically go back to before the Neolithic era. At that time the population was very sparse. Human beings lived in small groups, often moving from place to place. It was right that meeting strangers should cause curiosity, but also fear. Today, however, reacting with those instincts is very inadequate to the complexity of globalization. In urban life we meet not individual strangers, but large numbers of strangers, every day. We repress suspicion and fear, because that is what social convention requires; but they accumulate in the unconscious. In more fragile people the perception of danger can become not relative but absolute. This corresponds to what psychopathology calls paranoia and in Jungian terminology total projection of the shadow.

2. Why can paranoia have collective and epochal aspects which other psychological problems do not have?

As I said apropos of September 11, paranoia has a menacing characteristic which distinguishes it from other mental disorders: it is psychically *very* contagious. It can "infect" the collective unconscious even more than the individual unconscious. Western psychiatry, which is oriented towards the individual, like the culture that produces it, says that "collective psychoses" belong to the past (Jaspers, 1913). Unfortunately, this is only partly true.

Let us make a comparison. Many psychotherapists are convinced that the most serious mental pathology of the 21st century is eating disorders. A change in one's relationship with the ideal measures of one's own body can become a veritable delusion: some girls are absolutely convinced that the ideal weight is only 30 kg (60 pounds). An anorexic girl who cultivates this delusion may infect a few friends; but she cannot found a movement which aims to renew society by purifying it with this physical ideal.

The situation is different if the delusion is paranoid, for it is much more contagious. Let us imagine a person who cultivates the delusion that a certain nation or ethnic group is conspiring to seize power in the world: and who therefore wants to renew society by eliminating it. Such a person may found a political movement with this as its programme. His message can be disseminated. And it can be strengthened by wars, social unrest, unemployment and inflation, evils, which activate the projection of the shadow. By discussing this factor we are certainly not replacing historical studies; but we are completing them with a psychological perspective.

*The Structure of Paranoia*

Let us sum up what psychiatry and depth psychology tell us about the constituent elements of paranoia. We find in it two phases which are para-religious, and therefore of interest to Jungian psychology:

1. The first is a sort of illumination. The subject experiences it as a new truth, which is suddenly revealed to him. It will no longer be called into question: it has a "religious" quality, it suddenly gives life meaning. Therefore it is non-negotiable. It becomes, according to descriptions, the "granite foundation" of an existence which formerly rested on a fragile base.

2. The subsequent phases are "consequences" of that premise: arguments and dogmas, policies and rituals. Seemingly, they are negotiable and can be discussed. It is as if, for the subject, the "granite foundation" derived from a Winnicottian "false self"; whereas the consequences inhabit the ego. Indirectly, this second phase too is dangerous: for it gives the illusion that it is possible to reason with the paranoiac. For this reason paranoia was one of the first syndromes classified by French psychiatry, which called it "Folie lucide". The *Harvard Guide to Modern Psychiatry* (Nicholi, 1978) refers to "successful paranoiacs". According to the handbook, this is an important phenomenon, but one that has not been sufficiently studied. Significantly, the book was published after the rapid rise and fall of Senator McCarthy in American politics. This consideration forcefully underlines the difference between paranoia and other disorders. Whereas other serious mental problems, such as depression and schizophrenia, make the subject slide down lower and lower, until he is excluded from society, paranoia, by contrast, can actually function as a multiplier of his abilities; or at least of his manipulations.

## *Chapter 11 of Mein Kampf*

In chapter 11 of Mein Kampf, Adolf Hitler describes step by step, in febrile tones, what for him was an absolutely new and unexpected "'vision": a poor, religious eastern Jew. At first he seems almost incredulous. Hitherto he had not been a convinced anti-Semite: he had met only integrated Jews, like the family doctor whom he still trusted. The vision is gradually transformed into a "revelation": that man is "other". At that moment what he calls "the granite foundation" of his doctrine is born (Hitler 1925, p. 238). Afterwards it will be possible to discuss, for example, the statistics provided by Nazism about Jewish participation in international crimes. It will not be possible to discuss the "granite foundation" of the "natural" incompatibility between Jews and Aryans. The wave that will culminate in catastrophe is not born of political conflicts: what is known as "scientific" racism derives from the paranoid imagination and its consequent projection. According to Norman Cohn: "The deadliest kind of anti-Semitism [...] has little to do with real conflicts of interest between living people or even with racial prejudice as such. At its heart lies the belief that Jews – all Jews everywhere – form a conspiratorial [my italics] body set on ruining and then dominating the rest of mankind". (Cohn, 1967, p.12).

The Slavs too are, for Hitler, constitutionally inferior, unsuited to a modern society. But what about the Czechs, who are so trustworthy? The Czechs are in fact the most dangerous of the Slavs. The proof lies in the fact that they behave seriously: they hide their aims behind loyalty (Hamann, 1996).

Has it not been proved that the Protocols of Zion, on which so much anti-Semitism is based, are a fake? No. "It is the liberal press that says that. And that is the most certain proof that they are genuine" (Hitler, 1925).

Not only the Jews, but also the Slavs and German liberals become containers of the shadow: not because of real facts but because of a "granite premise". It exhausts the entire horizon of meaning from the outset and includes all arguments from the beginning. Even counter-arguments become confirmations, in a circular process: paranoid "absurd consistency" or "inversion of causes".

Shortly before he died, projection of the shadow became so total in Hitler that he issued an order of destruction even for Germany (Hitler, 1945). The future belongs to the Slavic peoples, he said. Germany has shown that it is not superior (Speer, 1969) and that it deserves this apocalypse. This would appear to be a Social Darwinist assessment: but it was also an extension of the paranoid projections. The tyrant attempts to purify his inner world – which is intolerable and unknown – by celebrating a ritual of the universal scapegoat.

### The Wolf and the Lamb

It is easy to trace this archetypal model back to the fable of the wolf and the lamb. The wolf "knows" (whether consciously or not) that he will devour the lamb. Both drink from the same stream, but the wolf is higher up. "Why do you dirty my water?" he asks menacingly. (We note that paranoid people too often have contamination phobias: racism is obsessed with the fantasy that racial interbreeding can produce genetic monstrosities). The lamb replies: "Mr Wolf, that's not possible: I'm drinking lower down, and water flows downwards". The wolf switches argument: "I've heard that you spoke ill of me a year ago." 'It can't have been me: a year ago I hadn't even been born yet." "Enough arguing," shouts the wolf. "If it wasn't you it must have been your brother." And he devours him. Thus he repeats another monstrosity typical of paranoiacs: the fusing of personal and collective responsibility. The only true aim is to release destructive tension by absolute projection of the shadow.

Of course, one question would remain open: in formulating the rationalizations whereby he will attack the victim come what may, does the paranoid-wolf know he is lying, or does he lie to himself as well and convince himself (a process called fantastic pseudology) (Delbrück, 1891)? Even studies of the most egregious paranoid people always leave some uncertainty. There is a grey area in which the two possibilities probably overlap. It is likely that the person who lies consciously is less dangerous: lying is a moral error, which can be understood and corrected. Paranoid delusion, by contrast, always has something incomprehensible and incorrigible about it.

## The Universality of Paranoid Potential

Hitler is an easy example, but any tyrant and even any politician can become a "successful paranoid person". Napoleon stated: "The prince must be suspicious of everything". (Balzac, 1838, maxim no. 276)

Many historians (Bullock, 1991) have stressed the parallels between Hitler and Stalin, and the fact that they copied each other. Other historians have noted how Stalinism applies the exterminationist principles of racism to the "class struggle". Incidentally, "class", like race, is very hard to define: so it is a useful potential container in any circumstance for projecting evils from which demagogy wants to "liberate" the masses.

In particular conditions, even in mature democracies the collective paranoid element can silence reason. John W. Dower (Dower, 1986) has analysed how, in some respects, the War in the Pacific was a continuation of the "war between races" practised during the nineteenth century in the West. Thus, among Americans and Japanese it became "normal" to remove parts of the body, as had happened in the past with the practice of "scalping". The photograph from *Life Magazine* in which a white middle-class woman thanks her marine fiancé for sending her the skull of a Japanese, was published in Life, a staid bourgeois weekly.

In theory, contemplating a skull on a desk might seem to resemble the meditations on human transience characteristic of the sixteenth and seventeenth centuries. In reality it is the exact opposite. Those old thoughts helped people to introject death, to achieve awareness of the fact that it concerns all of us, and that the polarities life and death should never be separated too much. Here, by contrast, warlike, racist rage tries to project it as far away as possible. Compared to the woman who observes it, death is "other"; in particular, the dead man is other, and it is obvious that he deserved to die. Compassion is replaced by splitting.

*Fig. 1: Arizona war worker writes her Navy boyfriend a thank-you-note*
*for the Jap skull he sent her*

## Part II: The Need for Enemies

*The Mass Media*

The projection of the collective shadow has always existed.

However, the modernization of the media of communication brings immense changes in mass psychology. In a positive sense, because it spreads knowledge; but also in a negative sense, because it lends itself to manipulation. The king was a king from birth: he didn't have to justify his power. But more modern regimes have to convince the population: so they are more tempted to find scapegoats. Today this simplification is often called populism.

Since the time of Gutenberg information has been constantly progressing. When the media of communication become mass media there is a quantum leap. On the one hand, at last most of the population can be informed. On the other hand, those who control the media have a strong temptation. How can one reach an increasingly large audience? By replacing complex debates about complex phenomena with simple analyses. And which is the simplest analysis? The one that clearly indicates someone who is to blame for problems. This scapegoat, however, must be different from the people who use the mass medium: the consumer public wants to feel comforted, not guilty. For this reason the invocation "deliver us from evil" stands at the centre of Christianity's most important prayer, the Lord's Prayer. It is the main preoccupation of the ordinary man: from the sacrifices of antiquity to the Roman Catholic confession and the ritual self-criticisms in communism. We can tolerate evil existing in us only in exceptional circumstances, and only for brief periods.

Towards the end of the nineteenth century, in the United States press, the information-providing daily newspaper is superseded by the sensationalist yellow press.

In the period between the two World Wars, information-providing radio is superseded by radio that spreads propaganda: first Fascist, then Nazi and Soviet.

In the second half of the twentieth century mass TV gradually replaces other sources of information. In the democracies, the absolute falsification of the repressive regimes is replaced by a "relative disinformation". The mass media of the dictatorships had disseminated *hard* paranoia, those of the TV tycoons devote themselves to a *soft* paranoia. In a mediocre television like that of Italy, this can be seen in the excessive presence of crime reports: although in a less radical way than political slander, they are offered to the ordinary man so that he can project evil away from himself.

## Pseudo-speciation

We know that opposite poles should never be moved too far apart. The paranoiac attempts the absolute separation of the binomial good-evil: and for this reason he fails. He radically rejects the otherness inside himself, the evil of which we are all partly carriers. So he does not want to look inside himself. The true paranoiac, then, does not turn to the analyst: his mental processes, so to speak, correspond to anti-psychology. Nothing significant is interior; everything is projected.

What is the threshold beyond which the next man (the "neighbor") becomes "something other"? Erikson (Erikson, 1968) has called it pseudo-speciation. Animals have instincts which enable them to recognize who belongs to another species. One does not socialize with an animal of a different species: therefore it can be killed and eaten. With those of the same species one forms groups. Indeed, one can mate and have children: belonging to a species is defined precisely by the fertility within it and by the sterility of mating with other species.

A dog barks at another dog; but then he sniffs him, recognizes him as similar, and lowers his hackles. Man too possesses instincts of this kind. But they have been overlaid by the infinite complexity of culture, which makes this simple certainty infinitely fluid. Our senses are "deceived" by colours, clothes, and especially languages which others speak and we don't understand. On meeting a new person we don't sniff them: we try to speak to them. If they speak an incomprehensible language, dress in an incomprehensible way, believe in a religion that seems to us absurd, our instinct takes the first steps towards pseudo-speciation. It considers them too other, and begins to lose the inhibition against doing them harm: as if they didn't belong to the human race but to another species. As if they were one of those animals that we traditionally kill without feeling guilt, in order to eat them. In this way, the human species has become the only one which, for reasons that are not natural but cultural, regularly kills members of its own species.

Pseudo-speciation is a psycho-zoological concept partly analogous to what, in Jungian terms, is a radical projection of the shadow. In the instability of our cultural defences, collective paranoia takes hold of us more easily than we think: it becomes the rule in racism, but also in nationalism. In genocide, but also in ordinary war. In the pogrom and in the lynching. The historians of genocide have noted a degeneration which is manifested especially in images. The enemy starts to be caricatured as an animal: a tendency so universal as to be practised even by anti-Fascist intellectuals.

*Fig. 2: from Simplicissimus, 1920: caricature of colonial French troops*

When this happens a slide towards genocidal conditions is taking place. Killing animals is considered much less serious than killing human beings: so the feelings of guilt culturally associated with murder are being erased in the collective imagination. With the intensification of racist propaganda, Nazism had circulated films in which the Jews were presented as rats. With the escalation of the war in the Pacific, Allied propaganda circulated illustrations in which the Japanese became monkeys. The military authorities often described the enemy as a "... subhuman beast...", "...a cross between the human being and the ape" (Dower, p. 53 and p. 71).

## More on the Mass Media

The ordinary citizen today knows the world through the mass media. It is natural that this Allied propaganda, too, should have some consequences. While in Europe it urged people to destroy Fascism and Nazism, regarding the Pacific war it had partly convinced people that it was necessary, simply, to destroy *all* Japanese. One study of this question shows that the cause of these convictions is not the presence of the enemy, but the projection of the shadow.

The genocide scholars Chirot and McCauley (Chirot – McCauley, 2006, p. 216) draw attention to an interesting aspect of the surveys carried out during the war among American soldiers: of those who fought against the Japanese, 42 per cent were of the opinion that the entire population of Japan needed to be eliminated; among those who were still being trained in the United States it was as high as 67 per cent. This seems to correspond to the fact that *the less you know your enemy*, the more your attitude towards him is moulded by collective paranoia. That this is indeed the case has been partly confirmed, in the United States too, by the fearful reaction to the September 11 attacks: the panic and the substantially paranoid rumours about new attacks was greater in the internal states of the country and less intense in the states situated along the two coasts, which were objectively more likely to be attacked, but were more used to having relations with other countries and which contained a higher proportion of immigrants, both Islamic and non-Islamic.

## Dominant Factors in Collective Projections

The end of the Cold War eliminated the West's real geopolitical adversary: the Soviet bloc. But it did not eliminate one of the most powerful factors in the collective unconscious: the need to identify evil and an enemy that represents it. Collective projections became more disorderly. In the two opposed blocs, it had been easier to identify the other one as the container of negativity.

About 30 years ago I wondered about the shifts in collective projections. Until the Eighties the rigid international contrast between the communist world and the liberal-capitalist one seemed to correspond to schizo-paranoid collective projections and the impatience of the puer. But with Gorbachev, the thaw had begun. A relative international cooperation seemed to be developing: significantly, environmentalism, which distributes responsibility among all people, was beginning to spread. A partly depressive way of thinking, perhaps more mature and inspired by the senex, was emerging. It is not sufficient to project evil on to the opposite front; we have to accept part of it ourselves: we are all responsible for the destruction of the planet. This analysis of mine was insufficient, as no doubt the one I am making now is too. In the Nineties a brief international cooperation did indeed continue. But soon Islamic fundamentalism again provided a container suited to global paranoid projections.

Paradoxically, it is in the secular modern countries that this collective projection tends to manifest itself as a belief that has no need of proof: as an undisputed belief, but of a negative kind. No longer seeing goodness, the man in the street – secular and now devoid of positive religiosity – constructs a "belief in evil": he "knows" that it exists, even when he has no proof of it.

*"Where there is a projection there is also a hook"*

Let us return to the formula "Where there is a projection there is also a hook". Projections do not originate in the void: there are almost always real reasons why the shadow is projected on to certain people or certain groups and not on to others. But the dimension of the evil that is attributed to them derives chiefly from our imagination.

On the tenth anniversary of the September 11 massacre, the New York Times published a Special Report: The Reckoning (www.nytimes.com/interactive/us/sept-11-reckoning/viewer.html). In the ten years following the attack Al Qaeda had succeeded in killing only about fifteen Americans; whereas the number of deaths due to war and the expenditure on opposing Al Qaeda seemed to be running out of control.

Meanwhile a paranoia of terrorism also fostered arms sales. The use of private weapons against other private citizens caused 10 000 times as many deaths in the United States as Al Qaeda did in the same period (2001 – 2011).

In present-day pacifist Germany it is worrying to see the rebirth of a paranoid nationalism called PEGIDA (Patriotishe Europäer gegen die Islamisierung des Abendlandes: Patriotic Europeans against the Islamization of the West). But what may particularly interest analysts like us is a geographical fact. Pegida originated in Dresden and has become widespread in the eastern Länder, where there are very few Islamic immigrants. It is much less widespread in the Western ones: the very Länder which have received most of the huge number of refugees who poured into Germany and were welcomed there in 2015. Let us try to express this in other words. The need to project the collective shadow not only does not correspond to the real political problems, but often seems actually to proceed in the opposite direction: where the real problem grows, the projections of the collective shadow decrease. The respect for the "reality principle" evidently helps the psyche. If this is lacking, the psychological infection of the masses is fostered. The origins of our concerns may be real: but this does not prevent most of our reactions from potentially being paranoid.

We may even attempt to measure the difference between a real problem and the collective reaction.

## The Paranoid Differential

We might describe the difference between a real problem and its "perception", which certain inquiries have turned into figures (Fig. 3), as the "paranoid differential".

Let us compare, within the EU countries, the real percentage of the Islamic population and the "perception" that the average citizen has of it (that is, the subjective conviction of how many Muslims there are in that country).

In Germany the proportion of Muslims in the population is 6%. The "perception" of the average citizen, however, is that it is 19%: that is, over three times the real figure. In France, too, the perception is excessive. The proportion of Muslims is 8%, whereas the public believes it is 31%: nearly four times as much. In Italy the proportion of Muslims is 4%: but the public thinks it is 20%: that is, 5 times the real figure. Italy – which the pre-globalization legend called a "non-racist country" – is the country where the unfavourable view of the Muslims is highest (61%, according to the Pew Center), even though it has one of the lowest proportions of Muslims, and therefore has less knowledge of them.

However, the biggest surprises come from eastern Europe, where the proportion of Muslims in the total population is close to zero. In Poland it is 0.1%: the public is convinced that it is 5%. In Hungary it is also 0.1%, but the public thinks it is 7%. If we call the real problem 1, "paranoid fantasy" multiplies it respectively 50 and 70 times. In short, the real element (the hook) is almost entirely absent, while the "paranoid differential" is almost everything: so the constant rise of racist movements corresponds more to the projection of the collective shadow than to the real figure. We will therefore be less surprised if images like Figure 4 are published in eastern Europe, which was subjected for nearly half a century to the paranoid vigilance of the communist police: not in Cologne, where local women really have been assaulted by immigrant refugees. The problem does not derive from sexual violence, but from the paranoid imagination. So it is no coincidence that it activates the image of the white woman contaminated by the dark skin: an archaic projection of the shadow, which history has often associated with lynching.

Fig. 4: Islamic rape of Europe

*Two collective problems: terrorism and the environment*

In the last two years I have participated in the IAAP international group concerned with Analysis and Activism. Typical subjects of discussion have been Islamic fundamentalism and the terrorism that it practises, but also the prejudices and exclusion that these factors cause towards the entire Muslim population in the world. Sometimes this collective frenzy has been contrasted with the lack of attention that is attracted by climate change. On 22nd March 2016 the European edition of the New York Times – one of the most objective of the mass media – devoted almost the whole of its front page to the Brussels attacks. Only a much smaller article pointed out that, according to new scientific reports, the predictions about climate change on which the Paris international agreements were based were over-optimistic. The figures for 2016 show that the melting of ice in the Western Antarctic seems to be proceeding much faster than was indicated by the 2015 figures (www.nature.com/nature). The mere return of El Niño endangers the lives of 60 million people (floods in the Pacific and South America, drought in Africa). The reports of the International Energy Agency (2016, www.iea.org/newsroomand-events/pressreleases/2016/june/energy-and-air-pollution.html)    and the World Health Organization say that deaths due to air pollution have reached 6.5 million a year: far more than the number due to HIV, tuberculosis and road accidents combined.

Numerical comparisons are always very artificial. Nevertheless the tragic attacks in Brussels killed 31 people, a figure similar to that for deaths due to road accidents in Europe on certain weekends. Although deaths due to terrorism are a tragic and rightly widely discussed novelty, a statistician friend of mine pointed out to me that the fact that I use a bicycle will continue to represent for me, and also for the majority of Europeans, a risk of death far greater than that posed by terrorism.

Terrorism, however, remains "the evil" – that is, the adversary that we need. In the short term, having an enemy is cathartic, for minds that cannot cope with the long term. But in the long term it has led to world wars.

By contrast, in order to deal with environmental problems we don't need to identify an enemy but to cooperate: this arouses few passions. It does not authorize projections accompanied by "football crowd" emotions. What it requires is self-criticism, both individual and collective: sacrifices, both material and psychological. It activates both consciousness and conscience. We must ask ourselves: how much does each of us contribute to the environment's sickness?

## Our Commitment

The life towards which Jung's psychology guides us does not lead to populist enthusiasms, but to slow maturation. If the most devastating collective paranoia in history was directed at the most integrated minority in Europe, the Jews, we should already be asking ourselves today what might happen tomorrow, when China will become the most powerful country in the world: a country whose population is almost double those of the United States and Europe put together, and which is physically, linguistically and culturally so different from them. I have lived in the biggest Chinatown in Italy and have seen the prejudice grow over the years, changing from peaceful coexistence to suspicion.

I would not like to end, however, with the paranoid projections on to Islam or China, but with an example of an anti-paranoid attitude.

When he was a guerrilla fighter, Pepe Mujica was wounded several times, arrested, and held in prison for over a decade. In his old age, he was transformed into a popular president of Uruguay. At the end of his term of office, El Pais asked him to talk about his imprisonment in a long interview. "I was a prisoner for 25 or 30 years", he said. Perhaps noticing that his interviewer was surprised, he added: "about half of that time, imprisoned by the military; the other half, a prisoner of my own rigid thought patterns" (that is, of revolutionary ideology). How easy it would have been to put all the blame on the dictatorship!

This, however, would have continued to encourage projections of the collective shadow, even though democracy has long since returned in his country. The true defence against paranoid infections, which continue over generations, is a consciousness which acknowledges responsibilities in everyone.

Translated from Italian by Jonathan Hunt

## References

Aa.Vv. The Reckoning, *The New York Times* www.nytimes.com/interactive/us/sept-11-reckoning/viewer.html?_r=0

Balzac, H. de (1838) *Maximes et pensées de Napoléon*, Éditions de Fallois, Paris 1999.

Bullock, A. (1991) *Hitler and Stalin: Parallel Lives*, n. ed. Fontana, London 1998.

Chirot, D., McCauley, C. (2006) *Why Not Kill Them All? The Logic and Prevention of Mass Political Murder*, Princeton University Press, Princeton.

Cohn, N. (1967) *Warrant for Genocide: The Myth of the Jewish World Conspiracy and the Protocols of the Elders of Zion*, n. ed. Serif, London 2005.

Delbrück, A. (1891) *Die pathologische Lüge und die psychisch abnormen Schwindler. Eine Untersuchung über den allmählichen Übergang eines normalen psychologischen Vorgangs in ein pathologisches Symptom*, Enke, Stuttgart.

Dower, J. W. (1986) *War without Mercy: Race and Power in the Pacific War*, Pantheon Books, New York.

Erikson, E. H. (1968) *Identity. Youth and Crisis*, n. ed. Norton, New York - London 1994.

Hamann, B. (1996) *Hitlers Wien: Lehrjahre eines Diktators*, Piper, München.

Hillman, J. (2004) *A Terrible Love of War*, Penguin, New York.

Hitler, A. (1925) *Mein Kampf*, Eher, München, I: *Eine Abrechnung.*

— (1974) *Mein Kampf: Eine kommentierte Auswahl*, ed. Christian Zentner, List, München.

— (1945) *Nero-Befehl*, in Dokumente zur Deutschen Geschichte VEB Deutscher Verlag der Wissenschaften, Berlin 1977, S. 109 (Nero Befehl *March 19 1945, www.ns-archiv.de/personen/hitler/nero-befehl/*).

International Energy Agency (2016), *Small increase in energy investment could cut premature deaths from air pollution in half by 2040, says new IEA report* 27th June, www.iea.org/newsroomandevents/pressreleases/2016/june/energy-and-air-pollution.html

Jaspers, K. (1913) *Allgemeine Psychopathologie*, n. ed. Springer, Berlin 1959. Eng. Ed.: (1997). *General Psychopathology – Volumes 1 & 2.*, Baltimore and London: Johns Hopkins University Press.

Millás, J. J. (2014), 'Retrato de Uruguay, el país que sorprende al mundo', *El País*, 24 March, elpais.com/elpais/2014/03/24/eps/1395660898_932004.html

Nicholi, A. M. (1978) *The Harvard Guide to Modern Psychiatry*, The Belknap Press of Harvard University Press, Cambridge (Mass.).

Nietzsche, F. (1881-84) *Also sprach Zarathustra: Ein Buch für alle und keinen*, Fritzsch, Leipzig.1886 *Jenseits von Gut und Böse*, Naumann, Leipzig. Eng. Ed.: (2005) *Thus Spoke Zarathustra*, Oxford: Oxford World's Classics.

Rogelj J., den Elzen M., Hoehne N., Fransen T., Fekete H., Winkler H., Schaeffer R., Sha F., Riahi K., Meinshausen M. (2016), 'Paris Agreement climate proposals need a boost to keep warming well below 2 °C', *Nature*, www.nature.com/nature/journal/v534/n7609/full/nature18307.html

Sophocles (ed. 2011) *Ajax*, ed. P. J. Finglass, Cambridge University Press, Cambridge

Speer, A. (1969) *Erinnerungen*, Ullstein, Frankfurt a. M. Eng. Ed.: (1970), *Inside The Third Reich*, New York and Toronto: Macmillan

Von Franz, M.-L. (1980) *Projection and Re-collection in Jungian Psychology: Reflections of the Soul*, Open Court, London.

# President's Farewell Address

*Tom Kelly*
President (2013 – 2016)

As I look back over the past three years, it seems as though I have been in somewhat of a time warp. On the one hand, it has gone by so very quickly that it seems like only yesterday we were in Copenhagen; on the other hand, the three years have been filled with so many IAAP events and activities throughout the world that I wonder how it was ever possible to fit all of that into three short years. And yet, here we are at the end of one administration and the beginning of a new one.

I have been particularly fortunate to have had such an extraordinary Executive Committee to work with. Each member, without fail, contributed tirelessly with their time, energy, thoughtfulness, care and creativity in building on the foundations that had been laid down for the IAAP by each previous administration. Because of the reduction in IAAP dues of 12% voted by the Delegates in Copenhagen, this administration was faced with the challenge of providing services for the IAAP with less income. Fortunately, what we lost in yearly revenue was more than compensated for by the good will, enthusiasm and countless hours of hard work by this team of seasoned colleagues.

While the Delegates have voted to maintain the yearly dues at the current rate for the next three years, I believe this is something that will need to be given serious consideration in the next administration. Managing such a large and complex organization as the IAAP requires an enormous amount of time and energy. As we move forward and need to rely increasingly on digital communication, it may not be manageable, or realistic, to expect analyst colleagues to be able to carry the entire responsibility for the functioning of the IAAP in addition to maintaining a clinical practice. In the past few years, this has, at times, been a challenge for all of the officers and for some members of the Executive Committee. I leave this question to future administrations but it is one that we will need to visit again.

Thanks to the revised Constitution of the IAAP voted on and accepted in Copenhagen, in this administration, it was possible to continue the work begun by the previous administration. The Education Committee, under the stewardship of Co-Chairs Misser Berg and Angela Connolly, revised the procedures and structures of the Ed Com to ensure the highest possible standards for the router program. Research into the effectiveness of the router program has been completed in this administration, thanks to the work of John

Merchant and the Curriculum Working Group of the Ed Com, chaired by Joy Norton, has worked assiduously in establishing a curriculum for routers that represents and respects the different branches of thought in analytical psychology.

In response to the interest and desire of some Group Members to become involved in the training of routers, the Ed Com established an Affiliate Candidate Program whereby training of the routers in a country is taken over entirely by an IAAP Group Member. Because it is not always possible for the Affiliate Candidates to then become members of that Group Member, there is collaboration with the IAAP for the screening interviews, intermediate exams and final exams. To date, three Group Members are actively involved in the Affiliate Candidate Program: CIPA Sicily, with a group in Malta; the Danish Society, DSAP, with a group from Estonia and Finland; and the Russian Society, RSAP, with a group in Belarus. In addition, a Group Member from London is actively exploring the possibility of offering training to Affiliate Candidates in Ireland.

The long-term goal of the Ed Com is to ensure quality training of routers in countries where there is no IAAP Group Member to initially form Individual Members who will, with time, form an IAAP Group Member without Training Status and eventually, a Group Member with Training Status. At the Meeting of Delegates on Wednesday afternoon, the Lithuanian Association for Analytical Psychology (LAAP), the Mexican Society of C.G. Jung (SOMEJ) and the Uruguayan-Argentinean Society of Analytical Psychology (SUAPA) were all voted into membership as IAAP Group Members with Training Status. In addition, the Chilean Society of Analytical Psychology (SCPA), The Colombian Society of Jungian Analysts (SCAJ), the Czech Association for Analytical Psychology (CAAP) and the Finnish-Estonian Group of Analytical Psychologists (FEGAP) were accepted as IAAP Group Members without Training Status. Each of these new Group Members represents the blossoming of seeds that were planted, supported and tended to by umpteen analysts from many different Group Members and by previous administrations of the IAAP. Each one also shows that the long-term goal of the Ed Com to establish independent Group Members throughout different regions of the world is working. At the next Congress in 2019, I think we can anticipate the formation of a Group Member from the China region. These developments are a testimony to the dedication and devotion of analyst members from many different Group Members around the world. They also reflect the vibrant and ever-growing interest in Analytical Psychology in different regions of the world. We can all be proud of this accomplishment.

We are, I believe, only beginning to recognize the bi-directional impact that work with professionals from different cultures will inevitably have on our theory and practice. Further exploration of this impact promises to reap further benefits for the membership of the IAAP and to challenge us to deepen our understanding of psyche and psychic process in new and innovative ways.

In this administration, we have worked very hard to improve communication with the membership of the IAAP. Thanks to the enormous amount of work by the Communications and Publications Sub-Committee, and particularly its Chair, George Hogenson, we have managed to provide regular information about forthcoming events and conferences hosted by IAAP Group Members. Communication with the Presidents of IAAP Group Members has also improved thanks to these efforts. In addition, the publication of the Newssheet twice a year provides the membership with personal reports from IAAP Group Members, Developing Groups and Router Groups as well as reviews of journals and interviews with members of the IAAP from around the world. This would be impossible without the dedication of Emilija Kiehl, editor of the Newssheet. Furthermore, the IAAP website has been totally revamped to make it more relevant, user-friendly and easy to navigate. After a number of unfortunate cyber attacks, the website has been rebuilt to prevent further unwanted and unwarranted intrusions of this nature. In this age of Internet communication, this requires constant prudence and surveillance.

I hope you will forgive me for listing only a few of the many accomplishments of my administration. I realize that I am talking to the converted here and that the people who really need to hear this are not present at this congress. Nevertheless, I hope you will take this back with you to your respective Group Members and provide them with information when they ask, "What does the IAAP do for me?"

In his closing statement at the end of the Congress in Barcelona in 2004, Murray Stein stated that the IAAP had matured and reached the phase of mid-life. Now, some twelve years later, the aging population of the membership of the IAAP is, I believe, cause for concern. The resultant anticipated decrease in income from membership dues will inevitably impose limits and restrictions on what the IAAP can continue to offer the membership. While there are increasingly more younger members in some parts of the world, this is not the case everywhere. Coupled with the growing governmental, legislative, professional and insurance restrictions imposed in different countries on the work we do, we are increasingly finding that the very profession we exercise is being challenged and, in some countries, even threatened. Long-term work on oneself is out of fashion in the current zeitgeist where instant gratification and brief internet-based encounters are favoured over long-lasting relationships, which require hard work in order to reap the benefits and lasting pleasures they can offer. Concurrent to this on the other hand, is the wave of aging baby-boomers who, now in the autumn of their lives, are seeking some kind of soul nourishment, often without knowing where to turn to face the challenges and needs of the last phase of life, such as establishing a meaningful connection to the spiritual in a way that is truly nourishing.

Analytical Psychology has a lot to offer in response to this crises of need, however, we too have to be in tune with the needs of the zeitgeist that come to expression in novel manners in order to remain relevant. This requires us to learn new and creative ways of responding to these needs as they express themselves today in our collective.

Many years ago, I had the pleasure of attending a dinner hosted by one of the IAAP Group Members in honour of the candidates who had terminated the formal training program and who were to be admitted into the membership of this Group Member. Without fail, each of the newly certified analysts shared how their training had been a deeply transformative and in some ways life-saving experience for them. It was a very moving experience and a gratifying one for these new analyst members but also for the entire membership of the Group Member in question. It was also an expression of confidence in their training model. Over the years, I have had the tremendous opportunity to attend a number of similar ceremonies in honour of recently graduated analysts in different parts of the world. Regardless of where and how these new analyst members had trained, the new analyst colleagues bore witness to the value of their training as a profoundly meaningful and transformative experience. My point here is that there is no one way to do training and no one training model that is perfect or that can be expected to meet the needs of everyone. What remains a constant however, regardless of the training model, is the personally transformative experience of work in the container of the personal analysis and in the container of the training.

One of Jung's great gifts was his understanding of the transformative effect of the creative process and of this as an expression of the aliveness of psychic energy.

As we move forward into the second half of the second decade of this new millennium, I believe we will be called on to revise our thinking about training and to open our minds, and even more importantly our hearts and souls, to the category of professionals called psychotherapists. The world is changing and unless we are ready to find new and creative ways of making available the uniqueness of what we have to offer, we are doomed to becoming redundant. I believe the growth in interest in analytical psychology around the world is testimony to our ability to meet this challenge in a meaningful, soulful and creative manner. This is yet another challenge that lies ahead for us all but also for the well-being of the IAAP. The research project begun by the Organizational and Advisory Working Party in this administration, under the leadership of Martin Stone, began to explore the current concerns of the membership of the IAAP in different parts of the world. I believe we need to continue this exploration in order to get a pulse of the membership and an intuition of their emerging concerns for the future.

This farewell address would be incomplete without an expression of heartfelt thanks for the many colleagues who have worked so hard for the IAAP over the past three years. First and foremost, my heartfelt thanks to the members of the Executive Committee: Marianne Müller, Angela Connolly, Toshio Kawai, who was also Chair of the Program Committee, Pilar Amezaga, Batya Brosh Palmoni, Fred Borchardt, Alessandra De Coro, Christine Hejinian, George Hogenson, Emilija Kiehl, Margaret Klenck and Robert Wimmer. A very special thanks is in order for my Honorary Secretary, Misser Berg, for her tireless energy but also for her excellent organizational skills and steadfast and reliable presence. My thanks also to our host Society, AJAJ, the Association of Jungian Psychologists, Japan, to Yasuhiro Tanaka, Chair of the Organizing Committee, and to his team for their care and attention to the many details this congress required and for their extraordinary hospitality.

There are far too many people to thank here, however, there is one more person who deserves my sincere thanks and appreciation. The demands of the work required as an Officer of the IAAP, the long working hours and frequent absences can be rather trying on one's personal and relational life. Throughout my many years on the Executive Committee, Michel Boivin, my life-long partner and soulmate has been a constant source of support and understanding and to him today, I offer my thanks and gratitude for his presence in my life. He will be happy to know that I will be absent much less often now.

I leave the leadership of the IAAP knowing that it is in very competent hands with Marianne Müller and the new Executive Committee. Marianne has all the qualities required to be a solid, steady, hard-working and competent leader. I wish her and her new team all the very best in the coming three years. She can count on the support and good will of the membership of the IAAP.

And finally, I wish the IAAP a long, healthy and creative life for many generations to come.

Thank you.

Tom Kelly

# President's Farewell
## at the 2013 Congress in Copenhagen[1]

### Joe Cambray

The three years since our last congress in Montreal have been a time of change and re-vision in the IAAP; for me these years have raced by, often with short nights and long days. Our having successfully reached this point in the congress and more broadly in our communal life is due to the openness, devotion, and hard work of many individuals and groups, certainly everyone on the various committees, sub-committees, working parties, etc., (as I will detail later), but also the many IAAP members who have been willing to meet, discuss substantive issue and sustain debate until all who wished to have the opportunity to be heard have had their chance to do so fully. The main precipitants for these communal discussions have been the revision of the constitution along with associated documents and the financial crisis beginning in 2008.

As undertaken in the previous administration, the revising of the IAAP constitution has been a six-year process ably chaired in this administration by Marianne Müller. Initially undertaken to help streamline and simplify the document, to eliminate errors that had accumulated over time with the various amendments, and thus to save costs on legal consultation, the project has had a life of its own. Whenever foundations are altered, even if done gently and with care, a good deal of dust arises and it takes time for this to settle before we can assess the value of the changes implemented. The early round of alterations certainly produced lively discussion, debate and various suggestions for other modifications. This has led over the three years to an intense process of compromise and negotiation, which I believe has strengthened the IAAP rendering it more open and democratic in its processes. Consequently, there seems to be an increased sense of interest, animation and vibrancy about the association that has the hallmarks of an emergent process.

Scrutinizing our foundational documents has not only revealed their fundamental soundness – the original vision largely holds true – but also seems to have breathed new life into our organizational processes. As you will see, in areas where things have been unstructured and a bit chaotic we have introduced more order and where

---

1 The President's Farewell by Joe Cambray at the 2013 Congress in Copenhagen did not appear in the Copenhagen Proceedings and we are taking the opportunity to publish this important document here.

things were too bound up in forms no longer functional, change and re-visions were applied. Rather like a marriage of conscious and unconscious, the emergent edge is between order and chaos; too much of either will stifle or dissolve the process. So it has been three years of organizational alchemy if you will.

Several new organs have arisen out of these developments, in particular the Education Committee and the Consultation Service. While these entities were already being conceptualized at the beginning of this administration having emerged from the work of the last several administrations, their evolution has been accelerated by the transformations underway in the association. Further, the IAAP is embedded in a changing world. Thus, the impact of the Zeitgeist has been felt in various ways, most notably in the struggle for financial recovery in much of the world since the market crashes of 2008. The consequences of the financial downturn directly affected many members' income and well-being. The Executive Committee (EC) has taken actions to assist our membership with a hardship clause to help members who cannot pay dues, and more generally with a recommendation to reduce the dues made possible through careful fiscal management. There has also been a broad trend towards increasing activities at a regional level, where various groups and individuals sharing languages and cultures have held events in common.

These regional activities have been a part of various approaches towards reconciliation among groups, a most heartening direction for the IAAP's future. Some of the presentations at this congress overtly discussed themes of reconciliation. In turn the IAAP EC has come to more fully value these regional groupings. In fact, being present at regional events has increased effective interactions between the EC and the membership. Through these interactions specific regional issues have come into focus for the EC and creative approaches to dilemmas have been pursued in a collaborative fashion, such as the potential training of new analysts within the broader Latin American region.

The new Education Committee, co-chaired in this administration by Honorary Secretary, Angela Connolly, and Vice President, Jan Wiener, combines and extends the Developing Group and Individual Membership Sub-Committees. In building this new committee, which is still under construction, regional groupings naturally arose, which have helped make the administrative tasks more manageable. These include fiscal oversight, coordinating resources and enhancing interactions and collaboration between those active in the various regions. In turn this has helped to form a strategic vision; the goal of the Education Committee extends beyond making new Individual Members (IMs) to helping the new IMs form and launch new Group Members, which eventually will take on training responsibilities, as we have just witnessed with our Russian colleagues. This is a unique task, which only the IAAP is capable of undertaking and is an important part of the IAAP's future in the global society.

In the process of articulating the vision of the new Education Committee, regional organizers work together with staff teams who travel and work on-site. These efforts are further supported by working groups who monitor and pursue curriculum development, research and evaluation, and cultivate communication and resources within each region. The staffing of these teams has opened up opportunities for the general membership to become more involved in this program. At the same time, strategic planning has clarified the need to set upper limits to the numbers of people being handled by the Education Committee at any one time to keep this in line with available resources and to respect budgetary constraints.

There is also much to be gained in non-material ways from the programs of the Education Committee. In an interconnected world we have come to value the importance of relational perspectives. And after all, Jung's interactive field model for analysis was one of the first theories of the relational field, which includes intrapsychic as well as interpersonal elements. Conscious and unconscious patterns of interaction together with implicit links to environments, the collective unconscious and the world, were all included in the field. From the IAAP's history of involvement in the various regions we can now extend the field to explore the bi-directionality of influence, which is emerging from our interactions with peoples from cultures that were not part of the first or second generations of Jungians. New visions are forming of how analytical psychology might be conceived and applied in differing cultures, which may in turn cause those in the older, established centers to review and revise theories and practices, all as part of our communal evolution.

The other new organ of the IAAP EC is the Consultation Service (CS). This has developed out of on-going concerns about good governance practices, mediation and the need for consultation that arises over time in various quarters. Previous administrations have sought vehicles to respond to these concerns and their fine work has been pioneering to the new service. While the range of potential uses for the CS is still being explored, it is evident that consultation can be of value to group members undergoing internal strife, or experiencing conflict with other group members; in fact the use of the CS has helped reduce the need for Committees of Inquiry and the expense associated with these. In addition, the CS has been of use to the EC when complex question about policies have required detail study of our history and documents. The CS can then offer advisory reports for the EC to consider. Furthermore the CS could be available to members considering forming new groups or groups seeking a change in status, such as from non-training to training, helping them to explore their choices in a reflective process. The role of the CS in helping consider regional issues is nascent but worthy of further consideration. As you can tell this is still fluid and a work in progress but it is already active with some success to date.

Another new development in this administration has been the production and dissemination of the Newssheet, so beautifully edited by Emilija Kiehl. This new, electronic communication tool allows high-lighting of groups on a regular semi-annual basis, so that we can come to know more about one another's thinking and activities along with images of people and places, thereby helping build more connections amongst us. In general your feedback has been quite supportive of this new direction, so this will likely continue.

In the midst of these changes, we have also sought continuity. Thus, hard copy versions of the Newsletter covering this administration together with the List of Members were sent out this summer to the entire membership. These publications provide valuable information about events in the community as well as a relatively up to date directory of membership. I hope you have received your personal copies and find them of value and interest.

To shift focus now, but in line with this Congress' theme, I would like to acknowledge the formative experiences Jung underwent 100 years ago at the end of 1913 into 1914. These of course were crafted over the following 15 or more years into the *Red Book*, which reveals the innovative and transformative processes, which molded young man Jung into the figure of *Jung* whom we so esteem today. By August of 1914 he was caught on the horns of a dilemma: were his visionary experiences a prelude to madness or was he undergoing a set of prophetic revelations – was he to be a prophet or a madman, neither very appealing to him. As I've suggested elsewhere, he finally found a transcendent third position in 1928 upon receipt of Richard Wilhelm's manuscript translation of *The Secret of the Golden Flower*. That exit was enshrined in his coining of a new concept, synchronicity, a most controversial subject, a new principle in Western thought that put visionary experience on an objective footing as part of the very nature of our universe and solidified the radical notion of an objective psyche. As we know Jung held back on publishing much about this new idea until the early 1950s just because it was so controversial, though he and Wolfgang Pauli had been discussing the conceptual basis for this in their correspondence since late 1934.

As we have celebrated, pondered and reflected upon the impact of the last 100 years from the originary events of this period, I have been musing as to where the visionary nature of the analytic enterprise might be emerging today. As I've outlined here the IAAP is certainly undergoing some valuable innovative changes, which while controversial at times, can be seen as within the spirit of the times. How then will we also keep the radical emergent, creative edge alive in our organizational life? In Murray Stein's 2004 President's Farewell address he helpfully spoke about the IAAP at mid-life; I now would like to ask about the possibility of re-visioning our association in terms of its relationship to the spirit of the depths; this might be read as a "re-birth" fantasy, a return to origins in the sense of visionary experience, not rote imitation, and at this time for our collective, not only for each of us as individuals as valuable as those personal experiences obviously are.

At first I was tempted to console myself with stories of the Baal Shem Tov, the ecstatic, mystical figure of Hasdic Judiasm, especially as told by holocaust survivor Elie Wiesel:

> When the great Israel Baal Shem-Tov saw misfortune threatening the Jews, it was his custom to go into a certain part of the forest to meditate. There he would light a fire, say a special prayer, and the miracle would be accomplished and the misfortune averted.

> Later, when his disciple, the celebrated Maggid of Mezeritch, had occasion, for the same reason, to intercede with heaven, he would go to the same place in the forest and say: "Master of the Universe, listen! I do not know how to light the fire, but I am still able to say the prayer," and again the miracle would be accomplished.

> Still later, Moshe-Lieb of Sasov, in order to save his people once more, would go into the forest and say: "I do not know how to light the fire, I do not know the prayer, but I know the place and this must be sufficient." It was sufficient and the miracle was accomplished.

> Then it fell to Israel of Rizhyn to overcome misfortune. Sitting in his armchair, his head in his hands, he spoke to God: "I am unable to light the fire and I do not know the prayer; I cannot even find the place in the forest. All I can do is tell the story, and this must be sufficient." And it was sufficient (Souls on Fire, p. 167-8).

But then as Wiesel himself continues in his comment:

> It no longer is [sufficient]. The proof is that the threat has not been averted. Perhaps we are no longer able to tell the story. Could all of us be guilty? Even the survivors? Especially the survivors? (ibid. p. 168)

Although we are in no way threatened with such a terrible catastrophe as the holocaust, the issue of trusting the efficacy of memory versus direct lived experience, as an essential aspect of our link to origins is something we all face, and perhaps our survival ultimately depends upon. Of course many of us in our practices attempt to offer analogous experiences as we have had in our own personal analyses, but with each generation and in each culture there are shifts and changes. In the generational transition of analytic culture remembering stories of our forbearers (analytic lineages) and spiritual ancestors including their struggles are crucial to our on-going organizational existence. But, it is also essential that we remain open to the creation of new narratives as they arise from our interactions as individuals and within and between groups. We need both history and the flexibility to change.

The emergent qualities of archetypal reality cannot be codified but must be engendered in the moment anew for each individual. But is this enough now or is the community itself something more than the sum of the individuals who compose it and susceptible to its own processes? If so, then within this is the possibility of communal renewal to be realized, or dismissed? Might we articulate a shared vision as a vital step?

At a mundane level while the IAAP has a mission statement, we do not as yet have a "vision statement" – there is a deeper challenge here, can we together dream and actively imagine a richer future for our association? Can our forms of training and education foster greater creativity, if so how? Can we continue to diversify while valuing our local differences, in effect complexifying our association without leaving it riddled with complexes? Without trying to define what makes us unique, can we cherish it and come to better appreciate this uniqueness in others, especially in our colleagues from various cultures with their own traditions and approaches? Might we also seek out fruitful dialogue with scholars and researchers who have overlapping passions that might spark with our own and ignite an imaginative fire like that of the Baal Shem-Tov? I would urge us to discover the cosmological vision we live in and expand it as best we can, not to just borrow it from modern science, psychology or theology or any preformed discipline, but as a true act of discovery, something I have come to see at the core of Jung's own creativity and worthy of supreme effort.

## Acknowledgements

To conclude my remarks I would like to offer thanks to the many who have helped me and this administration achieve what we have been able to do, and then to introduce you to our newest members and organizations. Over the years it has been my great good fortune to come to know a number of my predecessors, past presidents, a significant number of whom have been at this Congress: Tom Kirsch, Verena Kast, Luigi Zoija, Murray Stein, Christian Gaillard, and Hester Solomon. Their labor and visions have provided a solid foundation on which to continue the work of building this organization.

The Executive Committee elected to serve in this administration has itself been a complex mixture of individuals from different cultures and analytic traditions; it has been an honor to serve with them. My fellow officers have been extraordinary in sharing their energy and ideas, working tirelessly for the greater good of the organization, I've been humbled by the intensity of their commitment to our common goals. I believe that those members of the EC who will go on in the next administration will continue with their own innovative work and that our deeply valued association is in good hands. Also thanks to our hard working Ethics Committee, so capably chaired by Ann Casement – the committee certainly had a mountain of documents to process in this administration and did so with care and precision.

In thanking the secretarial staff without whom we would most certainly have floundered long ago, I wish to recognize the outstanding contribution of the presidential secretary, Mariuccia Tresoldi, whose tireless devotion to the IAAP has been most inspiring. And I would like to make a special acknowledgement of Yvonne Trueb for the long and devoted service she has provided to the IAAP. Many of you know her from your communications with her, whether to pay dues, to make changes to your data on the website, or any of a million other transactions. Yvonne is retiring, and so with deepest gratitude for years of service we wish her great happiness as she goes forward. Yvonne is currently training her replacement, Selma Gubser (you may recognize her surname as she is married to our accountant, Daniel Gubser) a very capable individual who already knows much about the structures of the IAAP. We also give thanks to Sibylle Koersten who has helped the secretarial staff and was key to finding the organization that gave us a second legal opinion on our revised constitution. Our support staff includes our webmaster, Don Williams, who has kept us afloat in cyberspace for which we are most grateful, together with his technical assistant Lucien Apostol; Emilija Kiehl whom I mentioned earlier has done a remarkable job editing and producing a number of publications, electronic and in hard copy.

The Program and Organizing Committees for this Congress have been outstanding. Thanks to our program chair, Robert Wimmer, for his light touch and guiding hand in the generation of the program and to Misser Berg, chair of the organizing committee who has been an incredible force bringing the many details of the congress into a remarkable and coherent whole. Misser, together with Pia Skogemann, are the innovators who have championed the idea of the use of electronic translation and together with DSAP have provided the readers and tablets to those of you who have requested them, the first time the IAAP has attempted to use such an alternative – this helped greatly to keep down the costs for the Congress and is the principle reason why the registration cost was able to be as low as it was. I would remind you to fill out the questionnaire that was in your registration packet, it has some questions about your experience with the various forms of translation. Your answers will help future Congress committees.

# Alphabetical List of Authors

(entries up to p. 210 appear in the print edition, beyond that only on CD)

## Haruki Murakami goes to meet Hayao Kawai

Two of Japan's foremost contemporary cultural spokespersons met for an informal conversation with remarkable results. While their extended talk took place at a particular location at a particular moment in history, much of the content is timeless and universal. After popular acclaim in Japan, the transcript now makes its first appearance in English.

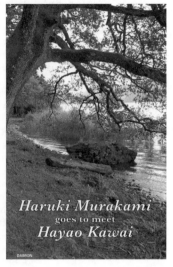

From the Contents:

The Meaning of Commitment
Words or Images?
Making Stories
Answering Logically versus Answering Compassionately
Self-Healing and Novels
Marriage and 'Well-digging'
Curing and Living
Stories and the Body
The Relationship between a Work and its Author
Individuality and Universality
Violence and Expression
Where are We Headed?

**Hayao Kawai** was Minister of Culture for Japan and decorated as a 'Person of Cultural Merit'. He originally studied mathematics, then trained to become a Jungian psychoanalyst and sandplay therapist in Zürich. Back in his native country, he went on to introduce Jung's psychology and sandplay therapy. Kawai became a well-known writer and television personality in Japan and also abroad; many of his works have been translated into other languages.

**Haruki Murakami** began to write at the age of 30 and blossomed into one of the premier writers of his generation. He has been awarded numerous honors in Japan as well as internationally, including the Franz Kafka Prize, the Jerusalem Prize and many others. He is known for his journalistic pieces, short stories and genre-defying novels, including *The Wind-up Bird Chronicle, Norwegian Wood, A Wild Sheep Chase, Wind/Pinball* and *1Q84*.

160 pages, hardcover, ISBN 978-3-85630-771-4

## English Titles from Daimon

# English Titles from Daimon

*Our books are available from your bookstore or from our distributors:*

AtlasBooks
30 Amberwood Parkway
Ashland OH 44805, USA
Phone: 419-281-5100
Fax: 419-281-0200
E-mail: order@atlasbooks.com
www.atlasbooks.com

Gazelle Book Services Ltd.
White Cross Mills, High Town
Lancaster LA1 4XS, UK
Tel: +44(0)152468765
Fax: +44(0)152463232
Email: Sales@gazellebooks.co.uk
www.gazellebooks.co.uk

Daimon Verlag - Hauptstrasse 85 - CH-8840 Einsiedeln - Switzerland
Phone: (41)(55) 412 2266    Fax: (41)(55) 412 2231
Email: info@daimon.ch
Visit our website: **www.daimon.ch** or write for our complete catalog